South Asia's Turn

South Asia's Turn

*Policies to Boost Competitiveness and
Create the Next Export Powerhouse*

**Gladys Lopez-Acevedo, Denis Medvedev,
and Vincent Palmade, Editors**

Contents

Part 3 THE WAY FORWARD

Boxes

Figures

Tables

Foreword

South Asia is at a turning point. The region is benefitting from a confluence of positive internal and external forces. South Asian countries are starting to receive the competitiveness dividends from the economic reforms and public investments in infrastructure and education carried over the past 25 years. Rising labor costs in East Asia are steering global investors toward South Asia as a possible cheaper alternative. At a time of declining global growth and trade, South Asia—home to a quarter of humanity—has the potential to boost global growth as both a major exporter and consumer market. This is good news, not only for South Asia but also for the world as a whole. But challenges to the region's competitiveness remain. More than one million young people are reaching working age every month and will need jobs; firm competitiveness is low; and countries in the region have not been particularly successful in integrating with each other.

This book, *South Asia's Turn: Policies to Boost Competitiveness and Create the Next Export Powerhouse*, looks in detail at the drivers and constraints impacting South Asia's competitiveness. It outlines the four policy levers that will help the region become more globally competitive across a broader spectrum of industries, accelerating growth and reducing poverty, especially for women.

One of these policy levers (improving the business environment) is well known, but much remains to be done. The other three (policies to better connect to global value chains, maximize agglomeration benefits, and strengthen firm capabilities) are much less discussed, and we hope this report will help policy makers focus more on them.

The report combines a critical mass of quantitative analysis, using the latest data and tools available, with a rich set of industry and company case studies to draw new insights on what South Asia needs to do to boost competitiveness. And it proposes a number of specific policy solutions drawn from relevant international good practices (including from within the region).

We very much hope that this report will help the countries of South Asia, individually as well as collectively, take a turn toward realizing their great competitiveness potential.

Annette Dixon
Vice President
South Asia Region
World Bank Group

Anabel González
Senior Director
Trade and Competitiveness Global Practice
World Bank Group

Acknowledgments

This report was prepared by a team led by Denis Medvedev and Vincent Palmade, both of the World Bank's Trade and Competitiveness Global Practice (GTCDR), under the guidance of Esperanza Lasagabaster (practice manager, GTCDR) and Martín Rama (chief economist, South Asia Region). Annette Dixon (vice president, South Asia Region), Anabel González (senior director, GTCDR), and Cecile Fruman (director, GTCDR) linked the team to the World Bank Group's overall strategy and steered them in that direction.

This report presents a combination of findings from a cross-cutting analysis of the dynamics of firms, clusters, value chains, and cities across the region, as well as detailed case studies of the apparel, electronics, automotive, and agribusiness industries. The full case studies are available online at www.worldbank.org/SouthAsiaCompetes.

Chapter 1 of the report was authored by Antonio Martuscelli and Gonzalo Varela; chapter 2 by Apoorva Gupta, Antonio Martuscelli, and Gonzalo Varela; chapter 3 by Filipe Lage de Sousa, Deeksha Kokas, and Giuliana de Mendiola Ramirez; chapter 4 by Filipe Lage de Sousa and Deeksha Kokas; chapter 5 by Michael Ferrantino and Gaurav Nayyar; chapter 6 by Xavier Cirera and Ana Cusolito, with inputs from Filipe Lage de Sousa; and chapters 7 and 8 by Gladys Lopez-Acevedo, Vincent Palmade, and Dominique van der Mensbrugghe. Bill Shaw streamlined, organized, and edited the narrative.

The agribusiness case study (attached to chapter 3) was authored by Soujanya Chodavarapu, Asa Giertz, and Peter Jaeger. The electronics case study (attached to chapter 4) was authored by Ashish Narain with support from Sriyani Hulugalle, Tim Sturgeon, and Daria Taglioni. The apparel case study (attached to chapter 5) was authored by Gladys Lopez-Acevedo, Raymond Robertson, and Atisha Kumar. The automotive case study (attached to chapter 6) was authored by Priyam Saraf with support from Michel Bacher, Amjad Bashir, and Sanjay Kathuria.

Major contributions were received from Alvaro Gonzalez, Atisha Kumar, and Siddharth Sharma, and the team benefitted from the advice provided by Ana Margarida Fernandes and Sebastian Saez. Guoliang Feng, Deeksha Kokas, and Lara Loewenstein provided invaluable research assistance. Rosanna Chan, Paramita Dasgupta, Tugba Gurcanlar, Luke Jordan, Bertine Kamphuis, Sanjay Kathuria, Eric Manes, Anna Reva, Fatima Shah, and Shahid Yusuf provided critical inputs during the inception phase. Tanya Cubbins and Isaac Lawson provided production and logistical support. Sections of the report draw extensively from a recently prepared World Bank report, *Stiches to Riches*. The peer reviewers were Shubham Chaudhuri (Macroeconomics and Fiscal Management, World Bank), Uri Dadush (Carnegie Endowment for International Peace), Navin Girishankar (Trade and Competitiveness, World Bank), Pravin Krishna (Johns Hopkins University), and Bill Maloney (Equitable Growth, Finance, and Institutions, World Bank).

The team is grateful to South Asia country directors and, most important, country authorities for their support as well as the dozens of companies, industry associations, and experts interviewed for this report.

Abbreviations

ADF	Agriculture Development Fund (Afghanistan)
AEPC	Apparel Export Promotion Council (India)
ASEAN	Association of Southeast Asian Nations
ASI	Annual Survey of Industries
BEPZA	Bangladesh Export Processing Zones Authority
BPO	business process outsourcing
CAGR	compound annual growth rate
CBU	completely built unit (automobiles)
CDE	constant differences in elasticity
CES	constant elasticity of substitution
CGE	computable general equilibrium
CIF	cost, insurance, and freight
CSR	corporate social responsibility
DTRE	duty and tax remission for export program
EPZ	export processing zone
EU	European Union
FAO	Food and Agriculture Organization (United Nations)
FDI	foreign direct investment
FOB	free on board
GCI	Global Competitiveness Index
GDP	gross domestic product
GSEM	generalized structural equation model
GTAP	Global Trade Analysis Project
GVC	global value chain
HTGL	Hi-Tech Gear Ltd.
IAMC	Integrated Assessment Modeling Consortium
IARI	Indian Agricultural Research Institute
ICP	International Comparison Project
ICT	information and communication technology
IIASA	International Institute for Applied Systems Analysis
ILFS	Infrastructure Leasing and Financial Services Ltd. (India)

ILO	International Labour Organization
ISIC	International Standard Industrial Classification
IT	information technology
LES	linear expenditure system
LPI	Logistics Performance Index
MAOTRI	Market Access Overall Trade Restrictiveness Index
MFA	Multi-Fiber Agreement
MFN	most-favored nation
MSSL	Motherson Sumi Systems Ltd.
NAFTA	North American Free Trade Agreement
n.e.s.	not elsewhere specified
NGO	nongovernmental organization
NTM	nontariff measures
OECD	Organisation for Economic Co-operation and Development
OEM	original equipment manufacturer
OLS	ordinary least squares
OTRI	Overall Trade Restrictiveness Index
PPP	purchasing power parity
R&D	research and development
SACU	Southern African Customs Union
SAR	Special Administrative Region
SEZ	special enterprise zone
SMEs	small and medium enterprises
TFP	total factor productivity
TPP	Trans-Pacific Partnership
TTIP	Trans-Atlantic Trade and Investment Partnership
USAID	U.S. Agency for International Development
USITC	U.S. International Trade Commission
WITS	World Integrated Trade Solutions
WTO	World Trade Organization

All monetary amounts are U.S. dollars unless otherwise indicated.

Overview

Which region will become the next global factory? As the workforce ages and labor costs rise in China and other East Asian countries, many eyes turn to South Asia. South Asia's potential is unquestionable: education levels are on the rise, more than one million young workers enter the labor market each month, and the population of the region's mega-agglomerations and sprawling cities is expanding monthly by roughly the same number. By 2030, more than a quarter of the world's working adults will live in South Asia. But despite flashes of brilliance across a handful of sectors, locations, and leading firms, this potential remains largely unfulfilled.

South Asia ranks below both its neighbors and various global benchmarks in attracting investment, penetrating tough markets, diversifying and upgrading its products, and regional integration. These forgone opportunities are also reflected in low scores across a range of measures of international competitiveness. With the growth rate of global trade having dramatically slowed down, how can South Asia improve its competitiveness, become an export powerhouse, create jobs, reduce poverty, and boost shared prosperity? This report proposes that the solution lies in improving productivity and looks for ways to

do so in the dynamics of firms, industry value chains, clusters, and cities across the region.

With some exceptions, South Asia has reaped few benefits from global integration

Despite the recent slowdown in trade, the global economy is more connected than ever. Participation in larger regional and global markets offers many opportunities to raise productivity: stronger competitive pressures weed out the least productive firms, while others improve by gaining access to knowledge and better inputs. Across the region, there are several examples of these channels at work, ranging from highly successful apparel industries in Bangladesh and Sri Lanka to India's software and business process outsourcing (BPO) sectors, and from productive agglomeration of light manufacturing firms in Sialkot, Pakistan, to Bangalore, India's becoming a global research and development (R&D) hub for major auto parts and electronics producers. South Asia's leading firms have risen to standards of global excellence, demonstrating that world-class levels of operational performance, efficiency, and innovation can be achieved with the right management, scale, technology, and worker training. Since 2010, on the strength of its services trade, South Asia's ratio of trade to gross domestic product (GDP) has consistently been better than China's, and—after controlling for size—India is more open to trade than the global average.

In the aggregate, however, South Asia's intraregional and global ties remain relatively weak. The ratios of merchandise trade to GDP and foreign direct investment (FDI) to GDP in the region are well below those of competitor countries. From 1990 to 2014, the region's FDI inflows were, on average, between 2.2 and 2.8 percentage points of GDP below that of countries in East Asia. Moreover, countries in South Asia receive little FDI from within the region. Trade integration is also low. From 1990 to 2014, South Asia's average ratio of exports to GDP varied from 17 to 21 percentage points below that of East Asia, and the average ratio of imports to GDP was 21 to 22 percentage points lower.

The region has also made little progress in diversifying its exports and moving up the value chain. Although South Asia has had some success in penetrating new markets, almost 80 percent of the region's export growth from 2001 to 2013 came from sales of the same goods to the same destinations, and the remaining 20 percent came from selling the same products in new markets. Exports remain highly concentrated in textiles and apparel in Afghanistan, Bangladesh, Nepal, Pakistan, and Sri Lanka; in minerals in Bhutan; and in animal and vegetable products in Afghanistan and Maldives. Overall, the region's export basket does not reflect a substantial transformation of production structures or innovative activities. Although the sophistication of exports has increased in India, it has remained low in the rest of South Asia; and quality (as measured by the prices its products fetch in international markets) has generally remained low and has declined for some countries.

Meanwhile, the global environment is becoming tougher. The demand for developing countries' exports has been limited by the slow recovery in the industrial economies and by the effect of the decline in commodity prices on resource-rich economies, while the benefits to many commodity importers have been eroded by declining remittances. New megaregional trade agreements, such as the Trans-Pacific Partnership (TPP) and the Trans-Atlantic Trade and Investment Partnership (TTIP), may divert trade and investment away from nonmembers. Against this background, it has become even more urgent for countries in South Asia to make overdue investments in boosting competitiveness to avoid falling further behind comparator countries in the global marketplace.

Productivity is the key to improved competitiveness

What lies behind South Asia's subdued competitiveness, and what strategies can help the region become more competitive? Porter (1990) has argued that different countries have become competitive with different mixes of endowments, factor prices, and policies. Although competitiveness can be buttressed in the short term by keeping costs low, the only sustainable path to improved competitiveness in the long term is increased productivity. Yet South Asia's growth over the past two decades seems to have been driven mostly by an accumulation of factor quantities rather than by improvements in their quality, efficiency, or productivity. Accelerating productivity growth should be at the top of policy makers' agendas in the region to ensure continued and sustained progress on job creation, growth, poverty reduction, and shared prosperity.

Across the globe, one mechanism for long-term improvement in productivity has been the movement of resources from agriculture to higher-productivity manufacturing and services. Between 1960 and 2013, the share of agriculture in South Asia's GDP decreased from 44 percent to 19 percent, while the share of industry rose from 18 percent to 29 percent. Similar to patterns observed in high-income economies, labor productivity differentials between agriculture and more modern activities play an important role in explaining the movement of labor across sectors, with the sensitivity of labor movement to productivity much higher in South Asia than in high-income economies. However, the movement of labor from agriculture to industry and services in South Asia has not been rapid enough to substantially reduce the large differences in productivity across sectors. In other words, the region has significant untapped potential, compared to the economies of the Organisation for Economic Co-operation and Development (OECD) for example, to reap productivity gains by a further reallocation of labor from lower- to higher-productivity activities.

Another important mechanism for productivity growth operates within sectors through the movement of resources from less-productive to more-productive firms. In South Asia, the high dispersion of productivity levels across firms and a strong bias of firm distribution toward small, inefficient, and slow-growing firms indicate that this mechanism has a strong potential to increase efficiency. Firms aged 25 years or more in Bangladesh, Bhutan, India, and Sri Lanka are only 50 percent to 90 percent larger than start-ups, while in China, Indonesia, and Vietnam similar firms are two to five times larger. According to some estimates, if the distortions that prevent the reallocation of resources to more-productive firms in India were reduced to the levels observed in the United States, productivity might increase as much as 60 percent.

Barriers to the growth of firms can also be found in government policy. Across the region, licensing and size restrictions (which have declined in importance but still exist), labor regulations that increase the cost of hiring and firing, financial sector regulations that favor small enterprises, and inadequate bankruptcy laws may have limited the ability of efficient plants to grow and enabled inefficient plants to survive. Taxes or labor costs that affect larger firms more than smaller firms may reduce the return on investment in large firms. Impediments to reaching foreign markets, whether from trade policy or the high cost of logistics, can also impede expansion.

The drivers of and constraints on productivity growth were analyzed in four case studies of critical industries—agribusiness, electronics, apparel, and automotive. These case studies show the links between the external environment of firms and their behavior within a well-defined industry in which industry dynamics (such as competition) can be analyzed and performance benchmarked. As such, they are of great help in understanding the relative importance of the external factors that drive or constrain a firm's performance and productivity. Also, and crucially, industry case studies assess industry-specific factors and policies that traditional cross-cutting analysis is ill-equipped to identify.

Business environment challenges remain a constraint on firm performance

On average, countries in South Asia score poorly on major indexes used globally to capture key aspects of competitiveness, such as the Global Competitiveness Index (GCI) published by the World Economic Forum and the World Bank's *Doing Business* report. In the most recent GCI rankings (2015–16), India is the only South Asian country in the top half of nearly 140 countries. In the World Bank's 2016 *Doing Business* report, all the South Asian economies, with the exception of Bhutan, are ranked in the bottom half. Ten years ago, a World Bank Investment Climate Assessment argued that South Asian countries underperform comparator countries on many investment-climate measures, including infrastructure and electricity supply, access to finance, employee skills, and corruption. Similar results emerge from the most recent round of Enterprise Surveys, in which an average firm in South Asia consistently ranks investment-climate constraints as more binding than does an average firm in China or Vietnam. Although performance varies substantially across countries and indicators—pointing to significant potential for improvement by leveraging best practices within the region—the overall gap puts South Asia's firms at a clear disadvantage compared to similar firms in other parts of the world. These challenges may be particularly daunting for the region's high potential firms, which would otherwise grow more rapidly and create more jobs.

The agribusiness case study shows that business environment issues (such as trade barriers, and restrictions on agricultural markets, products, and prices as well as blanket subsidies) remain the main impediments to the inclusive and sustainable development of the sector.

Growth of the region's cities and clusters offers multiple opportunities to raise firm productivity

Economic activity in South Asia is highly concentrated. In most countries a small number of districts account for a large share of economic activity. In India, for example, the five largest districts account for 18 percent of total employment. However, the degree of geographic concentration of manufacturing in South Asia has not changed substantially in the last two decades: the share of total employment held by the top five districts has remained relatively constant, while which districts are in the top five has changed. This indicates that more-productive locations have generally not been successful in attracting additional resources at the expense of less-productive locations, although congestion in the major economic centers has not reached sufficiently high levels to push a substantial share of economic activity out to the periphery. In the three South Asian countries with adequate data, district or state borders tend to be "thick"—impediments to efficient allocation of resources among districts are stronger than those within districts.

Agglomeration economies—the benefits that accrue to firms and workers from locating close together in cities or clusters—matter for firm productivity: a 10 percent increase in district employment leads to a 0.2 to 0.9 percent increase in the total factor productivity (TFP) of the district's firms. The effect operates primarily through two channels: localization (firms in the same industry locate close together to benefit from a specialized labor pool) and urbanization (firms from different industries locate close together to benefit from a diverse supplier network, common infrastructure, or large number of workers). Unlike in high-income countries, firms in South Asia appear to benefit relatively more from a wide diversity of workers available in a single location (urbanization economies) rather than a concentration of highly specialized workers (localization economies). These results suggest that cities, with diverse labor pools catering to a range of industries, may currently be more effective vehicles of supporting firm productivity in South Asia than clusters, which cater to a specific sector, although the two are not mutually exclusive. For example, a number of top firms in South Asia's automotive sector fostered innovation by locating near their customers, enabling their engineers to work with those of their clients and gradually building their capacity from simpler to more complex components.

The electronics case study shows that South Asia needs urban areas that provide thick markets for skilled labor, large tracts of industrial land, and world-class logistics to become competitive.

Increasing prominence of global value chains provides a pathway to greater efficiency

Participation in global value chains (GVCs) and exposure to international markets more generally are associated with higher levels of firm productivity in South Asia. Access to foreign markets, either through trade or the licensing of foreign technology, brings stronger outcomes for adoption of information and communication technology (ICT) and innovation, and these in turn have a robust positive relationship with firm-level productivity. Greater exposure to international trade makes firms more viable participants in GVCs, which in turn can further enhance productivity in a virtuous cycle. For example, a number of South Asia's leading firms in the automotive sector learned by becoming domestic suppliers to multinationals entering the region and then leveraged that experience to access international markets on their own. Although it is also true that more-productive firms may elect to join GVCs, evidence suggests that GVC participation and deeper global integration more generally have positive productivity effects on firms.

With more than 20 percent of its exports coming from GVC products, South Asia has the second-highest rate of GVC participation among developing regions. This ranking largely reflects, however, the region's strong performance in apparel. Bangladesh has one of the highest GVC participation rates in the world precisely because it exports little besides garments. India's participation in GVCs is low because it has a more diversified range of exports. In addition, the location along the value chain of each country's firms varies substantially: firms in Pakistan tend to be more upstream, while Sri Lankan and Bangladeshi firms are much further downstream. Final apparel producers in Sri Lanka and Pakistan have been more successful at penetrating higher-income markets than firms in Bangladesh and India, while firms in Pakistan and Bangladesh have shown a greater ability to penetrate high-income markets in intermediate apparel. Overall market sophistication declined, however, between 2000 and 2010 in all four countries, either because of increased sales to middle-income markets or because of more intense competition in high-income markets, or both.

Value chains tend to cluster regionally because of transport and other transaction costs and the need for timely delivery. Bangladesh and Sri Lanka have the highest shares of final apparel goods (86 percent and 44 percent of apparel exports, respectively) in the region and source many apparel inputs from Pakistan and India, which focus relatively less on final products (18 percent and 6 percent of apparel exports, respectively). In 2013, two-thirds of India's exports of knit and crochet fabric were destined for Sri Lanka and Bangladesh, while nearly half of

Pakistan's exports of woven cotton denim were destined for Bangladesh and Sri Lanka. An East Asia–South Asia regional value chain is also emerging, especially in intermediate apparel: 70 percent and 24 percent of South Asia's imported apparel inputs come from East Asia and South Asia, respectively. South Asian GVC activity is more integrated with East Asia than is that of any other region in the world, except East Asia itself.

Despite the importance of GVCs for firm productivity and overall export growth, South Asia lags on many capabilities that matter for GVC participation. Countries in South Asia are, on average, more wage competitive and closer to markets than are members of the Association of Southeast Asian Nations (ASEAN) or members of the Southern Africa Customs Union (SACU), but compare unfavorably with them on policy variables such as human capital, institutions, logistics, and trade barriers on imports of intermediate inputs. Bangladesh, Maldives, and Pakistan charge high tariffs on intermediate apparel goods, and all countries except Sri Lanka impose high tariffs on finished automobiles. Nontariff barriers are also pervasive, particularly in the automotive sector in Pakistan. Trade facilitation could be substantially improved; the ability to access imported inputs in a timely manner is particularly important for sectors in which South Asia has already developed an advantage (apparel in particular) as well as sectors of emerging opportunity (such as electronics). Restrictive product market regulations—such as limits on storage, processing, and marketing of agricultural produce, price caps and minimum support prices on key agricultural commodities, fragmented approaches to food safety standards and their poor enforcement, and gaps in harmonization of local norms with international automotive standards—inhibit South Asia's ability to increase its participation in GVCs in the agribusiness and automotive sectors.

The apparel case study shows how import barriers affect exporters and prevent the region from realizing its great potential.

Improving firm capability and leveraging technology can substantially raise firm productivity

With the exception of a few global leaders, firm capabilities in the region tend to be limited. On average, South Asia's firms overemploy relatively scarce capital and underemploy abundant labor. Given the prevailing wage rates and marginal products of workers, the optimum level of labor use in Indian and Sri Lankan firms is 1.7 and 2.2 times current employment levels, respectively, while estimates for Nepal and Pakistan suggest underuse on the order of 14 to 16 times the existing workforce. Thus, most firms in South Asia do not operate close to optimum efficiency, given the prevailing factor prices, bringing down aggregate productivity. Potential reasons for this less-than-rational behavior include limited managerial capacity, labor market rigidities (particularly with regard to firing workers), and spatial distortions that prevent firms from locating close to a ready supply of workers or vice versa.

Although the region's top firms make investment in creating knowledge and providing skills and training to their workforces a priority, on average firms in South Asia underinvest in knowledge. Overall public and private investment in R&D in the region is low and is increasingly falling behind Latin America and the Caribbean and East Asia. Investment in R&D within the region varies greatly, with a higher incidence of firms conducting R&D in Bangladesh and India (above the rates observed in Africa and Eastern Europe and Central Asia) and a much lower incidence in Nepal and Pakistan (below the rates of Africa and Eastern Europe and Central Asia). In general, larger firms are more likely to engage in R&D activities. With the exception of Bangladesh, access to licenses to use foreign technology increases R&D, while financial constraints significantly inhibit R&D investment.

Adoption rates of ICT also vary across the region. Indian firms score very high on multiple dimensions of technology use: nearly 100 percent of registered firms have computers and an Internet connection, which corresponds with the average for OECD countries. ICT use in Pakistan is consistent with that of global peers but is very low in Bangladesh and Nepal. Despite widespread Internet use, however, the adoption of e-commerce and other online business tools is limited, with the difference particularly stark in India. Size, export status, and, to a lesser extent, import status are important determinants of ICT adoption at the firm level. Complementary factors—technology and skills—are also important determinants of ICT adoption. Last, access to finance and to financial institutions is critical to the adoption of e-commerce. The region's moderate achievements on many of these dimensions may explain the limited penetration of some technologies and hint at missed opportunities to improve productivity performance.

Patterns of investment in innovation inputs, including ICT, managerial practices, and R&D, are reflected in innovation outputs. Within the region, close to 80 percent of firms in Bangladesh and India engage in technological innovation, well above the average in Eastern Europe and Africa. On the other hand, only about 20 percent of firms in Nepal and Pakistan invest in new products or processes. Moreover, the acquisition of knowledge capital (such as R&D, investments in equipment, and training) is highly concentrated in a few firms, and mature, exporting, and foreign-owned firms tend to be the most innovative. Compared to other regions, a much larger share of innovation in South Asia takes place in-house, limiting productive collaboration across firms and possibly explaining higher rates of imitation instead of radical innovation.

Returns to innovation in Bangladesh, India, and Nepal are positive and statistically significant. A 1 percent increase in innovation intensity increases firm productivity by 0.6 to 1.4 percent, an impact that is two to five times stronger than the magnitudes commonly estimated for OECD countries. Even among the leaders, however, most innovation consists of the imitation of existing products or processes. Few firms engage in disruptive innovative activities such as introducing new products to the country or to the world. Most of the firms in the region tend to innovate to upgrade the quality of their products, although the introduction of new products is slightly more frequent in India. And most innovation is done in-house (more so than in Africa or Eastern Europe and Central Asia), which may limit the potential for new products.

The automotive case study shows how protections from global good practices (high import tariffs and obsolete safety and emission standards) limit the spread of world-class firm capabilities.

Faster growth of exports and jobs is within reach if productivity improves

South Asia has tremendous potential to increase incomes and gain market share in exports through policies that enhance productivity. In a scenario under which productivity growth contributes about 2 percentage points per year to increases in regional GDP (consistent with South Asia's best historical performance), South Asia becomes the world's fastest-growing region for exports. By 2030, it could more than triple its share of global exports of electronics and motor vehicles, and come close to doubling its already significant market share in apparel. Further investments in port infrastructure, improvements in customs processes, and behind-the-border services (such as warehousing and transportation); more rapid implementation of improvements in port-to-port trade and transportation costs; and a reduction in the domestic cost of trade could boost export growth by more than 1 percentage point per year over the projected baseline and lead to additional unskilled wage gains of as much as 17 percent.

Turning to job creation, the report examines the intensely competitive apparel market. Productivity-enhancing measures that produce a 10 percent cost advantage over Chinese apparel could lead to a 13 percent to 25 percent rise in South Asian countries'

apparel exports to the United States. Given the high labor intensity of apparel manufacturing and the large sensitivity of South Asia's labor supply, especially women, to higher wages, a 10 percent price advantage over China in the U.S. market could translate into employment gains of 8.9 percent in Pakistan—by far the biggest winner—followed by Bangladesh (4.2 percent) and India (3.3 percent). These would be well-paying jobs: the wage premium of the apparel sector over agriculture ranges from 8 percent to 27 percent, depending on the country, and is even higher for women. Moreover, jobs created in textiles and apparel are particularly likely to attract low-skilled women. These results not only point to the critical importance of implementing productivity-enhancing measures in the apparel sector but also caution that inaction may lead to a decline in market share. Competitors that have pursued more aggressive apparel-friendly policies (such as Vietnam and Cambodia) can stand to gain much more than the South Asian countries in market access. The prospect of new megaregional trade agreements, such as TPP and TTIP, for which South Asian countries have thus far remained on the sidelines, giving an additional boost to the region's main competitors further underscores the urgency of reform.

Policies to boost competitiveness and productivity

In order to realize these gains and more, the region's policy makers should reexamine their policies and priorities for competitiveness and productivity. This report highlights not only policies to improve South Asia's investment climate but also three policy areas that have so far been less prominent in discussions of competitiveness and productivity but that—as shown by the empirical results and the industry case studies—have the potential to raise productivity across the region. These include policies to maximize the benefits of agglomeration economies, better connect to GVCs, and boost firm capabilities. In the critical case of the agribusiness value chains (which constitute one-third of South Asia's GDP), additional policy areas include the need to reform agricultural markets, price regulations, product standards, and blanket subsidies.

Deriving the maximum productivity benefits from South Asia's rapid urbanization requires policies that leverage agglomeration economies while minimizing the adverse impacts of congestion. The removal of policy-induced distortions that limit the flexibility of labor, capital, and land markets could enable firms that are more productive to grow. In particular, policies to increase the flexibility of labor markets, especially for women (who face particularly high discrimination in South Asia's labor markets) are likely to substantially reduce the misallocation of labor and improve productivity. Policies directed at improving urban governance and bridging the region's infrastructure gap will ensure that firms and workers are matched more easily. Achieving these goals will require tackling congestion issues head-on. In particular, investments in roads and public transit, provision of quality affordable housing and other basic infrastructure services, and reducing the negative social impact of agglomeration (such as crime) should be high on the policy makers' agenda.

When large-scale solutions are difficult or costly, improved infrastructure could be delivered through industrial zones or clusters. Although a number of traditional approaches to industrial zones in South Asia have not delivered the expected benefits, there are encouraging examples of new approaches from within and outside the region, such as India's Scheme for Integrated Textile Parks and China's plug-and-play industrial zones. The location of a cluster often makes all the difference, and countries in the region could make further efforts to identify and develop industrial areas close to ports, resolve pending issues in existing industrial zones, and ensure provisions for worker housing. Providing access to R&D and testing facilities, waste dumping, and recycling facilities would make these zones more attractive to small and medium enterprises.

Strengthening the participation of the region's firms in GVCs calls for taking the specific steps that matter most to global buyers as well as making broad-based investments in GVC capabilities. The former include improving fundamentals such as cost, quality, and lead times, particularly relevant to the shift toward lean retailing and just-in-time delivery in many industries. However, other factors are also growing in importance. Buyers who attempt to reduce the complexity of their supply chains increasingly value sellers who offer accompanying services such as input sourcing, product development, and financing (known as full package services). Buyers also take into account social and (to a lesser extent) environmental compliance, which has become more important to their bottom lines because of pressure from corporate social responsibility campaigns by nongovernmental organizations, compliance-conscious consumers, and, more recently, the increase of accidents in apparel factories.

Improving broader-based GVC capabilities requires policy actions such as facilitating imports for use by exporters (for example, through better-functioning duty drawback schemes); reducing average rates of protection and harmonizing tariff schedules across intermediate and final goods; improving standards and product market regulations; and strengthening trade logistics to reduce customs clearance and transit times—all areas where the region falls short of its Southeast Asian competitors and global benchmarks. At the firm level, improving firm capabilities to adopt new technology (including better managerial practices) and to innovate will be critical to accelerating the introduction of new products, improving product quality, and moving into higher value segments within existing or new GVCs.

For innovation, managerial capabilities, technology adoption, and worker skills, the report's findings suggest different priorities across the region. In Nepal and Bangladesh, the focus should be on efforts to foster the adoption of the Internet and computers, which will require overcoming infrastructure challenges as well as improving the provision of complementary skills such as technological training and human capital. In India, where the use of ICT is already widespread, the focus should be on improving ICT practices, particularly in e-commerce and other online business tools. India has a large software development industry and a relatively high number of information technology engineers; access to finance and the establishment of broad-based financial transaction platforms online could be critical to increasing the use of the Internet for commercialization.

A possible explanation for South Asia's growing gap in R&D investments compared to other regions is low returns to R&D in the absence of complementary factors: managerial capabilities, worker skills, and finance. Therefore, investing in these should be a policy priority throughout the region. Modernizing training institutions and expanding access to on-the-job training can lead to higher efficiency and lower costs, and

programs that support improving firm capabilities through technology extension, managerial training, and access to consulting services, networking, and information can have large and long-lasting productivity benefits. In addition, countries with higher innovation rates in the region should focus on breaking the pattern of inward innovation development by supporting cooperation among firms and institutions to generate novel and, if possible, radical innovations. For countries with lower innovation rates, policy should focus on increasing the number of firms engaged in incremental innovation in order to boost productivity, profits, survival rates, and sales growth.

Reference

Porter, M. 1990. "The Competitive Advantage of Nations." *Harvard Business Review* 68 (2): 73–93.

South Asia's Competitiveness Challenge and Opportunity

The Region's Competitiveness Potential Remains Largely Unrealized | 1

Which region will become the next global factory? As the workforce ages and labor costs rise in China and other East Asian countries, many eyes turn to South Asia. South Asia is still largely rural—agriculture accounts for a large share of employment and a substantial fraction of gross domestic product (GDP)—and it has not been particularly successful in integrating economically within itself or with the rest of the world. Yet more than one million young workers enter the labor market each month, and by 2030, 26 percent of the world's working adults will live in South Asia. This is the region's greatest opportunity and greatest challenge.

In the meantime, the global environment is becoming tougher. The commodity boom is over, putting the brakes on demand and tightening fiscal belts in resource-rich countries. Although commodity importers benefit from improved terms of trade, many also receive reduced remittances, limiting the benefits to the current account. Slowing global growth and an even more pronounced slowdown in global trade make it more challenging for firms to enter and expand in export markets. New megaregional trade agreements (such as the Trans-Pacific Partnership (TPP) and the Trans-Atlantic Trade and Investment Partnership (TTIP)) promise welfare gains to members but may divert trade and investment from nonmembers. Against this background, it has become even more urgent for countries in South Asia to make overdue investments in boosting competitiveness and raising productivity to avoid falling further behind comparator countries in the global marketplace.

There are many examples of excellence in the region. Exports of goods and services are higher, relative to GDP, than in China. At the sectoral level, the software industry in India, the garment sector in Bangladesh and Sri Lanka, and the Sialkot cluster in Pakistan are global success stories. And at the firm level, there is no shortage of global champions (for example, US Apparel, Orient Craft, Pacific Jeans, and MAS in apparel; Tata Motors, Bharat Forge, and Hi-Tech Gear Ltd. in the automotive sector; Fauji Foundation, Dilmah, and KRBL Ltd. in agribusiness; and Dixon Technologies and Micromax in electronics). Yet so far the region as a whole has made relatively little progress in integrating economically within itself or with the rest of the world, diversifying and increasing the sophistication of its exports, moving up the quality ladder, and improving its ranking on many competitiveness benchmarks. It has yet to realize the substantial benefits of economic integration and achieve its full potential—both relative to its endowments and its global competitors—while the window of opportunity may not remain open for long. The following discussion develops this observation in more detail.

Pockets of excellence are evidence of vast untapped potential

South Asia, and India in particular, is already well known for having achieved excellence and preeminence in the information and communication technology (ICT) industry. Less well known is that South Asian countries, locations, and firms have become major players in important manufacturing industries. These successes include:

- The apparel industries in Sri Lanka and Bangladesh, which are as big (on a per capita basis) as those in China and Vietnam;
- The light manufacturing cluster in Sialkot, Pakistan, which, despite all odds, has achieved a dominant global market share in products such as soccer balls and surgical instruments;
- Indian auto-parts firms, which are becoming global players through exports to and acquisitions of firms in leading markets such as Germany;
- Global electronics and auto-parts firms that have established their global research and development (R&D) centers in India; and
- Leading agribusiness firms developing, in partnership with governments, new crop varieties for the domestic and international markets (such as tea in Sri Lanka and rice and mint oil in India).

These cases were selected for the in-depth case studies in this report to analyze the drivers of competitiveness as well as the constraints that limit the competitiveness of firms, locations, industries, and countries at a time when South Asia is uniquely positioned to take advantage of rising production costs in East Asia.

Difficulties in attracting investment and penetrating global markets

Trade and investment integration can increase productivity. Opening up local markets to foreign trade and investment increases competition, which encourages labor and capital to move from less-productive to more-productive firms (Melitz 2003). Further, increased competition may induce firms to improve their efficiency (Helpman and Krugman 1985), to focus on their core competencies (Bernard, Redding, and Schott 2011) and reduce managerial slack (Hicks 1935), or to invest in new technology (Aghion et al. 2005). Finally, openness facilitates access to better inputs and technology (Atkin, Khandelwal, and Osman 2016), particularly important for those developing countries whose import substitution policies previously reduced firms' ability to purchase imported inputs.

Despite the well-known benefits of economic integration, South Asia's intraregional and global ties are relatively weak. Foreign direct investment (FDI), for example, is low (figure 1.1). Over the period 1990 through 2014, the region's FDI inflows were, on average, between 2.2 and 2.8 percentage points of GDP below that of countries in East Asia (see tables 1A.1 and 1A.2). Particularly in the latter part of this period (2011–14), as panel b of figure 1.1 shows, FDI inflows in all countries (except Maldives) were substantially below the average of countries at similar levels of development.

The flow of intraregional investment in South Asia shows the lack of regional investment integration. Globally, South–South cross-border investment has increased, and a recent market survey showed that multinationals in other regions allocate a significant share of outward investment to countries within their region. By contrast, countries in South Asia receive little FDI from within the region. In particular, despite the lower transaction costs of investing in nearby, familiar markets, Indian multinationals tend to invest outside the region (Gomez-Mera et al. 2015).

Some of the blame for low FDI inflows can be traced to burdensome regulations

FIGURE 1.1   Countries in South Asia attract less foreign direct investment than global peers

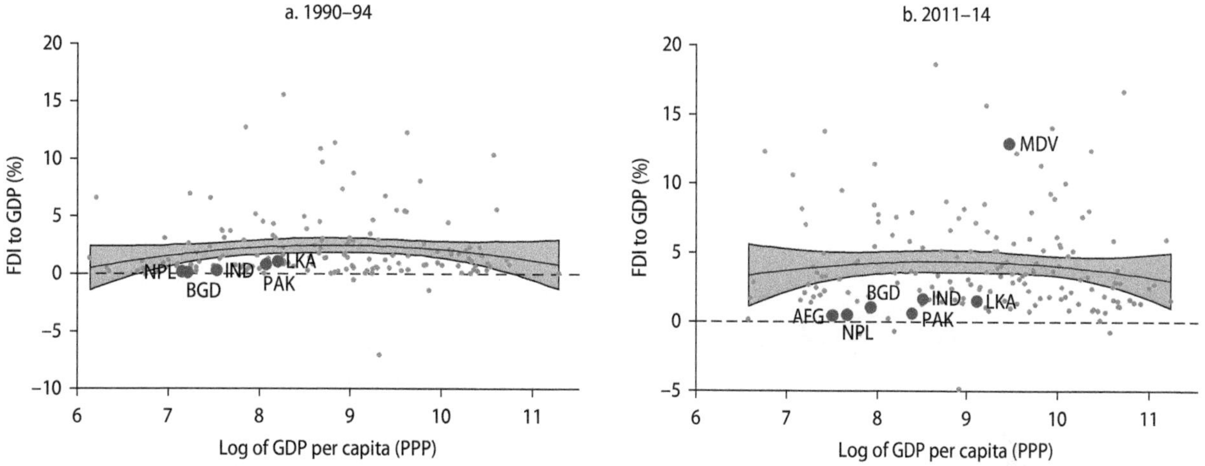

a. 1990–94

b. 2011–14

Source: World Bank calculations based on World Development Indicators database.
Note: FDI = foreign direct investment; PPP = purchasing power parity. Shaded area corresponds to the 95 percent confidence interval.

governing FDI. Nepal, for example, has failed to attract substantial FDI because of the complicated process required to repatriate profits, high entry barriers (with a long negative list), and insufficient guarantees of investor protection. The lack of readily available land with adequate access to infrastructure services has constrained foreign investment, particularly in Bangladesh. For example, in 2011, Samsung's large intended investment in electronics in Bangladesh fell through because adequate land was not available in an export processing zone. By contrast, Indian states compete for investment by major original equipment manufacturers (OEMs) by offering land combined with tax incentives, although there is some risk that such competition will lead to suboptimal investment locations and industry fragmentation.

Trade integration is also low. As shown in figure 1.2, from 1990 through 2014, South Asia's average ratio of exports to GDP varied between 17 and 21 percentage points below that of East Asia, and the average ratio of imports to GDP was 21 to 22 percentage points lower than the countries of East Asia and the Pacific Region (Maldives, with a

highly developed tourism export sector, being again the exception).[1] Countries in the region have become more integrated in the global marketplace, however: the region's share of merchandise trade increased from $1.15 of every $100 traded globally in 2000–04 to $1.82 in 2014, an increase of nearly 60 percent. Nevertheless, growth in the region has been more inward-oriented than that in East Asia.

South Asian countries can be divided into two groups by their performance in merchandise exports. Although exports increased at double-digit rates from 2000 through 2013 in Afghanistan, Bangladesh, Bhutan, and India (15, 13, 16, and 14 percent per year, respectively), growth was slower in Maldives, Pakistan, and Sri Lanka (2, 8, and 5 percent per year, respectively) and exports fell 1 percent per year in Nepal (see table 1.1). Regardless of whether countries belong to slow- or fast-growing groups, however, their share of the global merchandise export market remains small. For example, India, with an 80 percent increase in its market share in the past decade and a half, has just reached 1.5 percent of the global exports market. Bangladesh, with somewhat slower growth of

FIGURE 1.2   South Asia's trade integration is relatively low

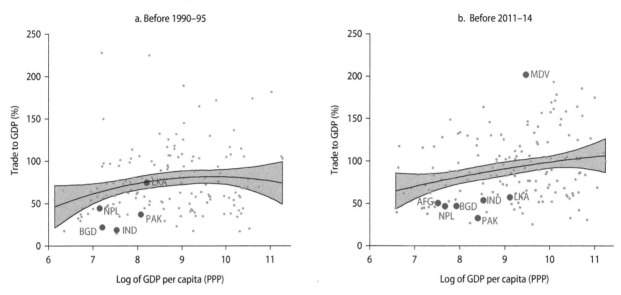

Source: World Bank calculations based on World Development Indicators database.
Note: PPP = purchasing power parity. Shaded area corresponds to the 95 percent confidence interval.

TABLE 1.1   Despite rapid growth, South Asia's share of global merchandise exports remains low

	Afghanistan	Bangladesh	Bhutan	India	Maldives	Nepal	Pakistan	Sri Lanka	South Asia
2000–04	0.002	0.107	0.001	0.814	0.003	0.010	0.139	0.074	1.149
2010–14	0.004	0.162	0.001	1.463	0.001	0.004	0.135	0.057	1.827
Absolute growth	0.002	0.055	0.001	0.649	−0.002	−0.005	−0.005	−0.017	0.678
Percent growth	121	52	112	80	−61	−54	−3	−23	59

Source: World Bank calculations based on UN COMTRADE database.
Note: Cell values in the first two rows indicate each country's share in global merchandise exports, expressed in percentage points. Cell values in the third row indicate the absolute change in market share, expressed in percentage points (difference between the first two rows). Cell values in the fourth row indicate the percent change in market share.

50 percent in its market share, has passed Pakistan to become the second-largest merchandise exporter in South Asia, with nearly 0.2 percent of the global merchandise market. Afghanistan and Bhutan more than doubled their global market share in the past decade and a half, but still account for less than 0.01 percent of the world market, combined.

The textiles and apparel sector is one exception to this general trend (figure 1.3). South Asia's share of global exports in garments rose from 7.4 percent in 2000–04 to 11.6 percent in 2010–14. More than half of that increase is accounted for by Bangladesh (due in particular to effective import facilities for exporters), about 40 percent by India, and the remainder by Pakistan. Gains in market share in other sectors are almost all below

1 percentage point and almost fully explained by increased exports from India.

In services, the region has recorded much better performance. Overall, South Asia's share of global services exports rose from 0.9 percent in the early 1990s to 3.6 percent in the early 2010s. Every country in the region except Nepal increased its share of global services exports; India and, at a substantially lower scale, Maldives more than doubled their shares of services exports (table 1.2).

Limited trade integration results from high trade costs. For example, Nepal charges high tariffs on yarn, a key input for most of its apparel exports. In India, high tariffs on inputs particularly affect the electronics sector, while tariffs on manmade fibers (combined with the problem of duty drawback

FIGURE 1.3   Outside of garments, South Asia's market share growth has been low

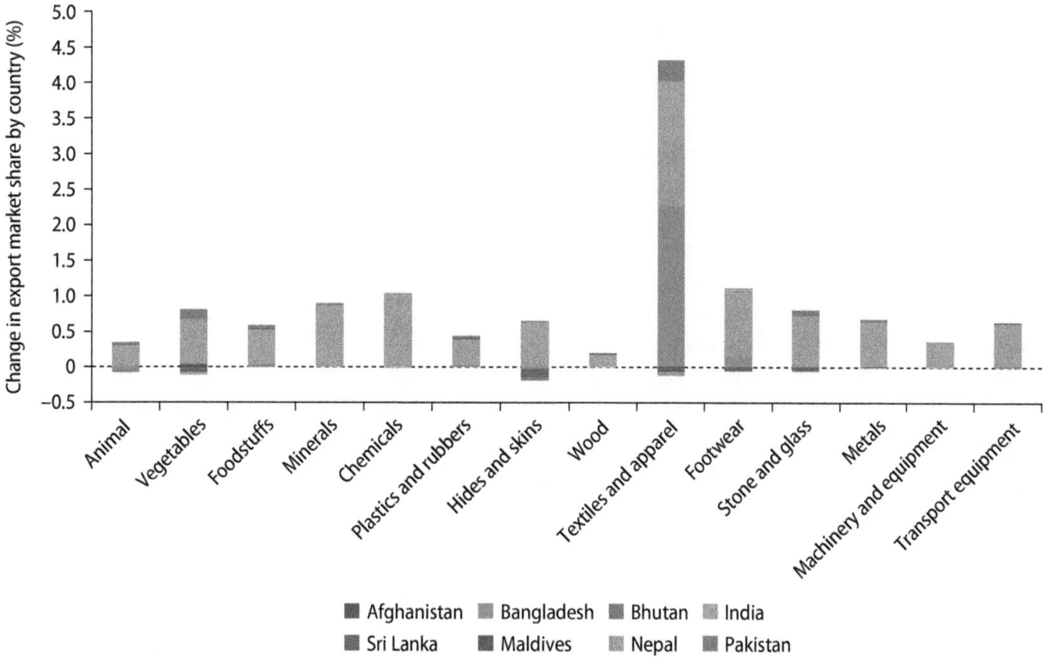

Source: World Bank calculations based on UN COMTRADE database.

TABLE 1.2   South Asia has more than tripled its market share in services since the 1990s

	Afghanistan	Bangladesh	India	Maldives	Nepal	Pakistan	Sri Lanka	South Asia
1990–94	—	0.05	0.54	0.01	0.03	0.17	0.06	0.87
2000–04	—	0.05	1.27	0.02	0.02	0.12	0.07	1.56
2010–13	0.08	0.06	3.16	0.05	0.02	0.13	0.08	3.58
Absolute growth	—	0.01	1.89	0.02	0.00	0.01	0.01	2.02
Percent growth	—	26	149	107	−13	10	8	129

Source: UN COMTRADE database.
Note: — = Not available. Cell values in the first three rows indicate each country's share in global merchandise exports, expressed in percentage points. Cell values in the fourth row indicate the absolute change in market share, expressed in percentage points (difference between rows 1 and 3). Cell values in the fifth row indicate the percent change in market share.

schemes for exporters) limit exporters largely to garments made of domestic cotton. Cotton is grown and harvested predominantly during the summer, which reduces capacity utilization. In addition to high tariff rates, South Asian countries impose high paratariffs, an extra tax on imported products that is typically complicated, subject to arbitrary enforcement, and applied irrespective of trade preferences. The addition of paratariffs brings the average import tax rates in Bangladesh and Sri Lanka to a level more than double that of the customs duty alone (Kathuria,

Portugal, and Shahid 2015). In Bangladesh, tariffs have declined and paratariffs have increased, making the latter the more important constraint on imports (Kathuria and Malouche 2016). In contrast, Sri Lanka's garment exporters have benefited greatly from zero tariffs on textile imports. In the services trades, Bangladesh, India, Nepal, and Sri Lanka are substantially more restrictive than high-income economies, and even China, according to the World Bank's Services Trade Restrictiveness Index,[2] although Pakistan's service restrictiveness is relatively low.

Steps already taken to reduce barriers to trade and investment in the region have paid substantial productivity dividends and hint at potential future benefits from further policy efforts to improve integration. In India, for example, the reduction in tariffs on auto parts and electronics greatly increased competition in the domestic market, raising standards among firms and enabling them to increase productivity further by working with demanding clients. More broadly, the sharp fall in the level and dispersion of tariffs in response to the 1991 balance of payments crisis induced firms to improve their efficiency and improved their access to imported inputs (Topalova and Khandelwal 2011).[3] The productivity benefits of reform were smallest in sectors in which burdensome regulations limited firms' ability to adopt new technologies,[4] greater for domestic than foreign firms (probably because foreign firms had already been exposed to competition), and largest in industries that also experienced the most deregulation and FDI liberalization. About a third of the rise in firms' product diversification was caused by increased access to better quality and a higher variety of imported intermediate inputs (Goldberg et al. 2010). Improved services policies after 1991 also boosted Indian firms' productivity. Policy changes that facilitated the operations of foreign services firms—particularly in banking, telecommunications, insurance, and transport—increased the productivity of foreign and local manufacturing firms that used those services (Arnold et al. 2015).

Little progress in diversifying the merchandise export basket

The composition of the export basket from South Asian countries has changed little in 15 years, which shows limited product innovation. Exports remain highly concentrated in textiles and apparel in Afghanistan, Bangladesh, Nepal, Pakistan, and Sri Lanka; in minerals in Bhutan; and in animal and vegetable products in Afghanistan and Maldives. Almost 80 percent of the region's export growth from 2001 to 2013 came from the intensive margin: sale of the same set of goods to the same destinations (figure 1.4, panel a). The remaining 20 percent came from the extensive margin, but almost entirely

FIGURE 1.4   Most export growth in South Asia has taken place along the intensive margin

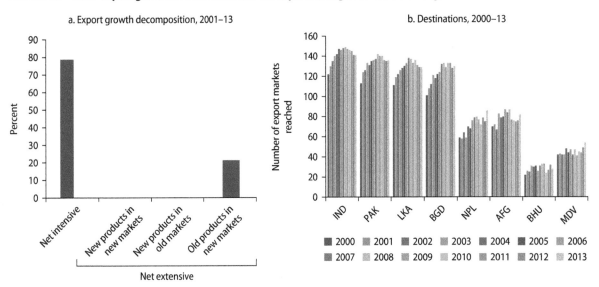

(continues next page)

FIGURE 1.4 **Most export growth in South Asia has taken place along the intensive margin** (continued)

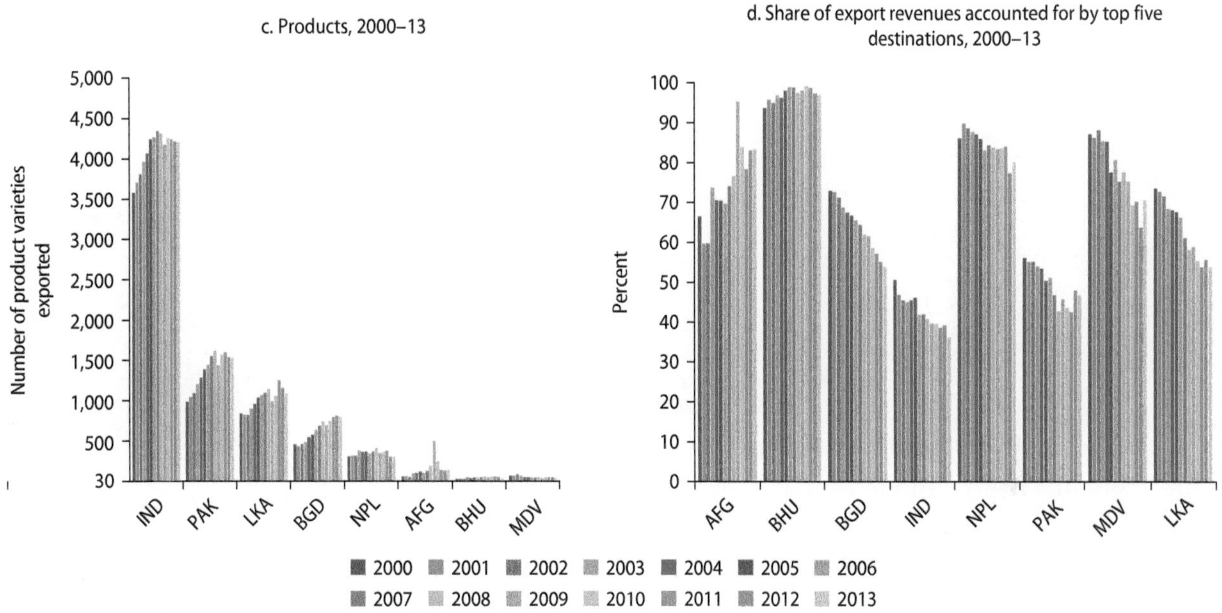

c. Products, 2000–13

d. Share of export revenues accounted for by top five destinations, 2000–13

| 2000 | 2001 | 2002 | 2003 | 2004 | 2005 | 2006 |
| 2007 | 2008 | 2009 | 2010 | 2011 | 2012 | 2013 |

Source: World Bank calculations based on UN COMTRADE database.

by selling the same set of goods to new markets. Although the number of product varieties exported increased in all countries except Nepal (figure 1.4, panel c), diversification into new products (either in old or new markets) accounted, on average, for only 0.07 percent of export growth. In some countries, most exports go to only a few destinations. For example, the top five export destinations account for 97 percent and 70 percent of export revenues in Bhutan and Maldives, respectively (figure 1.4, panel d). In contrast, India's top five markets purchase only 36 percent of the country's exports (figure 1.4 panel d).

Elusive sophistication and low quality of exports

On average, the sophistication of merchandise exports from South Asia (as measured by the Export Sophistication Index [EXPY] indicator) is higher than expected given the region's income level.[5] With the exception of India, however, countries in the region have not been successful in further increasing export sophistication. Although India

leapfrogged both Vietnam and Indonesia on this metric between 2000 and 2014, sophistication did not increase in Bangladesh and Sri Lanka, rose steadily but from a low level in Pakistan, and declined in Bhutan (figure 1.5, panel a). Even in India, one measure of export quality and sophistication, PRODY,[6] has remained low. A recent International Monetary Fund (IMF) study finds that the average level of sophistication for India's manufacturing exports is lower than that of the rest of Asia, in sharp contrast to India's performance in the services sector (IMF 2015). The average sophistication of the countries that purchase exports from South Asia, as measured by the weighted average of the buyers' per capita incomes, has declined over time (figure 1.5, panel b), both because South Asia is moving toward relatively poorer trading partners (figure 1.5, panel c) and because its existing trading partners are growing less rapidly than average (figure 1.5, panel d).

Quality, as measured by the price that exporters of a particular product fetch in international markets compared with other producers, is generally low and has declined

FIGURE 1.5   Average export sophistication in South Asia has been on the decline

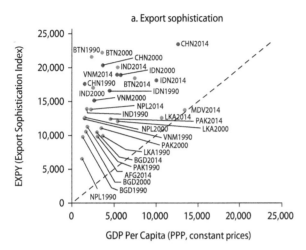

a. Export sophistication

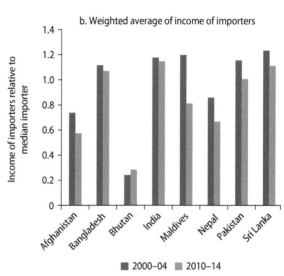

b. Weighted average of income of importers

Note: PPP = purchasing power parity.

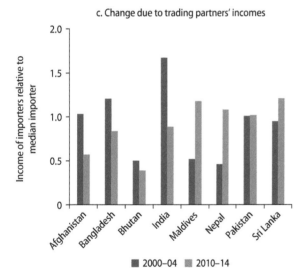

c. Change due to trading partners' incomes

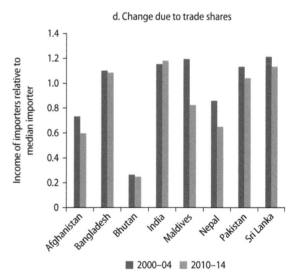

d. Change due to trade shares

Note: Trade weights are fixed at the 2000–04 level.
Source: World Bank calculations based on UN COMTRADE database.

Note: Partner incomes are fixed at the 2000–04 level.

for some countries.[7] For example, some Sri Lankan apparel (such as brassieres) was at the higher end of the price spectrum at the turn of the century, but now fetches prices in the lower fifth of the distribution (figure 1.6, panel i). In tea, for which the country has a built-in brand name, Sri Lankan exporters secure prices just above the median (figure 1.6, panel j). Nepali carpets are in the middle of the distribution of prices (figure 1.6, panel e), while mineral water exports are in the lowest tenth (figure 1.6, panel f). Pakistani cotton moved from the bottom quartile to the second quartile of the distribution of prices, advancing six positions in the ranking (figure 1.6, panel g); trousers, however, are sold at the very bottom of the distribution (figure 1.6, panel h). Key Bangladesh exports have lost ground along the quality ladder, moving six positions down the quality ladder in cotton t-shirts between 2000 and 2013 (figure 1.6, panel b).

FIGURE 1.6   Export quality is generally low and has declined for some countries

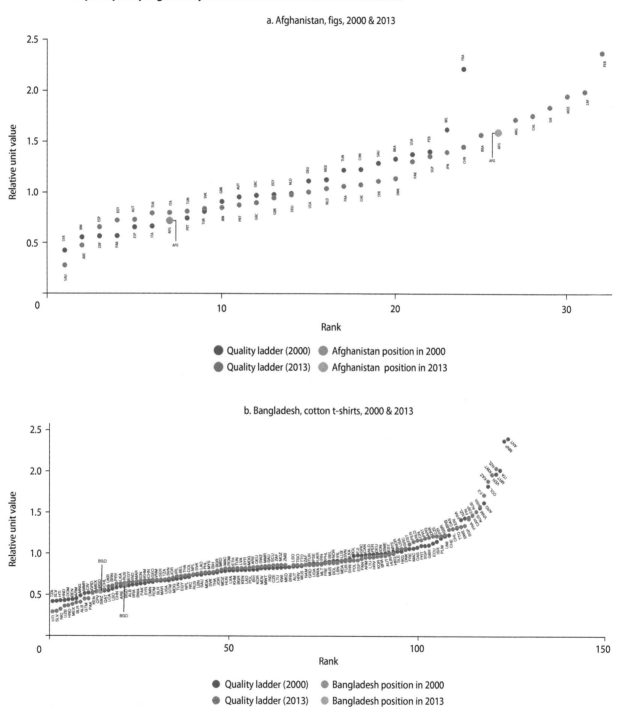

a. Afghanistan, figs, 2000 & 2013

b. Bangladesh, cotton t-shirts, 2000 & 2013

(continues next page)

FIGURE 1.6   **Export quality is generally low and has declined for some countries** (continued)

c. India, cars of 1000–1500cc, 2000 & 2013

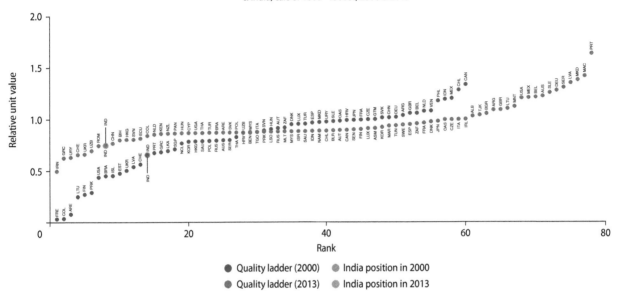

d. Maldives, tilapia, 2000 & 2013

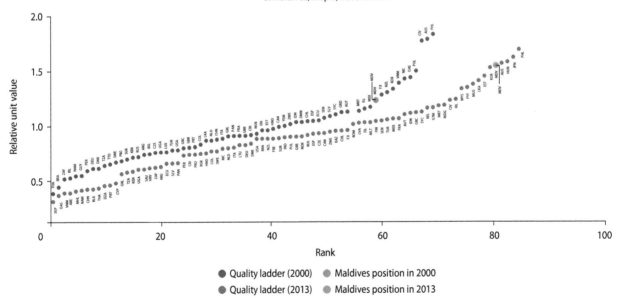

(continues next page)

FIGURE 1.6   Export quality is generally low and has declined for some countries (continued)

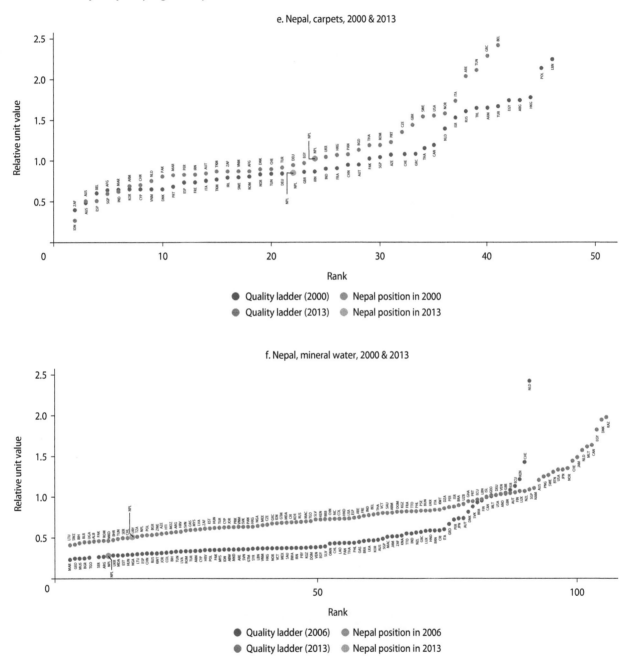

e. Nepal, carpets, 2000 & 2013

f. Nepal, mineral water, 2000 & 2013

(continues next page)

FIGURE 1.6 **Export quality is generally low and has declined for some countries** (continued)

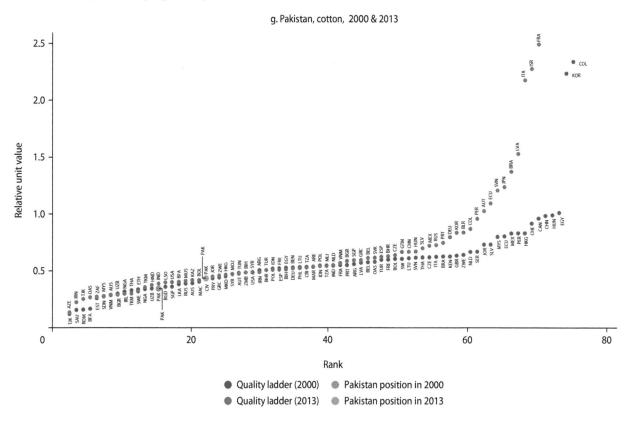

g. Pakistan, cotton, 2000 & 2013

- Quality ladder (2000)   Pakistan position in 2000
- Quality ladder (2013)   Pakistan position in 2013

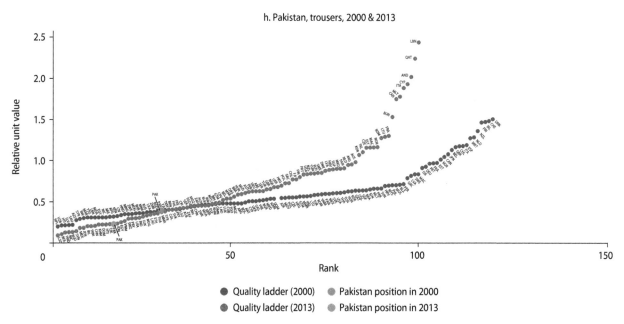

h. Pakistan, trousers, 2000 & 2013

- Quality ladder (2000)   Pakistan position in 2000
- Quality ladder (2013)   Pakistan position in 2013

(continues next page)

FIGURE 1.6 **Export quality is generally low and has declined for some countries** (continued)

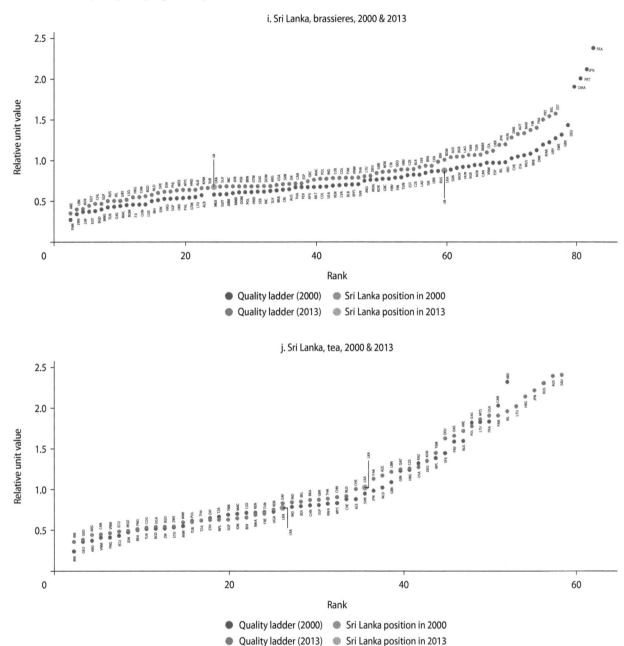

i. Sri Lanka, brassieres, 2000 & 2013

j. Sri Lanka, tea, 2000 & 2013

Source: World Bank calculations based on UN COMTRADE database.

Indian cars and cell phones also secure low prices relative to those of competitors. There are some exceptions in agricultural products, however. In Maldives some exports of fish are priced at the high end of the market—tilapia exporters, for example, receive 50 percent more than the price received by the median exporter of the same product (figure 1.6, panel d). Similarly, figs from Afghanistan have substantially moved up the quality ladder between 2000 and 2013 (figure 1.6, panel a).

Annex 1A

TABLE 1A.1   Per capita income and ratios of FDI, imports, and exports to GDP by region, 1990–2014

Variables	FDI/GDP	FDI/GDP	Imports/GDP	Imports/GDP	Exports/GDP	Exports/GDP
GDP per capita (PPP, constant 2005)		6.91e-05***		0.000199***		0.000750***
		(1.07e-05)		(2.92e-05)		(2.51e-05)
Europe and Central Asia	0.705	0.0880	−11.63***	−12.98***	−8.802***	−13.82***
	(0.521)	(0.533)	(1.425)	(1.432)	(1.348)	(1.230)
Latin America and the Caribbean	0.622	0.985*	−15.10***	−12.91***	−14.36***	−9.476***
	(0.552)	(0.562)	(1.526)	(1.541)	(1.443)	(1.324)
Middle East and North Africa	−1.688***	−2.729***	−16.64***	−18.68***	−9.538***	−17.09***
	(0.652)	(0.694)	(1.820)	(1.878)	(1.721)	(1.613)
North America	−2.259	−4.128***	−35.99***	−40.89***	−29.72***	−48.19***
	(1.485)	(1.520)	(4.119)	(4.159)	(3.895)	(3.573)
South Asia	−2.855***	−2.266**	−21.09***	−21.21***	−23.57***	−17.62***
	(0.858)	(0.893)	(2.325)	(2.396)	(2.199)	(2.059)
Sub-Saharan Africa	0.178	0.881*	−14.41***	−11.90***	−20.93***	−11.50***
	(0.516)	(0.530)	(1.425)	(1.464)	(1.348)	(1.258)
Constant	2.238**	1.368	54.82***	51.91***	47.44***	37.05***
Year dummies	Yes	Yes	Yes	Yes	Yes	Yes
Observations	4,062	3,979	4,154	4,075	4,154	4,075
R-squared	0.034	0.043	0.055	0.069	0.090	0.260

Source: World Bank calculations based on World Development Indicators database.
Note: Standard errors in parentheses. PPP = purchasing power parity.
*** $p < 0.01$, ** $p < 0.05$, * $p < 0.1$.

TABLE 1A.2   Changes in FDI, imports to GDP, and exports to GDP by region, 1990–2014

Variables	ΔFDI/GDP	ΔFDI/GDP	ΔImports/ GDP	ΔImports/ GDP	ΔExports/ GDP	ΔExports/ GDP
GDP per capita (PPP, constant 2005)		5.29e-05***		0.000216***		0.000833***
		(1.21e-05)		(4.29e-05)		(4.04e-05)
Europe and Central Asia	1.888***	1.428**	−3.495*	−4.859**	−2.665	−7.906***
	(0.586)	(0.599)	(2.093)	(2.105)	(2.083)	(1.984)
Latin America and the Caribbean	0.684	0.860	−12.61***	−10.71***	−11.97***	−6.366***
	(0.618)	(0.630)	(2.238)	(2.256)	(2.227)	(2.126)

(continues next page)

TABLE 1A.2   FDI, imports to GDP, and exports to GDP by region, 1990–2014 (continued)

Variables	ΔFDI/GDP	ΔFDI/GDP	ΔImports/GDP	ΔImports/GDP	ΔExports/GDP	ΔExports/GDP
Middle East and North Africa	−0.397	−0.906	−5.583**	−5.603**	−0.998	−7.491***
	(0.731)	(0.771)	(2.641)	(2.714)	(2.629)	(2.557)
North America	0.973	−0.450	−5.025	−10.26*	−3.048	−23.23***
	(1.644)	(1.685)	(5.925)	(5.999)	(5.896)	(5.653)
South Asia	−0.669	−0.366	−4.277	−4.890	−16.20***	−10.54***
	(0.998)	(1.041)	(3.475)	(3.598)	(3.458)	(3.391)
Sub-Saharan Africa	1.660***	2.196***	−0.633	2.479	−10.02***	0.495
	(0.580)	(0.599)	(2.102)	(2.175)	(2.092)	(2.050)
Constant	−1.592	−2.283*	4.477	1.022	6.143	−6.049*
Year dummies	Yes	Yes	Yes	Yes	Yes	Yes
Observations	3,892	3,811	3,896	3,830	3,896	3,830
R-squared	0.007	0.012	0.012	0.018	0.016	0.119

Source: World Bank calculations based on World Development Indicators database.
Note: Standard errors in parentheses. PPP = purchasing power parity
*** $p < 0.01$, ** $p < 0.05$, * $p < 0.1$.

FIGURE 1A.1   Export Orientation Index—Rankings for South Asia region countries and comparators

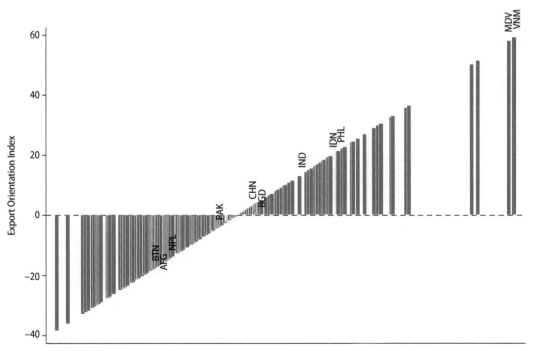

Source: World Bank calculations based on World Development Indicators database.

FIGURE 1A.2   Import Orientation Index—Rankings for South Asia region countries and comparators

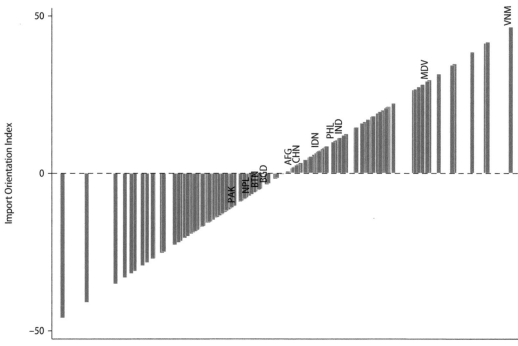

Source: World Bank calculations based on World Development Indicators database.

Notes

1. A slightly different picture emerges if, when measuring the export and import orientation of countries in South Asia, we control for some nonpolicy determinants of openness. For example, larger countries tend to trade less with the rest of the world because their domestic trade opportunities are larger than those of small countries. Similarly, landlocked or island states face higher transportation costs and therefore tend to trade less. Once size and whether a country is landlocked or an island state are taken into account, most countries in South Asia remain less integrated into the global marketplace, both in terms of export and import orientation, than the average. However, India, the largest economy in the region, appears to be more integrated than the average (see plots of these Export and Import Orientation Indexes in figure 1A.1 and figure 1A.2).

2. The Services Trade Restrictions Database (used to calculate the indexes) collects and makes publicly available information on services trade policy assembled in a comparable manner across 103 countries, five sectors (telecommunications, finance, transportation, retail, and professional services) and the key modes of service supply from the perspective of a foreign supplier who wishes to provide services to consumers in a particular country, with a focus on policy measures that discriminate against foreign services or service providers. See Borchert, Gootiiz, and Mattoo (2012) for more details.

3. A similar result was previously reported by Amiti and Konings (2007) for Indonesia.

4. This is consistent with cross-country evidence presented by Bolaky and Freund (2004) that the growth effect of trade depends on a country's business regulations.

5. In the EXPY indicator, each export good is assigned the value of the average per capita income of other countries exporting that good; the country's EXPY is the average of these values, weighted by the good's share of total exports (Hausmann, Hwang, and Rodrik 2006). The EXPY indicator has to be interpreted with caution, because it reflects the final product exported rather than the element of production carried out

locally. In today's increasingly fragmented production processes, a country may export a sophisticated product, such as a computer, but contribute only low-skilled assembly activities using high-tech parts manufactured elsewhere.

6. PRODY is an income level associated with a given good, calculated as a weighted average of the per capita GDP of countries producing the good, with weights derived from revealed comparative advantage calculations.

7. The unit values secured by exporters are used here as a proxy for product quality because true product quality is unobserved. It is worth mentioning, however, that differences in unit value may also reflect differences in manufacturing costs observed across firms or even across countries (see the discussion in Khandelwal 2010).

References

Aghion, P., N. Bloom, R. Blundell, R. Griffith, and P. Howitt. 2005. "Competition and Innovation: An Inverted-U Relationship." *Quarterly Journal of Economics* 120 (2): 701–28.

Amiti, M., and J. Konings. 2007. "Trade Liberalization, Intermediate Inputs, and Productivity: Evidence from Indonesia." *American Economic Review* 97 (5): 1611–38.

Arnold, J., B. Javorcik, M. Lipscoomb, and A. Mattoo. 2015. "Services Reform and Manufacturing Performance: Evidence from India." *Economic Journal* 126 (590): 1–39.

Atkin, D., A. Khandelwal, and A. Osman. 2016. "Exporting and Firm Performance: Evidence from a Randomized Experiment." NBER Working Paper 20690, National Bureau of Economic Research, Cambridge, MA.

Bernard, A., S. Redding, and P. Schott. 2011. "Multiproduct Firms and Trade Liberalization." *Quarterly Journal of Economics* 126 (3): 1271–1318.

Bolaky, B., and C. Freund. 2004. "Trade, Regulations, and Growth." Policy Research Working Paper 3255, World Bank, Washington, DC.

Borchert, I., B. Gootiiz, and A. Mattoo. 2012. "Guide to the Services Trade Restrictions Database." Policy Research Working Paper 6108, World Bank, Washington, DC.

Goldberg, P., A. Khandelwal, N. Pavcnik, and P. Topalova. 2010. "Imported Intermediate Inputs and Domestic Product Growth: Evidence from India." *Quarterly Journal of Economics* 125 (4): 1727–67.

Gomez-Mera, L., T. Kenyon, Y. Margalit, J. Reis. and G. Varela. 2015. "New Voices in Investment: A Survey of Investors from Emerging Countries." Washington DC: World Bank.

Hausmann, R., J. Hwang, and D. Rodrik. 2006. "What You Export Matters." NBER Working Paper 11905, National Bureau of Economic Research, Cambridge, MA.

Helpman, E., and P. R. Krugman. 1985. *Market Structure and Foreign Trade: Increasing Returns, Imperfect Competition, and the International Economy*. Cambridge, MA: MIT Press.

Hicks, J. R. 1935. "Annual Survey of Economic Theory: The Theory of Monopoly." *Econometrica* 3 (1): 1–20.

IMF (International Monetary Fund). 2015. "Make in India: Which Exports Can Drive the Next Wave of Growth?" Working Paper 15119, IMF, Washington, DC.

Kathuria, S., and M. Malouche. 2016. *Strengthening Competitiveness in Bangladesh—Thematic Assessment: A Diagnostic Trade Integration Study*. Washington, DC: World Bank.

Kathuria, S., A. Portugal, and S. Shahid. 2015. "Barriers to Regional Integration in South Asia: The Case of Para-tariffs." World Bank, Washington, DC (unpublished manuscript).

Khandelwal, Amit. 2010. "The Long and Short (of) Quality Ladders." *Review of Economic Studies* 77 (4): 1450–76.

Melitz, M. J. 2003. "The Impact of Trade on Intra-industry Reallocations and Aggregate Industry Productivity." *Econometrica* 71 (6): 1695–1725.

Topalova, P. and A. Khandelwal. 2011. "Trade Liberalization and Firm Productivity: The Case of India." *Review of Economics and Statistics* 93 (3): 995–1009.

Improving Competitiveness Requires Raising Productivity Rather Than Keeping Costs Low | 2

Competitiveness occupies a central position in government and industry agendas in South Asia.[1] However, current performance—whether measured as participation in global markets or using common competitiveness benchmarks—has been subdued. For example, the region possesses several key advantages in the apparel sector: it has an abundant supply of workers, labor costs are one-half to one-quarter those of China, and it is a top cotton producer in an industry in which textiles make up close to 70 percent of production costs. Some leading apparel firms in South Asia have achieved world-class operational performance by investing in training and technology, reaping economies of scale, and in India and Pakistan by integrating vertically to avoid barriers to sourcing high-quality inputs on the global market. Nevertheless, although South Asia increased its share of the global apparel market from 7.5 to 12.3 percent from 2000 to 2012, it continues to lag well behind China, which accounts for 41 percent of the market (table 2.1). Despite higher labor costs, China is able to attract buyers by offering a wide range of apparel at short lead times, while high productivity limits total costs. No country in South Asia has thus far succeeded in offering a comparable package of goods and services.

The comparison of South Asia's and China's apparel industries illustrates the difficulty in defining national competitiveness, because different countries have become "competitive" with different mixes of endowments, factor prices, and policies (Porter 1990). If competitiveness is defined as purely gains in global market share, countries can remain competitive in the short term by keeping production costs low through controlled exchange rates, rigid factor markets, and similar policies. However, such policies and the larger focus on gaining a bigger slice of the pie are quite likely to be a zero-sum game (Krugman 1994). A better strategy for improved competitiveness is to reduce the transaction costs for firms to compete domestically and globally by providing efficient infrastructure services, a smoother business environment, and more effective public services. Still, reducing these costs has its limits.

On the other hand, investing in productivity-enhancing measures can pay continuous dividends over the long term. Porter (1990, 76) ties competitiveness to the efficiency with which firms combine factors of production (total factor productivity or TFP) and argues that the "only meaningful concept of competitiveness at the national level is productivity." This report adopts a similar perspective: productivity is what drives

TABLE 2.1 **South Asia lags well behind China in apparel exports despite much lower labor costs**

Country	Rank in top 15 apparel exporters	Apparel exports as a share of world apparel exports (percent)	Apparel exports as a share of country exports (percent)	Average apparel monthly earnings (US$/per hour)
Bangladesh	2	6.4	82.8	0.51
India	7	3.5	5.2	1.06
Pakistan	13	1.2	19.0	0.58
Sri Lanka	14	1.2	44.8	0.55
China	1	41	7.1	2.60

Source: World Bank calculations using UN COMTRADE data and household surveys.
Note: Data are for 2012.

competitiveness in the long run, and boosting productivity leads to rising living standards through higher wages and returns on investment. Productivity in South Asia has been less studied than various cost factors, so the following discussion focuses on three major challenges to productivity growth in the region.

At the macro level, the contribution of TFP to growth in South Asia has declined in recent years, and factors subject to diminishing returns—quantity rather than quality of labor and non–information and communication technology (ICT) investment—have been the main drivers of growth. This calls for greater focus on improving productivity to sustain and accelerate growth, create jobs, reduce poverty, and boost shared prosperity. The main forces that can increase productivity growth are increased integration with the global economy, the movement of resources from agriculture to higher-productivity manufacturing and services, and the movement of capital and labor from less-productive to more-productive firms within narrowly defined economic activities.

At the sectoral level, the movement of labor from agriculture to industry and services (structural transformation) has not been rapid enough in South Asia to markedly reduce the large differences in productivity across sectors. While countries in the region are at different points along this transformation, South Asia is overall in its early stage, leaving significant untapped potential to reap productivity gains by further reallocation of labor from lower- to higher-productivity activities.

At the firm level, large productivity differences exist among South Asian firms, and much of the region's resources are locked away in small, low-productivity firms that neither grow nor exit, indicating the existence of barriers to market entry and exit (Cabral 2007; Li and Rama 2015; Tybout 1996). The consequent "misallocation" of resources accounts for a large share of the difference in productivity between South Asia and high-income economies (Hsieh and Klenow 2009; Hsieh and Olken 2014; Pagés 2010).[2] The following discussion develops these observations in more detail.

Macro challenge: Contribution of TFP to growth is low and declining

Gross domestic product (GDP) in South Asia more than quadrupled from 1990 to 2014, and most countries enjoyed rapid growth in output and per capita income (figure 2.1). However, the contribution of TFP to GDP growth has been mixed, as indicated by the four countries for which data are available to divide GDP growth into its components: changes in the quantity of labor, the quality of labor, ICT capital, non-ICT capital, and TFP (figure 2.2).[3]

Two main messages emerge from this analysis:

- The contribution of TFP gains to economic growth in the region has declined across the four countries for which data are available. In India and Pakistan, the contribution of TFP to GDP growth has declined dramatically since 2011 and

FIGURE 2.1   Growth in real GDP and real GDP per capita in South Asia has accelerated

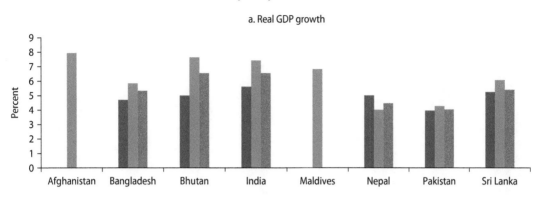

a. Real GDP growth

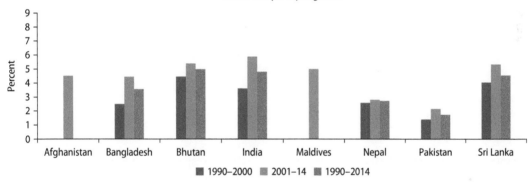

b. Real GDP per capita growth

■ 1990–2000   ■ 2001–14   ■ 1990–2014

Source: World Bank calculations based on World Development Indicators database.
Note: Afghanistan's growth for both GDP and GDP per capita is calculated over 2002–14 based on data availability.

FIGURE 2.2   South Asia's growth has been largely driven by factor accumulation

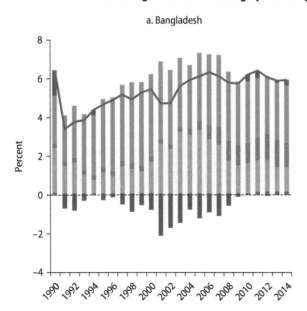

a. Bangladesh

b. India

(continues next page)

FIGURE 2.2   South Asia's growth has been largely driven by factor accumulation (continued)

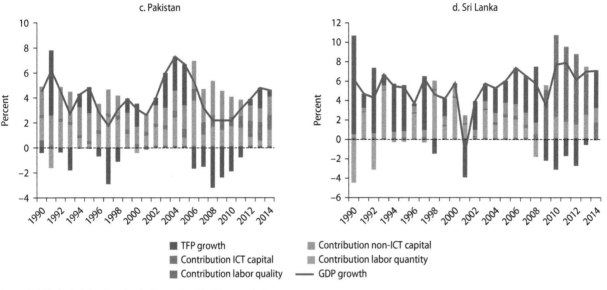

Source: World Bank calculations based on Conference Board Total Economy database.
Note: ICT = information and communication technology; TFP = total factor productivity.

FIGURE 2.3   Agriculture has given way to industry and services in South Asia

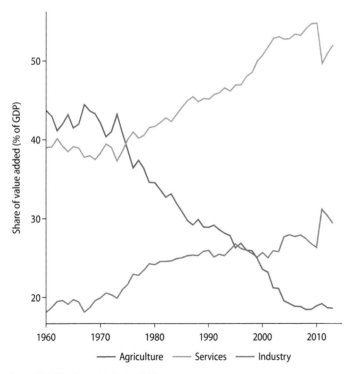

Source: World Development Indicators database.

2006, respectively. In Sri Lanka, although the contribution of TFP picked up in 2014, it has declined from its high levels before 2009. In Bangladesh, TFP has played a negligible role in GDP growth during the entire period of analysis.[4]

• Non-ICT investment and increases in the number of workers have been the leading forces behind growth in all four countries. Although investment in ICT has increased its contribution to growth in India, and substantially so in Sri Lanka, most of the growth is still accounted for by more labor (rather than higher-quality labor) and non-ICT investment—both factors subject to diminishing returns.

Sectoral challenge: Slow pace of structural transformation

As in other countries at similar stages of development, resources in South Asia are moving from agriculture to manufacturing and services (figure 2.3). This shift in economic activity from lower-productivity, traditional sectors to more modern and productive ones is known as structural transformation. Between 1960 and 2013, the average share of agriculture in GDP in South Asia fell from 44 percent to 19 percent, while the share of industry increased from 18 to 29 percent. Over the same period, real GDP per capita of the region nearly quintupled.

Individual countries are at different points along this transformation, but the overall trend is quite consistent (figures 2.4 and 2.5). An increase in real GDP per capita has been associated with a decline in the share of agriculture in employment and value added and concomitant increases in the shares of services and industry.[5] Maldives, a small island economy, has traditionally had a large services sector owing to tourism and has not experienced much structural change in the last decade. The share of value added of industry, however, appears to plateau at certain levels of income (at least in the larger countries), consistent with the views of structural transformation in the literature (Herrendorf, Rogerson, and Valentinyi 2013). The share of employment in agriculture has been consistently higher than the share of value added at all levels of GDP per capita for the four countries with adequate data. This suggests that agricultural productivity has not improved substantially over the decades. The share of services in employment and value added in this sector is high in South Asia, particularly considering the relatively low income levels. The share of services in GDP appears to rise relatively early in the development process, at below $700 per person in 2005 prices. This pattern differs from the experience of mature industrialized countries such as the United Kingdom, France, and the United States, where the share of the services sector reached high levels only at high levels of GDP per capita (Verma 2012).

Workers in South Asia are moving from agriculture to the higher-productivity manufacturing and services sectors, a transition that has been associated with increases in aggregate productivity.[6] However, the share of agriculture in total employment in the region remains high at over 50 percent, despite the fact that labor productivity in industry and services is several times that of agriculture. For example, in India average labor productivity in industry from 2004 to 2013 was approximately 5 times, and services 6.5 times, the level of productivity in agriculture, illustrating the potential for major productivity gains in the region from accelerating the process of structural transformation.

Differences in labor productivity play an important role in pulling labor to more productive sectors, above and beyond the "natural" rate of structural transformation (table 2.2).[7] In other words, movement from agriculture to industry and services is significantly faster in periods when the difference in productivity between the two sectors is larger. In this way, the process of structural transformation in South Asia is similar to the experience of the countries of the Organisation for Economic Co-operation and Development (OECD), although there are differences due either to the two groups of countries being at a different stage of the same path, or to the paths being somewhat different. In either case, the response of employment to differences in sectoral productivity levels is much higher in South Asia than in OECD economies, indicating that boosting productivity growth in manufacturing and services in South Asia carries a much greater potential for accelerating structural transformation, increasing nonfarm employment, and raising income growth.

Firm challenge: Firm growth is low and resources are trapped in small firms

In addition to structural transformation (resources moving from less- to more-productive sectors), productivity growth can be driven by movement in resources from less-productive to more-productive firms within narrowly defined economic activities. When this mechanism does not function as effectively as it could—due, for example, to

FIGURE 2.4   As incomes grow, resources shift from agriculture to industry and services

Employment and share of value added by sector for Bangladesh, India, Pakistan, and Sri Lanka, 1975–2013

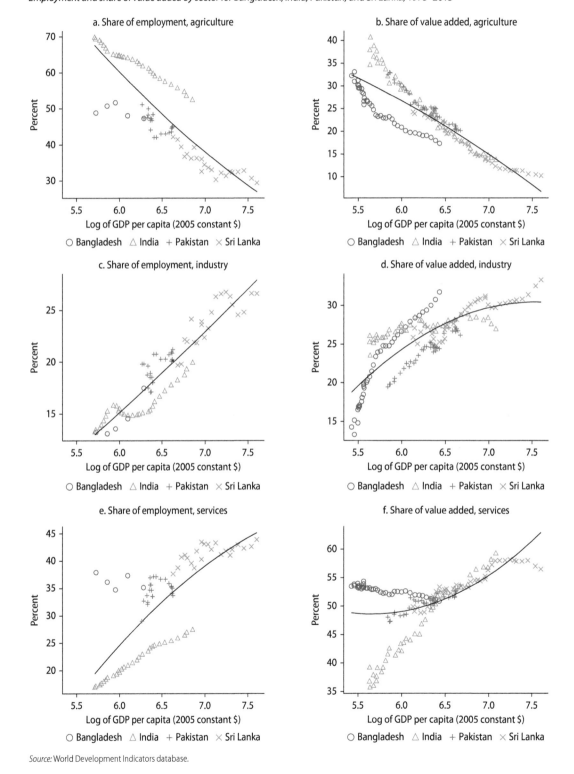

Source: World Development Indicators database.

FIGURE 2.5   As incomes grow, resources shift from agriculture to industry and services

Share of value added by sector in Afghanistan, Bhutan, Maldives, and Nepal

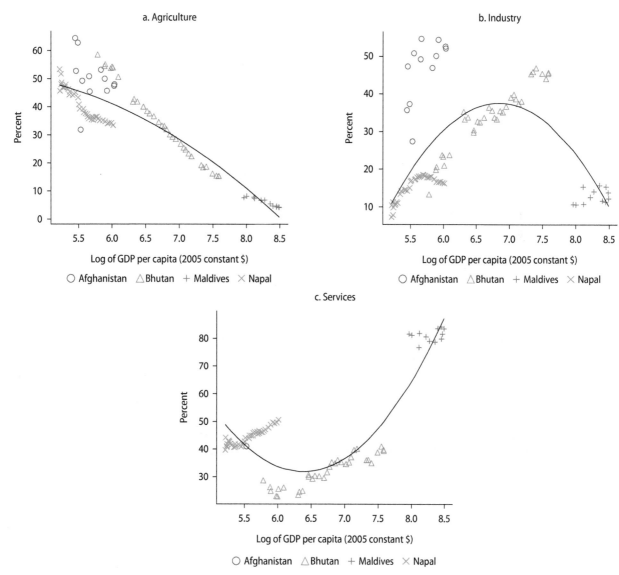

Source: World Development Indicators database.

barriers to competition—the economy suffers from misallocation of resources (box 2.1).

Evidence shows that the misallocation can substantially reduce aggregate productivity. In a seminal study, Hsieh and Klenow (2009) measure resource misallocation in China and India by comparing productivity dispersion among firms in these countries with the U.S. market.[8] They find that firms in China and India produce the same products with vastly

different levels of productivity, with a range that is much wider than that in the United States. Reducing these productivity gaps to the level of efficiency observed in the United States would increase TFP by 40–60 percent and 30–50 percent in India and China, respectively, and output would increase by twice as much if investment increased in response to higher productivity. Conversely, a more rapid expansion of less-efficient firms in the early

TABLE 2.2 **Labor productivity drives structural transformation**

	From agriculture to industry	From agriculture to services
OECD countries		
Intercept	0.14	0.08
	(0.09)	(0.08)
Lag employment share	0.97***	0.97***
	(0.00)	(0.01)
Labor productivity differential	0.18*	0.17*
	(0.08)	(0.07)
Observations	730	730
India, Pakistan, and Sri Lanka		
Intercept	15.68***	16.53***
	(4.15)	(4.77)
Lag employment share	0.84***	0.83***
	(0.05)	(0.05)
Labor productivity differential	4.43***	3.70**
	(1.25)	(1.21)
Observations	70	70

Source: World Bank calculations based on World Development Indicators database.
Note: Standard errors in parentheses, country fixed effects included but not shown. OECD = Organisation for Economic Co-operation and Development.
$*p < 0.05, **p < 0.01, ***p < 0.001.$

BOX 2.1 Barriers to competition and productivity dispersion

Consider a fictional example of an economy with two firms.[a] One operates at low productivity, but manages to survive in the market because it has political connections through which it secures subsidized credit. The other firm has no political connections, borrows at the market rate, and therefore faces higher costs. However, the second firm has higher productivity, which enables it to compete with the first firm. If labor and capital were to move from the firm with low productivity to the firm with high productivity, aggregate output would be higher, and the difference between productivity levels in the two firms would be lower. Thus, the misallocation of capital results in low output per worker, on average, across the two firms.

Barriers to competition in the real world also can create and perpetuate substantial misallocation of resources. For example, informal, low-productivity retailers in Brazil hold a large share of the market because they are subject to less stringent labor market regulations, and thus lower labor costs, than higher-productivity supermarkets (McKinsey Global Institute 1998). Subsidized loans and differential tax-code treatment in Japan are used "to keep mom-and-pop retailers from going out of business" (Lewis 2004, 14–15). And, prior to reforms, severe restrictions on foreign direct investment (FDI) in retail prevented investment by global best-practice retailers in India.

a. This example is taken from Hsieh and Klenow (2009).

1990s reduced TFP growth in Indian manufacturing by 2 percent over the 1987–94 period (Hsieh and Klenow 2009).

Although the detailed data required to replicate the Hsieh and Klenow (2009) analysis for other countries in the region are not available, indicators of productivity differences among firms compared to India can be calculated for a few sectors in Bangladesh, Nepal, and Sri Lanka. The results show substantial scope for improving productivity in Nepal by shifting labor and capital to higher-productivity firms in food and beverages (firms in the lowest 10 percent of the TFP distribution are more than five times less productive than those in the highest 10 percent) and other manufacturing, but less scope (relative to India) in Sri Lanka and Bangladesh (table 2.3).[9] The results also hint at the importance of competition: in Bangladesh and Sri Lanka, firms in the apparel sector, which is significantly exposed to competition through exports, show less productivity dispersion than firms in India.

Some authors explain high productivity dispersion—and, consequently, lower overall productivity—as the result of a disproportionately high number of small, unproductive firms that neither grow nor exit, releasing resources into the economy (Li and Rama 2015). For example, the share of manufacturing firms with fewer than 10 employees in India is almost visually indistinguishable from 100 percent and the most common observation in the sample is a firm with a single employee (Hsieh and Olken 2014). By contrast, in the United States, the most common observation in the sample is a firm with 45 employees. Moreover, the dominance of small firms in India appears to be the same as, or perhaps even greater than, it was more than twenty years ago (figure 2.6). Evidence from the

TABLE 2.3 Productivity dispersion across South Asia's firms tends to be large

Coefficients of variation by sector and country

Sector	Bangladesh	Sri Lanka
Food and beverages	0.64	1.56
Textiles	1.79	—
Apparel	0.65	0.98
Basic metals	2.75	—
Other manufacturing	1.49	2.95

Source: World Bank calculations based on World Bank Enterprise Surveys (Bangladesh 2013, India 2014, Sri Lanka 2011).
Note: Dispersion in each sector is normalized to India (i.e., India's dispersion is normalized to 1.00). — = not available.

TABLE 2.4 Small firms dominate the distribution across South Asia

Distribution of firms by number of employees, South Asia and comparator countries

Country	Year	Small (5–19)	Medium (20–99)	Large (100 or more)
Afghanistan	2014	69	26	5
Bangladesh	2013	37	36	27
Bhutan	2015	71	25	4
China	2012	55	32	13
India	2014	43	44	13
Indonesia	2009	88	10	2
Nepal	2013	82	16	2
Pakistan	2013	44	40	16
Philippines	2009	52	35	13
Sri Lanka	2011	76	18	6
Vietnam	2009	45	36	18

Source: Calculations based on World Bank Enterprise Surveys.
Note: Distributions may not total 100 percent due to rounding.

FIGURE 2.6 **Size distribution of firms in India is heavily biased toward small firms**

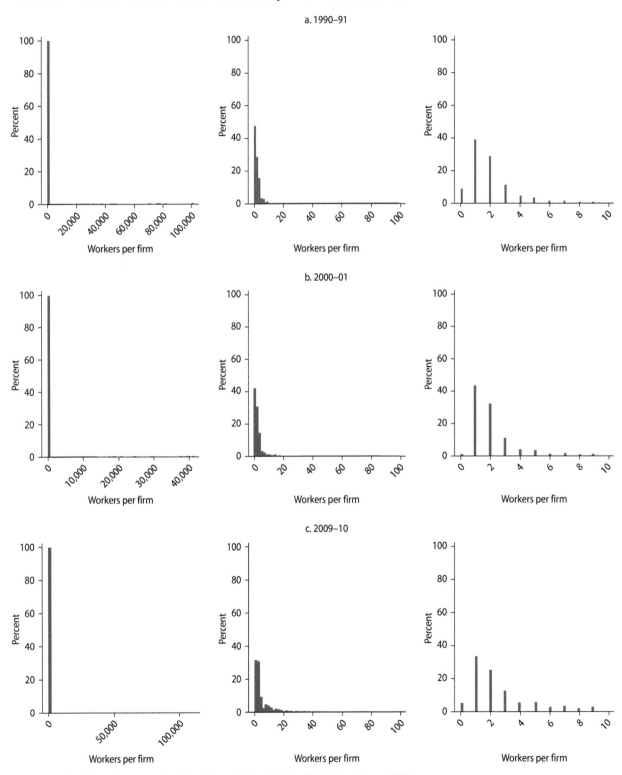

Source: World Bank calculations based on combined Annual Survey of Industries (ASI) and National Sample Survey (NSS) data.

World Bank Enterprise Surveys indicates that the importance of small firms in South Asia is greater than in comparator East Asian countries (table 2.4).[10] Countries with higher levels of GDP per capita tend to have a smaller share of firms with only a few employees (see figures 2A.1, 2A.2, and 2A.3).

There are many reasons why small firms may be less productive than larger ones: economies of scale, access to finance, better employees, and stronger business practices. Larger firms tend to innovate more, particularly in process and organization, because they can more easily secure financing for risky projects and because of the potential for economies of scale in research and development investments (see Del Mel, McKenzie, and Woodruff 2008; Cohen and Klepper 1996, and Ayyagari, Demirgüç-Kunt, and Maksimovic 2007). Larger firms also tend to invest more in administration and adopt better management and overall business practices, which are highly correlated with firm performance (Bloom and Van Reenen 2007; Bloom et al. 2013).[11] Regardless of the channel, productivity does appear to be lower in small than in large firms in Asia. For example, in both India and China, value added per worker in small firms is much lower than in large firms (figure 2.7).[12] This pattern is also documented by Hsieh and Klenow (2009), who argue that the relationship between productivity and size is stronger in China and India than in the United States due to distortions that prevent firms from achieving optimal size (which is also consistent with Banerjee and Duflo's (2006) contention that Indian policies constrain its most efficient producers and coddle its least efficient ones). Moreover, India's productivity growth between 1993 and 2007 was associated with productivity gains within large manufacturing plants (those with 200 or more workers) rather than with gains within small firms or with reallocation between plants (Klenow, Sharma, and Bollard 2011).

Another symptom of resource misallocation in the region is the difficulty firms face in growing. In India, manufacturing plants that are 40 years old are only 40 percent larger than manufacturing plants that are less than 5 years old, while in the United States older plants are more than seven times larger than younger ones (Hsieh and Klenow 2014). The same conclusion holds more broadly across the region: Firms aged 25 years or more in Bangladesh, Bhutan, India, and Sri Lanka are only 50–90 percent larger than firms aged less than 5 years.

FIGURE 2.7 Labor productivity is lower in small firms in India and China

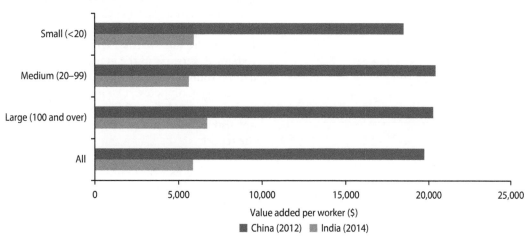

Source: World Bank calculations based on World Bank Enterprise Surveys.
Note: In India, value added per worker for all firms is calculated from a sample of 4,774 firms; for large firms from a sample of 1,144; for medium, of 2,378 firms; and for small firms of 1,252. For China, the sample sizes are 1,349, 579, 587, and 183 firms, respectively.

By contrast, older firms in Vietnam, Indonesia, and China are on average 4.5, 4.8, and 2.4 times the size of younger firms, respectively (figure 2.8). One explanation for this is that in India and China, within narrowly defined industries, larger plants have higher marginal products of labor and capital, while in the United States the difference is much smaller (Hsieh and Klenow 2009). A higher marginal product of labor in large firms likely indicates distortions that prevent firm growth; in a world without distortions, firms would continue to expand until the marginal product of labor or capital equalizes across firms.

Barriers to the growth of firms can likely be found in economic policy. Across the region, licensing and size restrictions (which have declined in importance but still exist), labor regulations that increase the costs of hiring and firing, financial sector regulations that favor small enterprises, and inadequate bankruptcy laws may limit the ability of efficient plants to grow and enable inefficient plants to survive. Problems in enforcing contracts in India, for example, make it costly to hire the right managers, which is crucial for firms' growth (Bloom et al. 2013). Taxes or labor costs that affect larger firms more than smaller firms may reduce the return on investment in large firms. Impediments to reaching foreign markets, both from trade policy and the high cost of logistics, can also impede expansion.

Four case studies of important industries in South Asia

Four industry case studies (agribusiness, electronics, apparel, and automotive) are an essential part of this report because they enable a better understanding of the drivers and constraints of South Asia's competitiveness. One of the case studies is featured at the end of each chapter of part 2. Extended versions of the industry case studies can be found online at www.worldbank.org /SouthAsiaCompetes. The main conclusions and recommendations from these case studies are also featured in the overview and part 3 of the report.

The industry case studies show the links between the external environment of firms and their behavior within a well-defined industry in which industry dynamics (such as competition) can be analyzed and performance benchmarked. They promote an understanding of the relative importance of the external factors that drive or constrain a

FIGURE 2.8   Firms in South Asia grow less rapidly than those in comparator countries

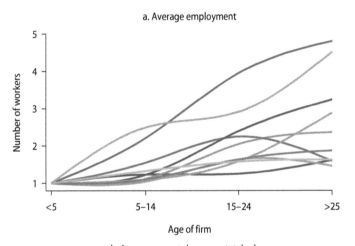

a. Average employment

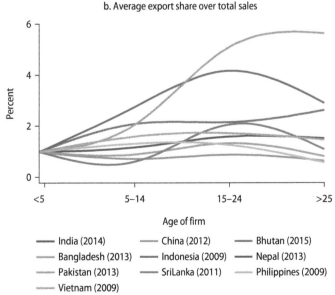

b. Average export share over total sales

── India (2014)	── China (2012)	── Bhutan (2015)
── Bangladesh (2013)	── Indonesia (2009)	── Nepal (2013)
── Pakistan (2013)	── SriLanka (2011)	── Philippines (2009)
── Vietnam (2009)		

Source: World Bank calculations based on World Bank Enterprise Surveys.
Note: Age cohorts of firms have been normalized with respect to the first age cohort, firms fewer than 5 years old.

firm's performance and productivity. Also, and crucially, the industry case studies assess the impact of industry-specific factors and policies that traditional cross-cutting analysis is ill-equipped to identify.

And indeed, the main finding from the four industry case studies is that industry-specific policies (also called product market regulations), are the main constraint to South Asia's realizing its great untapped competitiveness potential. These policies include restrictions on trade, prices, products (through standards), and markets that have protected firms from exposure to global good practices (in automotive and agribusiness) or have limited firms' capacity to adopt these practices (in apparel and electronics).

Manufacturing case studies were selected because the region's performance has been lagging in manufacturing relative to services. The following manufacturing sectors were chosen because they are important and representative of different types of manufacturing industries:

- Agribusiness (including agriculture) accounts for one-third of South Asia's GDP and is crucial for all countries. Increasing income and urbanization create the prospect of significant growth. Livelihoods in rural areas can be improved by linking farmers to processors and traders who are willing to pay a premium for higher-quality products as well as by providing off-farm job opportunities. The case study is featured at the end of chapter 3, "Business Environment Challenges," because it shows how, despite much attention and reform, business environment issues, especially industry-specific product market regulations, which have generally been overlooked by policy makers, continue to be a big challenge in South Asia.

- Electronics is one of the largest and fastest growing industries in the world and has played an important role in the development trajectories of several newly industrialized economies. Surprisingly, South Asia is not currently a significant player in the sector despite very competitive labor costs and the fact that leading firms are achieving world-class productivity in the region. The case study is featured at the end of chapter 4, "Productivity-Boosting Agglomeration Economies," because it shows that South Asia is missing urban ecosystems that provide thick markets for skilled labor, large tracts of industrial land for clusters to thrive, and world-class logistics to import and export seamlessly.

- Apparel is the largest globally traded labor-intensive industry in the world. With rising labor cost in East Asia, South Asia has an historic opportunity to capture its fair share of the global apparel market (having only 12 percent compared to 41 percent for China alone), in the process pulling millions out of poverty, especially women. The case is featured at the end of chapter 5, "Limited Success in Linking to Global Value Chains," because it shows how, despite the reforms of the 1990s, trade barriers continue to stand in the way of South Asia's realizing its great potential in apparel.

- Automotive is one of the most important industries globally and in South Asia, contributing 19 million direct and indirect jobs in India alone. The potential for South Asia to become globally competitive in this sector is shown by the experience of Indian auto-parts manufacturers who became world leaders by having first acquired technical and managerial skills from leading original equipment manufacturers established in India, followed by a process of serving increasingly discerning customers in competitive export markets. The case is featured at the end of chapter 6, "Firm Capabilities," because it shows how firm capabilities are acquired and spread through competitive exposure to global good practices.

The country coverage of each industry case study (as shown in table 2.5) was determined on the basis of its importance and data availability. For each industry case study, we also included relevant good practice benchmarks from outside South Asia, mostly from East

TABLE 2.5 Country coverage of the four industry case studies

	Afghanistan	Bangladesh	Bhutan	India	Maldives	Nepal	Pakistan	Sri Lanka	China	Vietnam	Thailand
Agribusiness	X	X	X	X	X	X	X	X			X
Electronics		X		X				X	X	X	
Apparel		X		X			X	X	X	X	
Automotive				X			X		X		

Asia, which shares many characteristics with South Asia and has been performing better.

The analytical approach for these case studies relied on both quantitative and qualitative analyses and was carried out using the following framework (see the online extended versions for more details):

- The first step assesses the competitiveness performance of the industry in each country by comparing its performance in output, trade, productivity, and cost with the other selected South Asian countries, as well as with the good practice comparator countries from outside the region (see table 2.5). This first step relies primarily on quantitative analysis using national statistics for output, World Integrated Trade Solutions (World Bank and UNCTAD 2015) for trade data, and enterprise surveys (national surveys and standardized World Bank Enterprise Surveys) for productivity and cost.
- The second step analyzes the drivers of productivity and cost at the firm and industry levels, including scale, skills, technology and innovation, agglomeration economies within clusters, and links along local and global value chains. This step combines results from enterprise surveys (including the innovation and labor force modules of the World Bank Enterprise Surveys) and in-depth firm interviews. It also includes, in the case of apparel, a survey of global buyers to understand what drives their decisions apart from cost and quality—for example, short lead times or compliance with social and environmental standards.

- The third step addresses constraints in the external environment of firms that limit their capacity or incentives to take advantage of these drivers. This step combines in-depth firm interviews with an analysis of the impact of external factors (such as infrastructure constraints and trade regimes) on firms' behavior and performance.
- The fourth and final step develops policy recommendations to remove the constraints and exploit the drivers of competitiveness. This final step is inspired by the policy choices taken by the more successful countries in the region and elsewhere such as, for example, the bonded warehouse regime that facilitated access to imported textiles for Bangladesh's apparel exporters. It also includes, in the case of apparel, an estimate (based on a gravity model) of how improved competitiveness, fostered by new policies, would affect output and jobs.

Annex 2A

The following model describes a simple process of reallocation of labor across different sectors, assuming a two-sector economy consisting of agriculture and industry. Employment in each sector can change because of a net addition of new workers as the labor force grows or an intersectoral migration of labor. This can be represented as follows:

$$L_t^A = (1+g^A)L_{t-1}^A + M \tag{1}$$

where L^A is the number of people employed in agriculture, g^A is the constant net rate of employment growth in agriculture, and M is the migration of laborers from industry to agriculture. Dividing equation (1) by total employment L, and assuming total employment grows at a constant net rate of g yields:

$$\frac{L_t^A}{L_t} = \frac{(1+g^A)L_{t-1}^A}{(1+g)L_{t-1}} + \frac{M}{L_t} \qquad (2)$$

Define m as the percentage of population that migrates from one sector to another: $m = M/L_t$. Assuming there are no frictions in the movement of labor from agriculture to industry (or, equivalently, that these frictions remain constant over time), intersectoral migration should be driven by the wage gap between the two sectors. For example, if the industrial wage rate is higher than the agricultural wage rate, workers should migrate from agriculture to industry. Further, the wage rate in a sector is equal to the marginal product of labor in that sector, which in turn is a function of labor productivity. Thus m can be written as:

$$m = f(w^A, w^I) = f(h(\omega^A, \omega^I)) = g(\omega^A, \omega^I) \qquad (3)$$

where w is the wage rate in a sector, and ω is the labor productivity. Equation (2) can therefore be expressed as follows:

$$\frac{L_t^A}{L_t} = \frac{(1+g^A)L_{t-1}^A}{(1+g)L_{t-1}} + g(\omega^A, \omega^I) \qquad (4)$$

This equation can be estimated using the following reduced-form model for OECD countries and the South Asian economies for which we have sufficient data on employment (India, Pakistan, and Sri Lanka). Proxying labor productivity in each sector with value added per worker yields the following:

$$\frac{L_{ikt}}{L_{kt}} = \alpha + \gamma\left(\frac{L_{ikt-1}}{L_{kt-1}}\right) + \beta(\log(VAPW_{ikt-1}) - \qquad (5)$$
$$\log(VAPW_{jkt-1})) + \delta_k Country_k + \epsilon_{ikt}$$

FIGURE 2A.1   Scatterplot of firms at the 25th percentile of employment distribution and income per capita

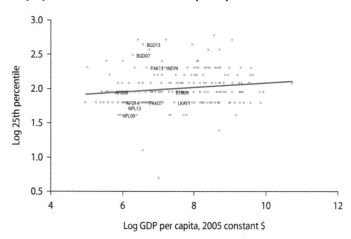

Source: Calculations based on World Bank Enterprise Surveys and World Development Indicators database.

FIGURE 2A.2   Scatterplot of firms at the 50th percentile of employment distribution and income per capita

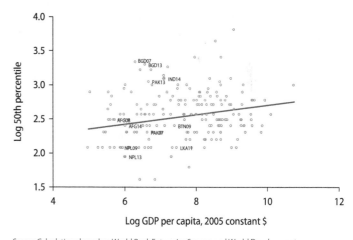

Source: Calculations based on World Bank Enterprise Surveys and World Development Indicators database.

where i represents agriculture and j represents industry or services, k represents the country dummy, and t represents time. $VAPW$ is the value added per worker calculated as the value added at constant prices divided by the number of workers. L_i/L is the employment share calculated as the number of employees in a sector divided by total employment.

FIGURE 2A.3   Scatterplot of firms at the 75th percentile of employment distribution and income per capita

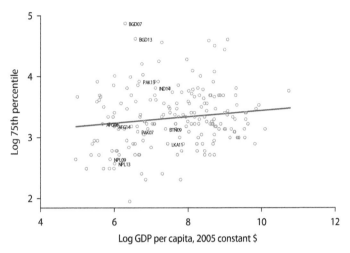

Source: Calculations based on World Bank Enterprise Surveys and World Development Indicators database.

Notes

1. The Indian government's Make in India initiative has industry competitiveness at its core. The Sri Lankan government has set up a National Productivity Secretariat to help enhance Sri Lankan productivity by energizing the sector to face international competition.

2. Hsieh and Klenow (2009), Pagés (2010), and others document that productivity dispersion between top and bottom firms is particularly large in developing countries. The positive correlation between firm size and productivity (although weaker in developing countries), and the fact that medium and large firms are underrepresented in South Asia, suggests that the preponderance of small firms drags down aggregate productivity, presenting a major opportunity for improving productivity.

3. It is worth mentioning that TFP is measured as the portion of output that is not explained by increases in physical capital stocks or in labor (both measured in quality and quantity). In fact, three important critiques have been leveled at this growth accounting framework. First, because TFP is measured as a residual, it provides an imperfect measure of shifts in the production function, which includes many determinants (particularly technical change, but also sustained political turmoil, external shocks, institutional changes, or measurement

errors). Second, the calculations are made by assuming a degree of competition in factor markets sufficient to ensure that factor earnings are proportional to factor productivity. Third, growth accounting cannot measure the fundamental causes of growth (policies, institutions, and history), but simply examines the proximate causes. Although these critiques have merit, the framework provides a simple and internally consistent way to organize data and is useful in generating insights into the process of economic growth.

4. Note that the analysis does not distinguish between a structural decline in TFP growth and a decline from idle or poorly allocated factors of production during cyclical periods of economic slowdown.

5. Sectoral employment shares data for Afghanistan, Bhutan, Maldives, and Nepal are available only for very few years and have not been used in this analysis.

6. The economic development literature has long recognized the role of structural transformation in boosting aggregate productivity. Baumol (1967), Dekle and Vandenbroucke (2012), Ngai and Pissarides (2007), Acemoglu and Guerrieri (2008), and others have shown that differential productivity growth across sectors will attract resources to more productive parts of the economy.

7. A simple reduced-form model is used to quantify the role of productivity in driving the process of structural transformation. The movement of labor from one sector to another is a function of productivity differentials across sectors (see annex 2A for a description of the model). The natural rate of structural transformation is measured by the coefficient on the share of employment lagged one period. The coefficient on the lagged employment share is always positive, significant, and significantly less than one, indicating a "natural" downward trend in the employment share of agriculture.

8. In theory, with no distortions firms producing similar products would have the same level of productivity. If that were not the case, then resources would move from the low-productivity firm to the higher returns of the high-productivity firm, driving the productivity of the former upward and of the latter downward. Given that factors omitted in the model may be responsible for productivity differences, the benchmark

for comparison is not zero productivity dispersion, but that of the United States—a relatively undistorted market.

9. As argued by Li and Rama (2015), because micro and small firms are generally underrepresented in datasets like the World Bank Enterprise Surveys, these indicators of dispersion of productivity likely underestimate true dispersion.

10. The World Bank Enterprise Surveys collect information about firms in different countries around the world in a harmonized way providing comparable cross-country information. The dataset includes only formal firms with at least five employees. The reader should keep in mind this truncation when interpreting results.

11. This conclusion holds even when restricting the sample to small and micro firms. Among these, the larger did better at business practices within a sample of small firms in Bangladesh, Chile, Ghana, Kenya, Mexico, Nigeria and Sri Lanka (McKenzie and Woodruff 2015).

12. Note that this calculation is based on the World Bank Enterprise Surveys, which do not include most micro firms, so it most likely underestimates productivity differences that would be observed if firms of all sizes were considered. Another important caveat is that differences in value added per worker between firms within different size classes may to some extent be explained by differences in average worker quality, as workers with higher abilities or skills may self-select into larger firms.

References

Acemoglu, D., and V. Guerrieri. 2008. "Capital Deepening and Nonbalanced Economic Growth." *Journal of Political Economy* 116 (3): 467–98.

Ayyagari, M., A. Demirgüç-Kunt, and V. Maksimovic. 2007. "Firm Innovation in Emerging Markets." Policy Research Working Paper 4157, World Bank, Washington DC.

Banerjee, A., and E. Duflo. 2006. "Growth Theory through the Lens of Development Economics." In *Handbook of Economic Growth*, edited by P. Aghion and S. Durlauf, vol. 1A, 473–552. Amsterdam: North-Holland Publishing Co.

Baumol, W. J. 1967. "Macroeconomics of Unbalanced Growth: The Anatomy of Urban Crisis." *American Economic Review* 57 (3): 415–26.

Bloom, N., B. Eifert, A. Mahajan, D. McKenzie, and J. Roberts. 2013. "Does Management Matter? Evidence from India." *Quarterly Journal of Economics* 128 (1): 1–51.

Bloom, N., and J. Van Reenen. 2007. "Measuring and Explaining Management Practices Across Firms and Countries." *Quarterly Journal of Economics* 122 (4): 1341–1408.

Cabral, L. 2007. "Small Firms in Portugal: A Selective Survey of Stylized Facts, Economic Analysis, and Policy Implications." *Portuguese Economic Journal* 6 (1): 65–88.

Cohen, W., and S. Klepper. 1996. "Firm Size and the Nature of Innovation Within Industries: The Case of Product and Process R&D." *Review of Economics and Statistics* 78 (2): 232–43.

Dekle, R., and G. Vandenbroucke. 2012. "A Quantitative Analysis of China's Structural Transformation." *Journal of Economic Dynamics and Control* 36 (1): 119–35.

Del Mel, S., D. McKenzie, and C. Woodruff. 2008. "Returns to Capital in Microenterprises: Evidence from a Field Experiment." *Quarterly Journal of Economics* 123 (4): 1329–72.

Herrendorf, B., R. Rogerson, and Á. Valentinyi. 2013. "Growth and Structural Transformation." NBER Working Paper 18996, National Bureau of Economic Research, Cambridge, MA.

Hsieh, C., and P. J. Klenow. 2009. "Misallocation and Manufacturing TFP in China and India." *Quarterly Journal of Economics* 124 (4): 1403–48.

———. 2014. "The Life Cycle of Plants in India and Mexico." *Quarterly Journal of Economics* 129 (3): 1035–83.

Hsieh, C., and B. A. Olken. 2014. "The Missing 'Missing Middle.'" *Journal of Economic Perspectives* 28 (3): 89–108.

Klenow, P., Sharma, G., and A. Bollard. 2011. "India's Mysterious Manufacturing Miracle." 2011 Meeting Paper No. 1176, Society for Economic Dynamics, Minneapolis, MN.

Krugman, P. 1994. *Peddling Prosperity: Economic Sense and Nonsense in the Age of Expectations.* New York: W. W. Norton & Co.

Lewis, W. 2004. *The Power of Productivity: Wealth, Poverty, and the Threat to Global Stability.* Chicago: University of Chicago Press.

Li, Y., and M. Rama. 2015. "Firm Dynamics, Productivity Growth, and Job Creation in Developing Countries: The Role of Micro- and

Small Enterprises." *World Bank Research Observer* 30 (1): 3–38.

McKenzie, D., and C. Woodruff. 2015. "Business Practices in Small Firms in Developing Countries." NBER Working Paper 21505, National Bureau of Economic Research, Cambridge, MA.

McKinsey Global Institute. 1998. *Productivity: The Key to an Accelerated Development Path for Brazil.* Washington, DC: McKinsey Global Institute.

Ngai, R., and C. A. Pissarides. 2007. "Structural Change in a Multi-sector Model of Growth." *American Economic Review* 97 (1): 429–43.

Pagés, C., ed. 2010. *The Age of Productivity: Transforming Economies from the Bottom Up.* New York: Palgrave Macmillan.

Porter, M. 1990. "The Competitive Advantage of Nations." *Harvard Business Review* 68 (2): 73–93.

Tybout, J. R. 1996. "Heterogeneity and Productivity Growth: Assessing the Evidence." In *Industrial Evolution in Developing Countries: Micro Patterns of Turnover, Productivity, and Market Structure*, edited by M. J. Roberts and J. R. Tybout, 43–68. Oxford: Oxford University Press.

Verma, R. 2012. "Can Total Factor Productivity Explain Value Added Growth in Services?" *Journal of Development Economics* 99 (1): 163–77.

World Bank and UNCTAD (United Nations Conference on Trade and Development). 2015. World Integrated Trade Solutions Trade Data.

Productivity Performance: Firms and Linkages

Although productivity can be measured at different levels—macro, sectoral, and geographic, for example—the most robust and intuitive representation is at the level of the firm. The focus on the firm as the unit of analysis and on firm dynamics as the driver of productivity growth goes back at least as far Schumpeter (1942), with competition playing a key role in forcing inefficient, unproductive, or unprofitable firms to either improve or exit and transfer their resources to more efficient, productive, or profitable firms, thus boosting economy-wide productivity.

Formally, there are two mutually reinforcing mechanisms, spurred on by competition in product and factor markets, that increase productivity. First, greater competition, from either domestic or international sources, pushes firms to become more efficient through learning from international exposure, investing in innovation, improving business practices, adopting better technology, including information and communication technology

(ICT), and improving the input mix. This is the *within-firm* component of productivity growth. Second, competition also induces inefficient firms to transfer resources to more efficient firms or exit altogether, boosting economy-wide productivity—the *between-firm* component of productivity growth (Cabral 2007). Resources can flow from less- to more-productive uses through improvements in standard factors such as infrastructure and business environment, but also as a result of participation in global value chains (GVCs) (Saia, Andrews, and Albrizio 2015) and agglomeration economies (Desmet and Rossi-Hansberg 2009; Michaels, Rauch, and Redding 2012).

The decomposition of changes in productivity into between- and within-firm components (with the former further broken down into contributions from firm entry and exit) has become a standard approach to thinking about productivity dynamics (Olley and Pakes 1996; Melitz and Polanec 2012). Unfortunately, none of the countries in the region carry out large, longitudinal firm surveys that would directly allow for this type of analysis.[1] Therefore, this report approximates the spirit of the decomposition by using cross-sectional firm data to consider elements that are likely to affect productivity across and within firms, in turn. This part begins with the business environment, agglomeration economies, and participation in GVCs as determinants of performance across firms, and then considers how input use, technology adoption, and innovation affect within-firm productivity.

Several broad conclusions emerge. South Asia scores poorly on many indicators of the quality of the business environment, which greatly constrains firms' productivity in general and particularly limits the growth of firms with high levels of productivity. Leveraging agglomeration and urbanization economies requires a reduction in the distortions in product and factor markets, particularly in the barriers that limit the flow of resources between districts and states.

Participation in GVCs can raise productivity through exposure to competition and knowledge spillovers from connections with lead firms; however, South Asian participation in GVCs is largely confined to apparel. Reducing trade barriers, increasing skills, and improving logistics would facilitate greater participation in GVCs. Finally, access to technology varies greatly across South Asian economies, ranging from extensive technology use in India to limited ICT adoption in Bangladesh and Nepal. Even among lead countries, however, the use of e-commerce and other productivity-enhancing online business tools is relatively low. Innovation tends to be concentrated in few mature firms and is likely to consist of imitating existing products rather than developing new ones. Greater investment in technology diffusion, improved resource management, and the development of skills that are complementary to technology could play a critical role in increasing innovation and thus boosting productivity.

Business Environment Challenges Continue to Weigh on Firm Performance | 3

Much of the macro and sectoral challenges to productivity in South Asia can be traced to a difficult operating environment for the region's firms. The business environment, also called the investment climate, has received a great deal of attention in the policy and empirical literature as a major constraint on firm productivity in the region. Most studies define the investment climate as the environment that affects entrepreneurs' ability to work efficiently, such as the degree of difficulty in accessing production inputs and dealing with regulatory and legal requirements and the level of security for running operations and obtaining payments. As argued by Hallward-Driemeier (2007), an inefficient business environment will lead to low and uncertain returns on investment, dragging down overall productivity and possibly more than offsetting technical improvements on the factory floor.

On average, countries in South Asia score poorly on two major indexes used globally to capture key aspects of the business environment: the Global Competitiveness Index (GCI) (World Economic Forum 2015) and *Doing Business* (World Bank 2016). In the most recent GCI rankings (for 2015–16), India is the only South Asian country in the top half of nearly 140 countries, in the

55th position, but lagging well behind China at 28. India is followed by Sri Lanka at 68, Nepal at 100, Bhutan at 105, Bangladesh at 107, and Pakistan at 126. Although all South Asian economies (with the exception of Bhutan) improved since 2014, many have yet to regain the ground they lost since 2007. Pakistan, for example, has lost 34 places and India, despite making major advances, still ranks 7 positions lower than it did in 2007.

When it comes to the components of the overall ranking, the most challenging areas in Bangladesh, Bhutan, Nepal, and Pakistan include inadequate supply of infrastructure and the effects of corruption, while in Sri Lanka the most problematic factors are inefficient government bureaucracy and limited access to finance. Although India has recently achieved better GCI scores on the macroeconomic environment, institutions, and infrastructure, its score remains hampered by inadequate electricity supply and poor technology readiness of its businesses.

In the World Bank's 2016 *Doing Business* report, all the South Asian economies, with the exception of Bhutan, are ranked in the bottom half of the "Ease of Doing Business," scale with an average ranking of 128 (figure 3.1). By contrast, many of South Asia's competitors are in the top half of the ranking, such as Thailand (49), China (84), and Vietnam (90).

FIGURE 3.1   South Asia countries lag behind comparators in business environment rankings

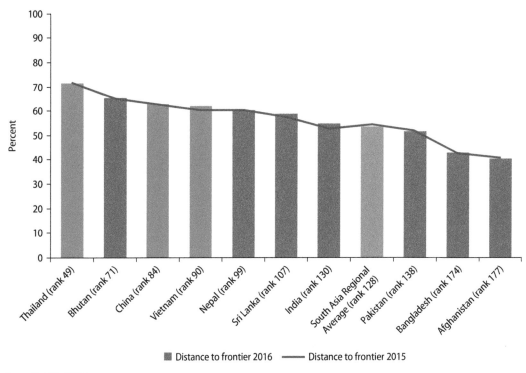

■ Distance to frontier 2016   —— Distance to frontier 2015

Source: World Bank 2016.
Note: The distance to frontier score benchmarks economies with respect to regulatory practice, showing the absolute distance to the best performance in each Doing Business indicator. An economy's distance to frontier score is indicated on a scale from 0 to 100, where 0 represents the worst performance and 100 the frontier. Tan bars represent countries in the South Asia region; blue bars represent countries outside the region.

Bhutan has the region's highest rank, at 71, followed by Nepal (99), Sri Lanka (107), India (130), Pakistan (138), Bangladesh (174), and Afghanistan (177). Compared to their 2015 rankings, only India and Sri Lanka improved—moving from 134 to 130 and 113 to 107, respectively—while all the other countries experienced a setback.

As measured by the *Doing Business* indicators, on average, the South Asian economies rank highest in Protecting Minority Investors, with India and Pakistan respectively ranked 8th and 25th globally. The region's next-best performing category is Starting a Business, but rankings here are well below those of comparators: India ranked 155 out of 189 economies, and although Sri Lanka ranked better (98), it nevertheless cost 18.7 percent of income per capita to set up a firm, compared to 6.4 percent

in Thailand and 4.9 percent in Vietnam. The areas with the most opportunity for improvement are Enforcing Contracts (where the region's average ranking is 143), Registering Property (136), and Resolving Insolvency (129). On average, resolving a commercial dispute through the courts takes 1,077 days in South Asia—almost twice the global average of 630 days.

The region also performs poorly in logistics rankings. According to the World Bank's Logistics Performance Index (LPI), in 2014 South Asia had the lowest logistics performance among all developing regions because of its poor quality of trade and transport-related infrastructure, time-consuming clearance processes, low quality of logistics services, and lack of timeliness of shipments compared to economies such as China, Vietnam, and Thailand. As with the GCI rankings, none of the South Asian economies placed in the top 50 of the LPI, while China is ranked at 30, Thailand at 31, and Vietnam at 48. Between 2007 and 2014, only Nepal and Sri Lanka were able to improve their logistics performance by gaining 25 places and 3 places, respectively, in the overall LPI rankings—but much ground still remains to be covered.

Poor logistics can sharply reduce efficiency. Lengthy and unpredictable delays in customs clearance can force firms to hold high inventories (regional firms in auto parts, textiles, electronics, and heavy engineering report maintaining on average 27 percent higher than necessary inventories to deal with uncertain delivery times) and can impose delays in production and increased turn-around times. Delays caused by poor road infrastructure and lengthy interstate clearance processes have similar effects. For example, in India, crossing two state borders between origin and destination can add as much as a week to the

uncertainty in delivery schedules (Jordan and Kamphuis 2014).

Moving from expert surveys and de jure requirements (such as the *Doing Business* report) to perceptions by firms (as shown in the World Bank's Enterprise Surveys) further underscores the pervasiveness of the challenges. In a 2006 Investment Climate Assessment, the World Bank argued that South Asian countries underperform comparators on many investment climate dimensions, including infrastructure and electricity supply, access to finance, employee skills, and corruption (World Bank 2006a). Similar results emerge from the most recent round of World Bank Enterprise Surveys in which an average firm in South Asia consistently ranks each investment climate constraint as more binding than does an average firm in China or Vietnam (table 3.1). Although performance varies substantially across countries and indicators—pointing to significant potential for improvement by leveraging best

TABLE 3.1   Firms in South Asia are at a disadvantage with respect to investment climate

Percent of firms that view an obstacle as a major or severe constraint

	Afghanistan (2014)	Bangladesh (2013)	Bhutan (2015)	India (2014)	Nepal (2013)	Pakistan (2013)	Sri Lanka (2011)	South Asia (average)	China (2012)	South Africa (2007)	Turkey (2013)	Vietnam (2015)
Access to finance	49	23	19	15	40	22	33	18	5	16	10	14
Political environment	76	76	12	16	85	34	13	28	1	3	13	3
Crime	58	8	1	5	14	35	7	10	1	38	8	5
Taxes	56	20	24	31	23	55	41	36	7	8	25	8
Corruption	62	49	4	36	42	64	15	42	1	17	12	5
Informality	33	9	10	17	29	12	28	14	7	11	14	11
Infrastructure	81	55	29	26	79	79	36	42	6	24	25	18
Electricity	66	52	14	21	69	75	26	35	3	21	18	4
Telecom	59	3	15	4	3	14	6	7	4	4	9	8
Transport	43	15	14	10	32	27	12	15	3	4	10	10
Labor regulations	11	3	15	11	3	12	13	12	1	6	6	4
Workforce education	53	16	14	9	9	23	16	13	2	9	10	8
Trade & customs	47	8	9	12	29	30	31	18	4	2	11	24

Source: World Bank calculations based on World Bank Enterprise Surveys.

practices from within the region—the overall gap puts South Asia's firms at a clear disadvantage compared to select comparators in other parts of the world.

Lessons from the case studies in this report echo the findings from the surveys. Difficulties in importing goods, poor trade logistics, and high protection rates have made participation in global markets more costly for firms across the region, while outdated standards and restrictive regulations have limited competition in the automotive and agribusiness sectors. Difficulties in accessing well-located and well-serviced industrial land and poor availability of skilled workers have also emerged as important bottlenecks to firm growth.

Although firms may have different capabilities to overcome various investment climate constraints, studies show that an average firm in South Asia experiences a sizeable productivity loss from the poor investment climate. For example, Hallward-Driemeier (2007) finds a significant negative effect on total factor productivity (TFP) and investment rates of garment firms across the region from customs delays, power outages, poor access to finance, and limited connectivity. In particular, the author shows that, if the business environment for firms in India were the same as that in China, firm productivity could be one percentage point higher. Analysis that approximates the approach of Hallward-Driemeier (2007) using the most recent round of World Bank Enterprise Surveys shows that, by and large, investment climate challenges continue to affect firm performance in the region. Across a wide sample of manufacturing firms in

Bangladesh, Bhutan, India, Nepal, Pakistan, and Sri Lanka, both output and value added per worker are systematically lower when firms face greater business environment constraints (table 3.2).

A restrictive business environment can be particularly damaging to firms that have the most to contribute to productivity growth and job creation. Many investment climate constraints can be particularly burdensome for small firms (Word Bank 2006a), limiting their ability to grow and create employment. Some evidence also shows that higher-productivity firms in the region may actually face greater constraints in accessing public services, suggesting that investment climate deficiencies are particularly binding on firms that would grow more rapidly and create more jobs in the absence of distortions (Carlin and Schaffer 2012).

The severity of investment climate obstacles in the region and their adverse impact on productivity have given rise to a series of wide-ranging reforms to address constraints in each aspect of the business environment: for example, a range of policy actions has been proposed to various regional authorities by the Asian Development Bank (2006), the Asian Development Bank and World Bank (2004), Afram and Salvi Del Pero (2012), Ferrari and Dhingra (2009), OECD (2009), and the World Bank (2006a, 2006b, 2008a, 2008b, 2009, 2010). Improving the investment climate is also high on the regional authorities' own policy agendas: nearly every country in the region is taking concrete steps to strengthen the business environment (box 3.1).

TABLE 3.2 South Asia's investment climate deficiencies constrain firm performance

	Output per worker (log)	Value added per worker (log)
Losses from power outages (log)	−0.024**	−0.038***
Losses in transit (log)	−0.079***	−0.036***
Improved access to finance	0.342***	0.403***
Observations	4,566	4,498
R-squared	0.039	0.027
Sector dummies (number)	20	19

Source: World Bank calculations based on World Bank Enterprise Surveys.
Note: ***$p < 0.01$, **$p < 0.05$, *$p < 0.1$.

BOX 3.1 Efforts to improve the investment climate in South Asia

In Bangladesh, the authorities initiated a number of reforms to address binding constraints on private sector growth in the recent years. New business-friendly legislation includes: (1) the Economic Zones Act of 2010, modernizing the country's economic zones agenda, including the institutional setup, and allowing for more efficient incentives and private participation; (2) the Competition Law, which is meant to uphold a level playing field for businesses; and (3) a new Value Added Tax Law that eases the compliance mechanisms for businesses and reduces discretionary exemptions. The authorities also introduced regulatory reforms that streamlined business registration and trademark and patent registration and simplified trade licenses and construction permits. A total of 56 regulatory processes have been reformed in recent years including company, investment, tax, and trademark registrations; trade licenses at local government levels; subordinate rules under three different tax laws for better contract enforcement; and dispute resolution. To foster trade competitiveness, the authorities have launched a trade information portal and introduced risk management in the clearance process, as well as taking preparatory steps to a new Customs Act, a national single window for trade, and making multimodal transport effective for trade logistics. Responding to concerns on fragmented policy coordination, these reforms are being carried out in the context of a formal, structured public-private dialogue.

In India, the authorities recently launched a new, ambitious program of regulatory reform. In 2015, the authorities eliminated the minimum capital requirement and ended the requirement of obtaining a certificate to commence business operations. Indian entrepreneurs no longer need to deposit $1,629 (100,000 Indian rupees)—equivalent to 111 percent of annual income per capita—in order to start a local limited liability company and can start business five days earlier than under previous regulations. Utilities in Delhi and Mumbai undertook significant business process reengineering, combining inspections and procedures to reduce the time required for companies to get connected to the electrical grid and get on with their business. In addition, the central government called for all states to automate registration processes, move toward effective single window systems, and implement risk-based inspection regimes that introduce self-certification and third-party audit schemes to lessen the burden of inspections on low- and medium-risk businesses.

In Sri Lanka, the authorities have recently taken steps to eliminate obstacles to foreign direct investment (FDI), including (1) up-front payment of the land-lease tax for foreign companies; (2) elimination of minimum investment requirements in ICT, R&D, and vocational training; and (3) implementation of online processing of business visas. Regulatory barriers to trade are being reduced through an agreement to ratify the World Trade Organization (WTO) Trade Facilitation Agreement (which is the basis for a medium-term trade reform agenda) and creation of the National Trade Facilitation Committee, which will be the body in charge of leading trade facilitation reform. Finally, a new Secured Transactions Act will enable the use of movable assets as collateral for bank loans, improving access to finance for small and medium enterprises (SMEs).

In Pakistan, the authorities have recently embarked on a two-year plan to improve the country's *Doing Business* ranking to the top 100 by 2018, by preparing a Doing Business Reform Strategy. The strategy provides reform recommendations for all the *Doing Business* indicators and provides institutions at the provincial and federal level with the mandate to carry out the reforms. The strategy is currently being implemented both at the federal and provincial levels,

(continues next page)

BOX 3.1   Efforts to improve the investment climate in South Asia (continued)

having been endorsed by an Ease of Doing Business Committee formed by the authorities. In addition, and complementing the big push on Doing Business, the Government of Pakistan also took a series of legislative actions and implemented regulations to improve access to credit, payment of taxes, and financial intermediation (capital markets and housing finance), as well as reforms in financial transparency and oversight of state-owned enterprises.

Although the importance of addressing investment climate constraints in the region is beyond question, the issues are well-known and policy pathways to address them have been mapped out by various institutions, including the region's own governments. There is little that the current study can add to the vast body of knowledge on the issue, save for emphasizing that industry-specific business environment issues in the form of product market regulations remain a critical constraint to productivity growth (the industry case studies, especially the study of agribusiness value chains in this chapter, show that these regulations restrict investment and competition). Therefore, the discussion in the following chapters focuses on newer, less-researched determinants and correlates of firm productivity in South Asia: agglomeration economies, value chains, and firm capabilities, including technology and innovation.

INDUSTRY CASE STUDY A

Industry-specific business environment issues in agribusiness

Agribusiness (including agriculture) accounts for one-third of South Asia's GDP, and its share is expected to double by 2030 as a result of income growth and urbanization, creating millions of productive jobs outside agriculture and positive backward links to farmers, most of whom are small and vulnerable.

Numerous examples show how leading private firms and market forces are needed to develop and diffuse the new higher-value products and services as well as to facilitate access by small-holders to knowledge, finance, and markets. Government-led arrangements, put in place to support farmers and achieve food security, are no longer relevant and are in fact counterproductive. Some of these arrangements (such as trade barriers, price caps on higher-value goods, restrictions on private agricultural markets, storage, and FDI in retail) discourage private investment and limit competition in the new high-value markets. Minimum support prices and government procurements encourage excessive production of low-value commodities, and large blanket subsidies lead to overuse of water and other unsustainable agricultural practices.

South Asia's great agribusiness opportunity

Agribusiness (agriculture, food processing, food retail, and restaurants) accounts for one-third of South Asia's GDP and is estimated to double in size over the next 15 years, reaching $1.5 trillion by 2030. The increase will be driven by income growth and urbanization, shifting the demand toward higher-value products (such as horticulture, livestock, and packaged and processed foods) and food-related services. Figure 3.2 shows that spending on food starts to grow significantly at South Asia's current GDP per capita level of $1,500.

Investments in agro-food processing result in input and income multipliers higher than in any other industry, and the employment effect is about 2.5 times that of other sectors (World Bank 2014). The increased demand for higher-value agricultural products and interactions with increasingly sophisticated buyers increase the productivity and income of poor farmers. Furthermore, some of the agricultural products with the highest growth potential, such as dairy products, can disproportionately benefit women.

South Asia has also the opportunity to develop its exports from a low base of

FIGURE 3.2   Food spending in relation to GDP per capita

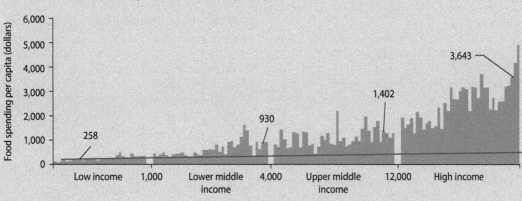

Source: International Comparison Project (ICP) Database, World Bank, Washington, DC (accessed October 2015).

FIGURE 3.3 **Horticulture yield**

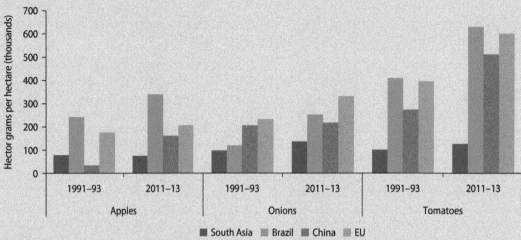

Source: FAO Database, United Nations, New York (accessed August 2015), http://faostat.fao.org/.

FIGURE 3.4 **Productivity in agro-food processing firms**

Output value per employee

Source: World Bank Enterprise Survey 2014.

3 percent of world agro-food trade compared to 14 percent for East Asia. Export bright spots already include basmati rice (India and Pakistan), dried fruit and nuts (Afghanistan), and branded tea (Sri Lanka).

Seizing these opportunities will require addressing three related challenges.

The productivity challenge
Agriculture yields remain low, especially in high-potential high-value products such as horticulture (figure 3.3). Postharvest losses are high due to a lack of storage capacity (India's Planning Commission estimated the warehousing shortage at 35 million tons), and productivity in agro-food processing firms is much lower in South Asia than in East Asia (figure 3.4).

The small-holder challenge
Agricultural production in South Asia is predominantly in the hands of small-scale farmers who are among the population's most vulnerable. Lack of market information and logistical difficulties prevent small-scale producers from accessing markets efficiently. If the product is to be exported, the logistics and financing requirements are usually beyond their capabilities.

The natural resources challenge
Agriculture's share of total fresh water use is very high (at, for example, 99 percent in Afghanistan and 90 percent in India), and competition for water is increasing with the growth in manufacturing and household consumption (FAO 2014). Much of the region's irrigation depends on groundwater. In India, for example, groundwater supplies 60 percent of the water used for irrigation, of which 15 percent is overexploited. (World Bank 2013). Climate change is exacerbating the need to improve water management and use.

How leading agribusiness firms can help address these challenges

Thirty-six leading agribusiness firms in South Asia were interviewed for this report.

Their experience sheds light on how, together with market forces and government support, they can help develop and bring to market superior products as well as improve farmers' access to knowledge, finance, and markets.

Developing and marketing new high-value products

Dilmah Tea is Sri Lanka's largest exporter of tea and the sixth largest tea company in the world, exporting premium tea to more than 80 countries. It started in 1974 with 18 employees and as of 2016 has 35,000. It has remained competitive because of its continuous investment in R&D and innovative marketing. KRBL Ltd., one of the world's largest exporters of basmati rice, successfully marketed the Pusa-1121 basmati rice developed by the Indian Agricultural Research Institute. This variety became a best-seller in the Persian Gulf and India. Higher prices led to rapid adoption by farmers—by 2013 the new variety accounted for 84 percent and 68 percent of basmati plantings in Punjab and Haryana, respectively.

Facilitating small-holder access to knowledge, finance, and markets

In Bangladesh, Aftab Bahumuki Farms Ltd. introduced contract farming for commercial broiler chickens on an experimental basis in 1991, working with a select group of 20 farmers. The number of farmers involved had increased to 650 by 2003. Begum (2008) found that contracted farmers achieved 30 percent higher net returns than noncontracted farmers. In Bhutan, Mountain Hazelnut Ventures was established in 2010 to plant and process hazelnuts. The company distributed tissue-cultured hazelnut plantlets and planting material to farmers. In three years of operation 2,000 hectares had been planted and 5,000 farmers trained. In India, Desai F&V, by taking control of the logistics and managing the process from fruit formation onward, succeeded in supplying remote urban centers with quality bananas and in exporting grade "A" fruit to distant markets in the Middle East. Pepsico provided potato varieties suitable for the processing of potato chips to thousands of Indian small-holders supplying its processing facilities.

Links with downstream producers can also improve farmers' access to finance. Access can be direct, through a variety of contract farming arrangements, with inputs provided on the basis of agreements to sell the output at a later date. There are indirect benefits as well, as banks are more willing to lend to farmers that have a contractual arrangement with a processor. Godrej Agrovet has helped 50,000 small-holders in eight Indian states access bank financing by guaranteeing prices and standardizing financing agreements between the banks and the farmers. The government and development partners can also help promote such arrangements as shown in Afghanistan (box 3.2).

How industry-specific business environment issues stand in the way

Agricultural policies put in place in the 1960s to support farmers and achieve food security are now limiting private investment and competition in the new high-value markets and encouraging excessive production of low-value commodities through unsustainable agricultural practices.

Barriers to trade

Average most-favored-nation rates applied on food products remain high in the region (at 33 percent in India and 26 percent in Sri Lanka compared to 16 percent in China and Vietnam). There are also instances of inverted tariff structures that discourage domestic production, such as in Afghanistan where tariffs on intermediate goods (10.2 percent) are higher than those on final goods (7 percent). Nontariff barriers (paratariffs, ad hoc quantitative restrictions, and cumbersome standards and custom procedures) have long been cited as major reasons for low intraregional trade. For example, revenue collection from supplementary duties exceeded revenue collection from customs duties in fiscal 2012/13 in Bangladesh.

Restrictions on agricultural markets

Outdated regulations, such as the 1939 Agriculture Produce Market Ordinance Act

BOX 3.2   Promoting access to finance and backward links in Afghanistan

In Afghanistan, the Agriculture Development Fund (ADF) began in 2010 as a $100 million project of the U.S. Agency for International Development (USAID) to provide much-needed long-term financing along agribusiness value chains. The ADF was rated the most successful USAID project in Afghanistan, with a more than 95 percent reimbursement rate and 60,000 farmers benefitting. The ADF is facing excess demand, and discussions are underway to scale it up. The key innovation of the ADF is to provide long-term loans to agro-food processors on the condition that they lend a portion of their loans to their suppliers-farmers. This approach leverages both the agro-food processors' knowledge as well as the business leverage they have over their suppliers to ensure proper use of the funds and repayment. By contrast, commercial banks in Afghanistan mostly cater to urban areas and lack such access and knowledge. The ADF has been operated by professionals with extensive experience in commercial banking and agribusiness and incorporates financial products that are fully compliant with Sharia.

in Pakistan and the 1956 Agriculture Produce Marketing Act in India, have hindered private investment in market and storage infrastructure as well as contract farming. The central government of India has promoted reforms (along the lines of a Model Agriculture Produce Marketing Act) since 2003, and while several states have introduced new legislation to modify the 1956 Act since, the changes have been partial and uneven; further, in many cases changes have not been fully implemented, largely preserving the status quo. Modern food retailers, which foster innovation and competition along the value chain, are also restricted by regulations (such as the FDI restrictions in India). Early reforms are promising. For example, the 2012 reforms by the Sindh province in Pakistan, which abolished notified market areas and market committees and allowed private markets and direct buying, led to the creation of the private chili trading platform in Kunri.

Restrictions on prices and inadequate product standards
Investment in higher-value food products is discouraged by price caps on items such as milk and meat in Punjab, Pakistan. Inadequate food safety certification systems can have a serious negative effect on exports. For example, India had to upgrade its testing facilities to resume the export of Alphonso mangoes to the European Union.

Minimum support prices and subsidies on fertilizers and water
The drive to food security in the 1960s and 1970s led to multiple public interventions to support the production of low-value commodities. By providing high returns and low risks, these measures discourage farmers from moving into higher-value crops. Minimum support prices and fertilizer subsidies are also backed by large government procurement and distribution systems plagued with inefficiencies. India's large subsidies get the most publicity because of their size ($38 billion dollars in the 2016 budget, excluding power and irrigation subsidies) and the fact that they are poorly targeted, but the subsidy bills of Bangladesh and Sri Lanka are also enormous—nearly as large as all public expenditures on agriculture. Pakistan subsidizes fertilizer through low urea prices. Large water subsidies (such as irrigation charges that cover only 10 percent of the cost of water in Punjab, Pakistan, and free power for water pumping in Punjab, India) lead to an unsustainable overuse of water.

The extended version of this case study is available online at www.worldbank.org /SouthAsiaCompetes.

Note

1. There are two exceptions in the case of India, but neither is fully satisfactory. India's Annual Survey of Industries (ASI) data are available with panel identifiers starting from 1998–99; however, firms with fewer than 100 employees are sampled only once every 4–5 years, making it difficult to determine whether a missing firm exited or was not sampled. The Prowess database by the Centre for Monitoring Indian Economy has data for more than 10,000 manufacturing firms dating back to 1990, but these are mostly large, publicly listed companies.

References

Afram, G., and A. Salvi Del Pero. 2012. *Nepal's Investment Climate: Leveraging the Private Sector for Job Creation and Growth.* Washington, DC: World Bank.

Asian Development Bank. 2006. *South Asia Economic Report.* Manila: ADB.

Asian Development Bank and World Bank. 2004. *Sri Lanka: Improving the Rural and Urban Investment Climate.* Washington, DC: World Bank.

Begum, I. A. 2008. "Prospects and Potentialities of Vertically Integrated Contract Farming in Bangladesh," PhD thesis, Department of Agricultural Development Economics, Hokkaido University, Japan.

Cabral, L. 2007. "Small Firms in Portugal: A Selective Survey of Stylized Facts, Economic Analysis, and Policy Implications." *Portuguese Economic Journal* 6 (1): 65–88.

Carlin, W., and M. Schaffer. 2012. "Understanding the Business Environment in South Asia." Policy Research Working Paper 6160, World Bank, Washington, DC.

Desmet, K., and E. Rossi-Hansberg. 2009. "Spatial Growth and Industry Age." *Journal of Economic Theory* 144 (6): 2477–2502.

FAO (U.N. Food and Agricultural Organization). 2014. Country Profiles, United Nations, New York.

Ferrari, A., and I. S. Dhingra. 2009. *India's Investment Climate: Voices of Indian Business.* Washington, DC: World Bank.

Hallward-Driemeier, M. C. 2007. "Improving the Climate for Investment and Business in South Asia," in *South Asia Growth and Regional Integration*, ed. S. Ahmed and E. Ghani. Delhi: Macmillan India Ltd.

Jordan, L. S., and B. Kamphuis. 2014. *Supply Chain Delays and Uncertainty in India: The Hidden Constraint on Manufacturing Growth.* Washington, DC: World Bank.

Melitz, M. J., and S. Polanec. 2012. "Dynamic Olley-Pakes Productivity Decomposition with Entry and Exit." NBER Working Paper 18182, National Bureau of Economic Research, Cambridge, MA.

Michaels, G., F. Rauch, and S. J. Redding. 2012. "Urbanization and Structural Transformation," *Quarterly Journal of Economics* 127 (2): 535–86.

OECD (Organisation for Economic Co-operation and Development). 2009. *Investment Policy Review: India.* Paris: OECD.

Olley, G. S., and A. Pakes. 1996. "The Dynamics of Productivity in the Telecommunications Equipment Industry." *Econometrica* 64 (6): 1263–97.

Saia, A., D. Andrews, and S. Albrizio. 2015. "Public Policy and Spillovers from the Global Productivity Frontier: Industry Level Evidence." Economics Department Working Paper No. 1238, OECD, Paris.

Schumpeter, J. 1942. *Capitalism, Socialism, and Democracy.* New York: Harper & Bros.

World Bank. 2006a. *The Investment Climate in South Asia.* Washington, DC: World Bank.

———. 2006b. *The Maldives: Sustaining Growth and Improving the Investment Climate.* Washington, DC: World Bank.

———. 2008a. *Afghanistan Investment Climate Assessment.* Washington, DC: World Bank.

———. 2008b. *Harnessing Competitiveness for Stronger Inclusive Growth: Bangladesh Investment Climate Assessment.* Washington, DC: World Bank.

———. 2009. *Pakistan Investment Climate Assessment.* Washington, DC: World Bank.

———. 2010. *Bhutan Investment Climate Assessment Report: Vitalizing the Private sector, Creating Jobs.* Washington, DC: World Bank.

———. 2013. *Turn Down the Heat.* Washington, DC: World Bank.

———. 2014. *India—Accelerating Agricultural Productivity Growth.* Washington, DC: World Bank.

———. 2016. *Doing Business 2016.* Washington, DC: World Bank.

World Economic Forum. 2015. *The Global Competitiveness Report 2015–2016.* Geneva: World Economic Forum.

Productivity-Boosting Agglomeration Economies Are Underleveraged | 4

Agglomeration economies arise when firms and people locate near one another (for example, in cities and industrial clusters). In South Asia, where the concentration of economic activity is relatively high, agglomeration economies have a major role to play in increasing productivity. However, distortions in goods and factor markets prevent resources from flowing to more productive firms, particularly across state and district borders. Therefore, despite the statistically significant effect of agglomeration on productivity—which today in South Asia operates mainly through urbanization (cities) rather than through localization (clusters)—the full productivity benefits of agglomeration economies are yet to be realized. The following discussion develops these observations in more detail.

Economic activity in South Asia is highly concentrated

Economic activity tends to be geographically concentrated. This is true in every country regardless of industry considered or concentration measure used. For example, Rosenthal and Strange (2004) show that in the United States, heavy geographic concentration of industries is not limited to sectors

highly dependent on particular raw materials (such as wood in the furniture industry), but extends to sectors in which distance or location is less important, such as the software industry. Michaels, Rauch, and Redding (2012) show that the transformation of the American and Brazilian economies over the last 100 years increased the concentration of resources in a few locations. Studies that control for geographical scale and borders, such as Duranton and Overman (2005), also show that economic activity is heavily concentrated.

South Asia is no exception. Measures of firm concentration (using the locational Gini, which is calculated in the same way as the Gini coefficient is used to measure income inequality) in manufacturing are quite high in Bangladesh (0.53), India (0.67), and Sri Lanka (0.48).[1] In India, the 5 largest districts account for 18 percent of total employment, a share that has not changed appreciably over time, although which districts were in the top 5 has changed (table 4.1).[2] In Bangladesh, the share of the 5 largest districts (which is much greater than in India in part because Bangladesh has only about 60 districts compared to India's nearly 400) increased more than 10 percentage points between 1995 and 2012, with most of the increase coming from

TABLE 4.1   Employment across South Asia is concentrated in a few districts

Share of top five districts as a percentage of total employment

Rank	District Name		District Name		
India		1991		2009	Rank in 1991
1	Greater Bombay	5.0	Madras	4.7	3
2	Nizamabad	4.1	Bangalore	4.4	4
3	Madras	3.3	Coimbatore	3.7	8
4	Bangalore	2.6	Mahendragarh/Gurgaon	2.9	77
5	24 Parganas (North)	2.5	Rupnagar/Patiala	2.8	6
	Total (top five)	**17.4**	**Total (top five)**	**18.5**	
Bangladesh		1995		2012	Rank in 1995
1	Dhaka	36.6	Dhaka	35.4	1
2	Chittagong	15.9	Gazipur	16.6	6
3	Narayanganj	8.6	Chittagong	16.2	2
4	Sirajganj	5.0	Narayanganj	9.3	3
5	Khulna	3.8	Sirajganj	2.8	4
	Total (top five)	**69.8**	**Total (top five)**	**80.4**	
Sri Lanka		1995		2009	Rank in 1995
1	Colombo	37.4	Gampaha	27.7	2
2	Gampaha	29.7	Colombo	24.1	1
3	Galle	3.9	Kurunegala	9.4	5
4	Kandy	3.8	Kalutara	7.2	9
5	Kurunegala	3.1	Kandy	5.9	4
	Total (top five)	**77.9**	**Total (top five)**	**74.2**	

Source: World Bank calculations based on Annual Survey of Industries (ASI) in India and Sri Lanka and Survey of Manufacturing Industries (SMI) in Bangladesh

areas outside Dhaka.[3] In Sri Lanka, the 5 largest districts account for three-quarters of total employment, a share that has declined somewhat since the mid-1990s.[4]

In most countries, modern manufacturing has tended to develop initially in very concentrated locations, often on a coast with access to international markets. As development proceeds, large coastal cities become congested and expensive, while at the same time the scale externalities they offer dissipate as manufacturing processes become more standardized. Manufacturing plants then move first to suburban or nearby satellite locations and thereafter to secondary cities in the hinterland. Yet the degree of geographic concentration of manufacturing activities in South Asia has not changed substantially in the last two decades (table 4.2).

The Raw Concentration Index in table 4.2 measures the degree to which the geographic pattern of employment in the industry departs from the geographic pattern of manufacturing employment in the country as a whole, with larger values indicating greater concentration of activity.[5] The Ellison-Glaeser (Ellison and Glaeser 1997) Index corrects for a potential bias in the raw index (the concentration value is larger in industries with a small number of very large plants) and allows for comparisons across industries. In any event, neither measure of agglomeration has changed significantly over time (with the exception of one year in India and two years in Sri Lanka), suggesting that more productive locations have generally not been successful in attracting additional resources at the expense of less productive locations, therefore inhibiting overall productivity growth. Ghani, Goswami, and Kerr (2012a) provide one explanation for this: the authors suggest that a compositional change may be under way, with larger plants moving out of South Asia's cities and

TABLE 4.2   Spatial concentration of manufacturing in South Asia has not changed much over time

	India: State		India: District		Bangladesh: District		Sri Lanka: District	
	Raw Index	EG Index	Raw Index	EG Index	Raw Index	EG Index	Raw Index	EG Index
1994	0.001	−0.000	0.006	0.005	—	—	—	—
1996	−0.013	0.001	−0.012	0.001	—	—	0.001	−0.009
1997	—	—	—	—	0.029	0.056	0.007	−0.011
1998	—	—	—	—	—	—	0.021	−0.001
1999	—	—	—	—	0.008	−0.025	0.030	−0.010
2000	0.009	0.018*	0.012	0.021**	—	—	0.026	−0.011
2001	—	—	—	—	−0.006	0.005	0.044	0.056
2002	—	—	—	—	—	—	0.044	0.056
2003	—	—	—	—	—	—	0.019	−0.023
2005	—	—	—	—	0.009	−0.036	—	—
2006	−0.009	−0.001	−0.013	−0.005	—	—	0.071**	−0.504
2007	—	—	—	—	—	—	0.073**	−1.660***
2008	—	—	—	—	—	—	−0.000	−0.330
2009	0.019	0.012	0.016	0.003	—	—	−0.004	−0.167
2012	—	—	—	—	0.047	−0.084	—	—
N	351	348	351	348	123	118	263	260

Source: World Bank calculations based on Annual Survey of Industries (ASI) in India and Sri Lanka and Survey of Manufacturing Industries (SMI) in Bangladesh; Ellison-Glaeser (EG) 1997.
Note: Table cells show the coefficients from a regression of concentration indexes on time dummies. A statistically significant positive (negative) coefficient indicates that spatial concentration in that year was significantly above (below) the mean. — = not available.
$*p < 0.1; **p < 0.05; ***p < 0.01.$

an increasing number of smaller service establishments moving in.

Agglomeration economies raise firm productivity

Evidence shows that agglomeration is positively associated with firm performance in South Asia (see, for example, Glaeser and Kerr 2009; Ghani, Kerr, and O'Connell 2011; and Mukim 2011). Proximity to cities had a positive impact on nonfarm employment in Nepal (Fafchamps and Shilpi 2005). Similarly, households in Bangladesh with better access to major urban centers achieved higher returns to nonfarm activities (Deichmann, Shilpi, and Vakis 2008). The concentration of high-return economic activities around Bangladesh's growth poles (Dhaka and Chittagong) led to higher productivity in the eastern part of the country (World Bank 2008). Therefore, the ongoing urbanization process in South Asia (as described in World Bank 2015) is likely to increase productivity due to agglomeration, which may reinforce an increase in productivity as workers move

from lower-productivity agriculture to higher-productivity manufacturing and services.

Evidence from the industry studies confirms the importance of agglomeration. The biggest benefits from agglomeration economies were found in the automotive industry, where geographic proximity to the customer has supported efforts to upgrade product, process, and function. There is a high, robust correlation between productivity and the propensity of automotive firms to be located next to other automotive firms. Although this correlation may arise in part from high-productivity firms electing to locate next to each other, interviews suggest that firms derive substantial benefits from clusters. The location of leading firms close to suppliers and clients also has been important in apparel and agribusiness; it is, however, too early to see agglomeration effects in the small electronics sector in the region.

Agglomeration is usually discussed in terms of localization (firms in the same industry locating close to one another) or urbanization (firms in diverse industries locating in the same area), as described in box 4.1. Other indicators have also been used to measure the productivity benefits of agglomeration: for example, two alternative measures of agglomeration at the plant level—market access and proximity to transport hubs—were correlated with productivity in four of the nine sectors in India investigated by Lall, Shalizi, and Deichmann (2004). In contrast, the authors find that measures of localization are correlated with productivity in only two sectors and measures of urbanization in none. These findings, however, rely on estimating the effects of agglomeration economies jointly with the estimation of the production function, potentially widening uncertainty around the estimates (see, for example, Van Beveren 2012; Combes, Duranton, and Gobillon 2011). Moreover, the correlation between measures of urbanization and market access can be high, as both indicators are calculated using the size of urban population in the same district.

In South Asia, much of the economic activity tends to cluster (localize) either naturally or in response to policy distortions. In India's automotive industry, the need to overcome logistical difficulties has largely determined the physical distribution of business activity. For example, in the early 2000s, Maruti Suzuki, India's largest carmaker, relied on some 400 major suppliers located across the country, some almost 2,500 kilometers away from its main plant in Haryana. Its total logistics costs were up to four times as high as its wage bill, and it had to carry large buffer stocks. By 2013, buffer stocks were brought down to zero and logistics costs slashed after almost all suppliers were required to build, warehouse, or locate within a few hours' radius of the plant. Today, approximately 80 percent of Maruti Suzuki's suppliers are located within a 100-kilometer radius. In Pakistan's apparel industry, leading firms and their suppliers in leather apparel—already clustered in Sialkot and benefitting from labor pooling, knowledge diffusion, and a critical mass of offerings to encourage international buyers to travel to this remote place—privately financed the construction of an international airport and exhibition center to further develop the cluster.

BOX 4.1 Agglomeration and productivity

Economic growth and geographical concentration of economic activities reinforce each other (Baldwin and Martin 2004; Martin and Ottaviano 2001) through the forces of localization and urbanization. Localization economies are the gains in productivity that result when firms in the same industry locate close to one another and benefit from sharing inputs, labor market pooling, and knowledge spillovers (Marshall 1920). Urbanization economies are the gains in productivity that result when firms in different industries locate in the same area (Jacobs 1969). The diverse range of industries in a particular location enables firms to access suppliers from different industries, benefit from research and development (R&D) spillovers, or access a generally higher-quality labor market.

Recently, other sources have been suggested, such as home-market effects (in which the concentration of demand encourages agglomeration) and economies of consumption (because consumers enjoy variety).

In a survey of the literature, Rosenthal and Strange (2004) report that the elasticity of productivity with respect to the size of the city or to the size of the industry generally lies between 3 and 8 percent. In a recent paper, Martin, Mayer, and Mayneris (2011) argue that, in the case of France, localization economies dominate urbanization effects—at least in the short term—and raise TFP by 5 to 10 percent. Much like this study, however, most of the empirical studies are based on developed countries, and there is little evidence for developing economies.

On the other hand, empirical evidence shows that urbanization economies appear to have had a larger impact on plant productivity in South Asia than localization economies (table 4.3). The estimation approach follows the two-step strategy of Martin, Mayer, and Mayneris (2011): first deriving plant-level estimates of total factor productivity (TFP) and then assessing the impact of various aspects of agglomeration economies while also controlling for geographical location (measured at the state level) and industrial diversity and the degree of competition (measured at the district or industry level).[6] Although statistically significant, the effects are relatively small and, in the case of India, seem to decline over time. In 1991, an increase of 10 percent in the number of employees in sectors other than that in which a firm operates was associated with a 0.5 percent increase in plant productivity in India; by 2009, the productivity impact fell to

0.2 percent.[7] In contrast, in Bangladesh the effect has ranged from 0.2 to 0.4 percent.

In Sri Lanka, the data allow for even more stringent controls by using plant fixed effects (table 4.4). With this specification, the impact of urbanization economies on plant productivity is positive, particularly in the earlier part of the sample. Looking at the overall picture from 1995 to 2009, a 10 percent increase in the number of employees in other sectors leads to an increase in productivity of 0.86 percent—higher than the cross-sectional estimates for India and Bangladesh. This suggests that our results using cross-sectional data could be underestimated, and the effects of urbanization economies in India and Bangladesh might be higher than the estimates show.

Further disaggregation of the results reveals that the impact of urbanization on firm productivity is greater for more-productive firms

TABLE 4.3 **Agglomeration economies are associated with higher firm productivity in India and Bangladesh**

	India						Bangladesh					
Variables	1991	1994	1996	2000	2006	2009	1995	1997	1999	2001	2005	2012
Localization	0.01	0.00	−0.01	0.01	0.00	0.01	0.06***	0.04*	0.01	0.03**	0.08***	0.02
Urbanization	0.05***	0.05***	0.00	0.03**	0.00	0.02**	0.03**	0.03**	0.03**	0.02**	0.04***	0.03***
Diversity	0.06***	0.03**	0.11***	0.05**	0.10***	0.03	−0.02	−0.12	0.01	0.08**	−0.18***	0.03
Competition	0.02**	0.02***	0.02*	−0.01	0.02*	0.01	−0.12***	−0.02	−0.02	−0.05**	−0.05**	−0.02
Observations	41,539	42,565	40,876	25,435	39,462	36,020	3,417	3,178	2,931	3,940	3,155	7,119
R-squared	0.05	0.05	0.02	0.03	0.04	0.03	0.03	0.02	0.01	0.02	0.03	0.01

Source: World Bank calculations based on ASI in India and SMI in Bangladesh.
Note: Constant and state dummies included but not shown.
***$p < 0.01$, **$p < 0.05$, *$p < 0.1$.

TABLE 4.4 **Agglomeration economies boost firm performance in Sri Lanka**

Variables	1995–2003	2006–09	1995–2009
Localization	0.0315	−0.0300	−0.0002
Urbanization	0.1916***	−0.0410	0.0855***
Diversity	0.1207**	0.0217	0.0560
Competition	0.0159	0.0420	0.0141
Observations	17,125	4,873	21,998
R-squared	0.0044	0.0027	0.0014
Number of firms	4,877	3,528	8,405

Source: World Bank calculations based on ASI.
Note: Constant term included but not shown.
***$p < 0.01$, **$p < 0.05$, *$p < 0.1$.

and is not significantly different from zero for less-productive firms.[8] For example, in Bangladesh, the impact of urbanization at the 75th percentile of the firm productivity distribution is more than twice as large as that at the 50th percentile (table 4.5). In contrast to earlier results, this approach also identifies significant positive effects of localization economies on firms' productivity, although results differ qualitatively for the two countries. Less-productive firms in Bangladesh benefit from localization effects, but the most-productive firms benefit in India. Results using other years show similar results.

Overall, these findings show that agglomeration economies matter in South Asia, and the magnitude of the estimated impact of agglomeration on firm productivity is similar to that found in previous research that focused on developed countries. But unlike the evidence for high-income countries, urbanization economies in South Asia seem to matter more than localization economies, although the two are not mutually exclusive. Evidence from the case studies documents the emergence of clusters in or around cities—for example, the apparel cluster in Lahore and the automotive clusters in Pune and Aurangabad. It is important to emphasize that these correlations do not indicate causality, because data limitations have prevented us

from addressing endogeneity when estimating the impact of agglomeration economies on productivity. Furthermore, the analysis did not take into account the potentially negative effects of agglomeration, such as congestion. Addressing negative externalities might indicate that agglomeration promotes productivity, regardless of whether the effects are through localization or urbanization.

Resources do not flow easily to more-productive firms

Despite the productivity-enhancing benefits of agglomeration, there appear to be significant barriers to resources moving freely across internal geographical borders in South Asian countries. Duranton et al. (2015) propose an empirically motivated counterpart to the misallocation measure of Hsieh and Klenow (2009), defining misallocation as the (negative of) correlation between firm productivity and some measure of firm size, whether output, employment, the use of capital, or land and other resources. With this definition, Duranton et al. (2015) are able to decompose overall misallocation at the country level into contributions from different factors of production, as well as to distinguish between misallocation of resources within entities (for example, states or districts) and between them.

TABLE 4.5   **More-productive firms derive greater benefits from agglomeration economies**
Estimation results at different percentiles of firm distribution

Variables	India (2009)			Bangladesh (2012)		
	25th percentile	50th percentile	75th percentile	25th percentile	50th percentile	75th percentile
Localization	−0.0060	−0.0010	0.0109*	0.0179***	0.0049	−0.0079
Urbanization	0.0107	0.0207**	0.0119*	0.0022	0.0280***	0.0674***
Diversity	0.0385***	0.0505***	0.0293*	0.0930***	0.0308	0.0220
Competition	0.0299***	0.0124*	0.0023	0.0231*	0.0063	−0.0150
State dummies[a]	Yes	Yes	Yes	No	No	No
Testing (*p*-value)	25 = 75	25 = 50	50 = 75	25 = 75	25 = 50	50 = 75
Localization (%)	0.7	25.5	2.3	4.7	17.7	22.6
Urbanization (%)	85.0	7.0	10.3	0.0	0.0	0.0
Observations	36,020	36,020	36,020	7,119	7,119	7,119

Source: World Bank calculations based on ASI in India and SMI in Bangladesh.
Note: Constant term included but not shown.
a. Model did not converge when using Bangladesh regional dummies.
***$p < 0.01$, **$p < 0.05$, *$p < 0.1$.

Calculating misallocation in this way for three South Asian countries for which requisite data are available reveals that, in most cases, district or state borders in the region are "thick"—that is, impediments to efficient allocation of resources between districts are stronger than distortions within districts. This holds true for all countries in markets for goods, and in India in markets for labor and capital as well (as evidenced by the relatively small contribution of the between-district component to overall efficiency plotted in figure 4.1). Moreover, the results in figure 4.1 show that across South Asia, factor (labor and capital) markets are more distorted than goods markets (as evidenced by more negative values for misallocation of output than for misallocation of labor and capital—a more negative number means less misallocation).

Although the empirically motivated measure of misallocation used here does not readily lend itself to calculating productivity gains from reduced misallocation (as done by Hsieh and Klenow 2009), regression analysis by Duranton et al. (2015) for India suggests that a 1 percent decrease in the index of employment misallocation could raise output per worker in manufacturing by about 0.3 percent and in services by about 0.9 percent (because labor is a relatively more important input in services

FIGURE 4.1 **"Thick" district borders prevent efficient allocation of resources**

Decomposition of total misallocation into between- and within-district components

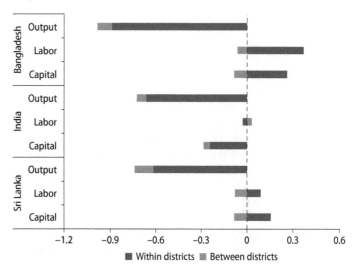

■ Within districts ■ Between districts

Source: World Bank calculations based on ASI in India and SMI in Bangladesh.
Note: A more negative number means more efficient allocation of resources (less misallocation); zero means no correlation between productivity and output or employment; a positive number means less-productive firms attract more labor or capital than more-productive firms. Numbers in the figure are averages across misallocation indexes calculated for each of the years for which data were available (Bangladesh: 1995, 1997, 1999, 2000, 2005, 2012; India: 1991, 1994, 1996, 2000, 2005, 2010; Sri Lanka: 1995–2003, 2006–09).

than in manufacturing). Therefore, reducing factor market distortions to improve the ability of more-productive firms to access inputs could have important consequences for overall productivity.

INDUSTRY CASE STUDY B

Better cities and trade logistics are needed for the electronics sector to thrive

Electronics is one of the largest and fastest growing industries in the world and has played an important role in the development trajectories of several newly industrialized economies. Surprisingly, South Asia is not currently a significant player in the sector despite very competitive labor costs and the fact that leading firms are achieving world-class productivity in the region.

Missing are urban ecosystems that would provide thick markets for skilled labor, the amenities that make them attractive to engineers together with large tracts of industrial land for clusters to thrive, and world-class logistics to enable the import and export of hundreds of components and products seamlessly. Some locations in South Asia are on the edge of being able to provide such conditions. Electronics clusters have emerged in Bangalore, Chennai, Colombo, and Delhi-Noida, with growing interest from leading global investors for Chittagong and Mumbai-Pune. Much progress has been achieved on the regulatory and policy fronts, but some issues related to "inverted tariffs" remain to be addressed in India. Progress has also been made to make customs and ports more efficient, but more efforts are needed to bring them to East Asia's level of efficiency. Similarly, efforts are being made to improve internal trade logistics. Governments are investing in skills in partnership with the private sector. The livability of large cities is a well-known challenge and steps are being taken to address it. In Bangladesh, a key constraint is the limited supply of large tracts of well-located and readily available industrial land for large investors and their suppliers.

The opportunity: South Asia on the edge of becoming globally competitive in one of the world's most important and fastest-growing industries

The electronics sector, one of the world's largest industrial sectors, has made a substantial contribution to global growth. Global trade in electronic products, including communications and information communication technology (ICT) equipment and electronics-based consumer products, was estimated at $1.4 trillion in 2012, having grown 5.9 percent per year between 2008 and 2012.[9] Electronics production is an important source of employment with 18 million people worldwide in 2010 (ILO 2014a).

The sector presents growth opportunities for developing countries. An important feature of the sector is that production is highly fragmented, with value often added in a variety of countries before goods and services make their way to end consumers. The ability to shift parts of the value chain to low-cost locations has created opportunities for developing countries to participate. Electronics companies from the developed world first started relocating to Malaysia, Singapore, Taiwan, and Thailand during the 1970s and early 1980s, followed by China, Indonesia, and the Philippines, primarily to take advantage of lower labor costs. In recent years, Vietnam has become an important producer for similar reasons. In 2013, information technology and electronics accounted for 7 percent of Vietnam's exports. Asia has been a major beneficiary and has become an important manufacturing hub, mainly due to its low labor costs, established supply base, and proximity to key final markets (ILO 2014b).

However, South Asia has yet to benefit from the global shift of electronics manufacturing. Other countries that started from a much weaker position have forged ahead and established themselves as new global players in electronics manufacturing exports. For example, electronics exports from South Asia are almost invisible compared to those from East Asian countries (figure 4.2). India is only the 14th-largest electronics producer globally, behind countries such as Mexico (8th), Brazil (10th), and Thailand (12th).

This is surprising both because of South Asia's growing labor cost advantage over East Asia and because leading firms in South Asia achieve productivity performance comparable to that of Chinese firms. Samsung reported to the authors that their Noida, India, plant ranks second in efficiency out of 30 comparable Samsung plants around the world. Similarly, the World Bank Enterprise Surveys (2011, 2012) show that productivity in the electronics sector is higher in Sri Lanka ($24,701) than in China ($22,382). Cost comparisons, obtained from a global manufacturer with facilities around the world, show that manufacturing costs in India are 80 percent of those in the United States and, importantly, slightly lower than those in China and Vietnam (figure 4.3).

What will enable South Asia to succeed in electronics?

Achieving low production costs at the plant level is not enough to be competitive in the electronics industry. An electronic product is the result of the assembly of hundreds of components, produced by skilled workers and engineers, from multiple suppliers in various locations and countries.

Industrial clustering is a key feature of the electronics industry because it helps reduce transaction and logistic costs among dozens of related firms. It also helps facilitate quality control and reduce transport-related uncertainties in the supply chain. For example, 76 suppliers from the Republic of Korea located

facilities next to Samsung following its investment in Vietnam, and similar dynamics can be observed at Samsung's main plants in Noida and Chennai, India. Clustering next to large cities provides access to a large pool of skilled workers and engineers as well as to the ancillary service providers required by this fast-moving, constantly innovating industry.

Thus by its nature, the electronics industry requires urban ecosystems that combine

FIGURE 4.2   Electronics production is low in South Asia

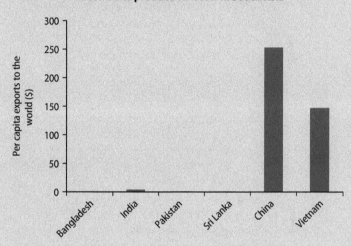

Source: World Bank calculations based on UN COMTRADE database and World Bank Enterprise Surveys.

FIGURE 4.3   India has a cost advantage in labor-intensive processes

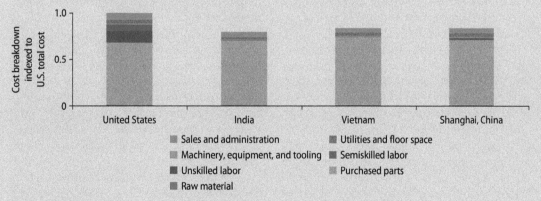

Note: Data drawn from auto parts manufacturer but representative of costs in electronics sector.

a deep pool of skilled workers, amenities that make their locations attractive to engineers, and large tracts of industrial land that can host clusters with very good internal and external connections, in particular to world-class ports. Because the industry is so globally competitive, it also requires a low cost of doing business and an enabling trade policy environment.

South Asia has made significant progress in regulation and trade policies, although some inverted tariff issues are left to be addressed in India (Subramanian and Modi 2015). The main challenge is to provide the urban ecosystems (including seamless internal and external trade logistics) for world-class electronics clusters to emerge and thrive.

Barriers to clustering

Although there is clustering around a few locations, access to land remains a challenge. The electronics industry in India initially grew in the 1990s around three major centers, Bangalore, Chennai, and Delhi-Noida. Bangalore emerged as a hub early on, with major public sector plants in defense and telecommunication. In recent times, Bangalore also has attracted private sector firms in computer and industrial products. The Delhi region, in particular, has a large concentration of small-scale factories making consumer electronic products and computers. More recently, Hyderabad, Chennai, and the industrial corridor between Mumbai and Pune have become important manufacturing locations.

Few industrial areas have been able to provide what investors require in the right locations. Interviews suggest that manufacturers seeking to link to global supply chains prefer to locate in areas that are close to ports, to speed up the movement of goods along supply chains and reduce dependence on local infrastructure. Setting up clusters in such areas—either as special enterprise zones (SEZs) or industrial parks—that are large enough to house lead firms and suppliers would help attract electronics manufacturers. Investors would also like to see world-class infrastructure developed around and within a cluster, especially to link it with a port and to major markets. Small and medium enterprises (SMEs) in particular require common facilities for R&D and testing, waste dumping, and recycling. Provisions for worker housing within or close to the cluster is important. Manufacturing facilities tend to be located outside urban areas to take advantage of lower land costs. However, ensuring an adequate supply of labor requires companies to pay to transport workers to the sites or to create facilities for them to stay nearby, both of which raise costs.

Clustering in South Asia is difficult because buying land in suitable locations is often an arduous and expensive task. Verification of title is complex, and procedures for purchasing land take time. It is difficult for large companies to assemble enough small plots of land. The scarcity of adequate land is also reflected in very high prices. Companies prefer to locate close to major markets or ports, but some Indian and Sri Lankan periurban areas are among the most expensive in the world (Saleman and Jordan 2013). The practical solution to these issues has been industrial zones, which played a central role in the development of manufacturing, and electronics in particular, in East Asia. The lack of readily available and well-located industrial land is probably the main constraint on the development of the sector in Bangladesh, which came very close to breaking into the global electronics industry, as Vietnam has done (box 4.2).

External and internal trade logistics issues

Countries that are able to achieve faster turn-around times gain a significant competitive advantage, especially for more innovative, cutting-edge products. This is where South Asia is at a disadvantage. Processing time is higher in India than in China, Singapore, and Taiwan (figure 4.4).

Although much progress has been made, South Asian firms continue to report long and unpredictable delays in customs clearance. In India, the average time reported to clear customs varied from 2 to 10 days for large firms, and 14 to 21 days for SMEs.

BOX 4.2   How Bangladesh missed the opportunity to break into the global electronics industry

In 2011, Samsung requested 250 acres in an export processing zone (EPZ) to develop an electronics hub in Chittagong, Bangladesh (a $1.25 billion investment, with jobs for up to 50,000 workers). The investment did not materialize because no tract of land that large was available in the area controlled by the Bangladesh Export Processing Zones Authority (BEPZA), and the use of the land in the mostly empty 2,500-acre Korean Export Processing Zone in Chittagong has been in dispute for more than 15 years. By contrast, Vietnam has been able to provide large, readily available tracts of land to large investors and their suppliers. Samsung was able to locate there with 76 of its Korean suppliers and now directly employs 100,000 workers.

Source: Ahsan 2014.

Remaining issues include ambiguities in product classification and difficulties in obtaining exemptions from import tariffs on raw materials and parts and components. Grievances also can take considerable time, and companies fear reprisals, such as losing their trusted-trader credentials. One firm stated that "[t]he customs bureaucracy is very difficult to handle when we import various equipment and that creates a big disincentive for anyone venturing into this market." Another interviewee said that "[t]o gain one rupee in customs duties the country is losing thousands."

Issues also remain with internal logistics. Indian firms reported that it takes 11 days for a container to travel from Shanghai to Mumbai but 20 days for it to travel from Mumbai to Delhi. A survey shows that a quarter of the journey is spent at checkposts, state borders, city entrances, and other regulatory stops (figure 4.5). In order to deal with the resulting uncertainty, firms in four industries (auto components, textiles, electronics, and heavy engineering) report maintaining inventories 27 percent higher, on average, than necessary. Total logistics costs, including inventory costs and lost sales, account for 14 percent of total costs for electronics firms, high by international standards (Jordan and Kamphuis 2014). The recently passed reform of the unified gross sales tax in India should improve matters considerably.

FIGURE 4.4   Process times for information technology hardware and electronics

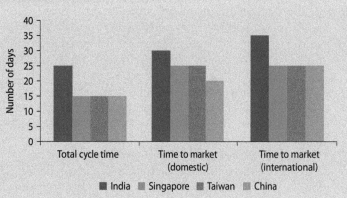

Source: D&B Analysis 2012.

Access to skilled workers

The availability of cheap and adaptable labor is one factor that makes South Asia attractive as a manufacturing destination. However, capitalizing on South Asia's advantage in workers requires significant investment in training and improving productivity. The returns can be large—international evidence shows that a 1 percent increase in training is associated with 0.6 percent increase in value added per hour (Dearden, Reed, and Van Reenen 2006). The question is who makes this investment? In South Asia, public investment in training has been low and of poor quality,

FIGURE 4.5 **Logistics issues in India**

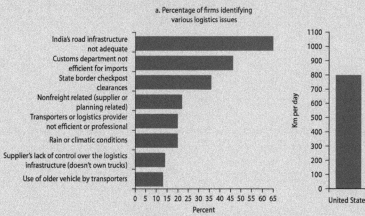

a. Percentage of firms identifying various logistics issues

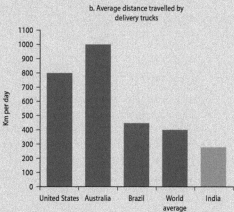

b. Average distance travelled by delivery trucks

Source: Jordan and Kamphuis 2014.

comparing unfavorably with other competitor nations. For example, vocational education programs in India can accommodate only 5 percent of secondary school graduates, while China has the infrastructure to train half of all secondary school graduates. The quality of training is also an issue. Across the region, the development of new programs and curricula is difficult in public institutions. Quality is further hampered by the lack of industry participation in training (BCG 2013). Samsung reported that it takes a full year of training to bring its workers in India to global standards. Tos Lanka, Sri Lanka's leading electronics company has also had to make large investments in training (box 4.3).

In China, the government supports vocational education with extensive industry participation. Curricula are flexible and, to make sure that faculty always keep abreast of the latest industry practices, the Chinese government has made it compulsory for vocational trainers to spend at least one month every year working in manufacturing companies. To facilitate access to labor, the government also supports employee housing next to or within well-located industrial parks that also have technical and vocational colleges and secondary schools. Vietnam provides subsidized training for employees. Programs include soft skills, technical English, technical skills, and on-demand training.

Further, companies can reduce annual taxable income up to 10 percent through spending on R&D. Sharing the costs of skills education between the state and private companies can significantly encourage investment, especially for companies with long-term plans.

South Asia is on the edge of breaking into the global electronics industry

As shown by the missed Samsung opportunity in Bangladesh (box 4.2), South Asia is very close to making it big in the global electronics industry. This will require continued improvements in urban ecosystems with respect to access to industrial land, internal and external trade logistics, and skilled labor.

Global investors are anticipating the shift and are on the move. Several multinational electronics firms (such as Samsung, HP, IBM, Motorola, Lenovo, Flextronics, and Foxconn) are present, or have announced plans to invest in the region (box 4.4), and many large firms have set up R&D centers with world-class capabilities in South Asian countries to support global operations. This activity has been encouraged by South Asia's large, fast-growing markets (the electronics market in India, for example, is expected to grow at 24 percent per year to reach a market size of $400 billion by 2020) (Ernst 2014) and the

---

BOX 4.3   How Tos Lanka is developing the skills of its workforce

Tos Lanka is Sri Lanka's largest electronic assembly company. It commenced operations at the Biyagama EPZ in 1998, with an initial investment of SL Rs 220 million. Tos specializes in the surface-mount technology assembly of printed circuit boards, electronic guitar tuners and effectors, and coils and electronic components for the automotive industry. The products are exported to Japan, the United States, and the European Union.

The factory has manual and automated electronic assembly lines, supported by chip mounting and wave soldering plants, together with extensive testing facilities. Female workers dominate the 240-strong workforce. The company has invested in training and development of staff to manufacture electronic products and components to international standards. Workers at Tos Lanka undergo training in Japan for a period of between three and twelve months. The majority of the workforce has been trained in Japan in quality-oriented manufacturing processes.

The company has also established its own R&D section and looks forward to accessing the huge Indian market through the Comprehensive Economic Partnership Agreement between India and Sri Lanka.

Source: Tos Lanka.

BOX 4.4   Foxconn enters India

Foxconn, the world's largest contract electronics manufacturer, has announced plans to open more than 10 plants and employ a million workers in India by 2020. This will include R&D and hi-tech manufacturing facilities and would represent a major diversification away from China, where it has the bulk of its manufacturing capacity. Foxconn has also announced a joint venture with Xiaomi of China to produce devices in Andhra Pradesh.

Source: Rai 2015.

---

potential of the South Asian diaspora, which has deep knowledge and extensive networks in the global electronics industry.

Indian exports of components and products have started to grow in areas such as mobile telephones, audio players, and display technologies. Indian companies such as Micromaxx, Deltron, TVS Electronics, and Sahasra are increasing their presence.

The extended version of this case study is available online at www.worldbank.org /SouthAsiaCompetes.

Notes

1. These are simple averages of locational Gini coefficients calculated at the two-digit International Standard Industrial Classification (ISIC) industry level.
2. Only two of the top five districts in 1991 remained in the top five in 2009, and employment in the five largest districts in 1991, which constituted 17.4 percent of total employment, amounted to a much lower 14.0 percent in 2009. For the purposes of spatial analysis, the report consistently uses India's 1989 districts, mapping new districts in later years to their 1989 "parent" districts.
3. Dhaka continues to dominate in levels, accounting for more than 35 percent of total employment.
4. Sri Lanka has 25 districts, but 7 of these had too few firms to carry out the analysis. Therefore data for these districts (Jaffna, Mannar, Vavuniya, Mullativu, Batticaloa, Ampara, and Trincomalee) have been combined into a single "residual" district, resulting in a total of 18 districts.
5. This index is calculated as $G_i = \sum_{s=1}^{N} \left(\frac{L_{i,s}}{L_i} - \frac{L_s}{L} \right)^2$, where i refers to a two-digit ISIC industry, s is location (district or state), and L is employment.
6. Localization economies are defined as the log of 1 plus the sum of all employees from sectors in region z other than the employees in plant i, while urbanization economies are defined as the log of 1 plus the sum of all employees in region z other than employees in sector s (1 is added to ensure the inclusion of all plants in the estimation; otherwise the existence of only one plant in a particular region would be discarded because log of 0 is not defined). More specifically, the indexes are defined as follows for each plant i, sector s, region z, and time period t:

$$Localization_{it}^{sz} = \ln\left(\frac{employees_t^{sz} -}{employees_{it}^{sz} + 1} \right)$$

$$Urbanization_t^{sz} = \ln\left(\frac{employees_t^z -}{employees_t^{sz} + 1} \right)$$

$$Diversity_t^{sz} = \ln\left(\sum_{s' \neq s} \left(\frac{employees_t^{s'z}}{employees_t^z - employees_t^{sz}} \right)^2 \right)^{-1}$$

$$Competition_t^{sz} = \ln\left(\sum_{j \in S_t^{sz}} \left(\frac{employees_{jt}^{sz}}{employees_t^{sz}} \right)^2 \right)^{-1}$$

7. Note that, due to data limitations, this report cannot adequately address the issue of input endogeneity (especially of capital) in the production function following the traditional approaches in the literature, such as Levinsohn and Petrin (2003) and Olley and Pakes (1996). However, Van Beveren (2012) showed that differences between most parametric or semi-parametric methods to estimate TFP (including Levinsohn and Petrin and Olley and Pakes) and ordinary least squares (OLS) are minimal. Therefore, the approach taken here is to estimate the production function by OLS, allowing the parameters for capital (α) and labor (β) to vary for each two-digit ISIC sector.
8. To assess this, the report estimates quantile regressions at the 25th, 50th, and 75th percentiles of the firm productivity distribution for the last available year.
9. World Bank calculations based on United Nations COMTRADE database. The classification of electronic products is from Sturgeon and Memedovic (2011).

References

Ahsan, Badrul. 2014. "Dearth of Land in BD Redirects FDI," *Financial Express*, November 16.

Baldwin, R. E., and P. Martin. 2004. "Agglomeration and Regional Growth." In Vol. 4 of *Handbook of Regional and Urban Economics*, edited by J. Vernon Henderson and Jacques-François Thisse, 2671–2711. Amsterdam: Elsevier B.V.

BCG (Boston Consulting Group). 2013. "People Productivity. Key to Indian Manufacturing Competitiveness." Boston Consulting Group. http://www.bcg.com/en-in/perspectives /28825.

Combes, P. P., G. Duranton, and L. Gobillon. 2011. "The Identification of Agglomeration Economies." *Journal of Economic Geography* 11 (2): 253–66.

Dearden, L., H. Reed, and J. Van Reenen. 2006. "The Impact of Training on Productivity and Wages: Evidence from British Panel Data." *Oxford Bulletin of Economics and Statistics* 68 (4): 397–540.

Deichmann, U., F. Shilpi, and R. Vakis. 2008. "Spatial Specialization and Farm-Nonfarm Linkages." Policy Research Working Paper 4611, World Bank, Washington, DC.

D&B Analysis. 2012. "IT Hardware & Electronics: Productivity & Efficiency Benchmarking." Government of India, Ministry of Science and Technology, Department of Scientific and Industrial Research, http://www.dsir.gov.in /reports/isr1/IT%20Hardware%20and%20 Electronics/4_9.pdf.

Duranton, G., E. Ghani, A. Grover Goswami, and W. Kerr. 2015. "The Misallocation of Land and Other Factors of Production in India." Policy Research Working Paper 7221, World Bank, Washington, DC.

Duranton, G., and H. G. Overman. 2005. "Testing for Localization Using Micro-Geographic Data." *Review of Economic Studies* 72 (4): 1077–1106.

Ellison, G., and E. L. Glaeser. 1997. "Geographic Concentration in U.S. Manufacturing Industries: A Dartboard Approach." *Journal of Political Economy* 105 (5): 889–927.

Ernst, Dieter. 2014. "Republic of India Manufacturing Plan Implementation: Fast Tracking India's Electronics Manufacturing Industry—Business Environment and Industrial Policy." World Bank, Washington, DC.

Fafchamps, M. and F. Shilpi. 2005. "Cities and Specialisation: Evidence from South Asia." *Economic Journal* 115 (503): 477–504.

Ghani, E., A. Grover Goswami, and W. R. Kerr. 2012a. "Is India's Manufacturing Sector Moving Away From Cities?" NBER Working Paper 17992, National Bureau of Economic Research, Cambridge, MA.

———. 2012b. "Highway to Success: The Impact of the Golden Quadrilateral Project for the Location and Performance of Indian Manufacturing." NBER Working Paper 18524, National Bureau of Economic Research, Cambridge, MA.

Ghani, E., W. Kerr, and S. D. O'Connell. 2011. "Spatial Determinants of Entrepreneurship in India." NBER Working Paper 17514, National Bureau of Economic Research, Cambridge, MA.

Glaeser, E., and W. Kerr. 2009. "Local Industrial Conditions and Entrepreneurship: How Much of the Spatial Distribution Can We Explain?" *Journal of Economics and Management Strategy* 18 (3): 623–63.

Hsieh, C., and P. J. Klenow. 2009. "Misallocation and Manufacturing TFP in China and India." *Quarterly Journal of Economics* 124 (4): 1403–48.

ILO (International Labour Organization). 2014a. "Better Work: Electronics Feasibility Study." ILO. http://betterwork.com/global/wp-conten /uploads/Better-work-Electronics-Feasibility -Study-Executive-Summary.pdf.

———. 2014b. *Ups and Downs in the Electronics Industry: Fluctuating Production and the Use of Temporary and Other Forms of Employment.* Geneva: ILO.

Jacobs, J. 1969. *The Economy of Cities.* New York: Vintage Books.

Jordan L. S., and B. Kamphuis. 2014. "Supply Chain Delays and Uncertainty in India: The Hidden Constraint on Manufacturing Growth." Working Paper ACS 14223, World Bank, Washington DC.

Lall, S.V., Z. Shalizi, and U. Deichmann. 2004. "Agglomeration Economies and Productivity in Indian Industry." *Journal of Development Economics* 73 (2): 643–73.

Levinsohn, J., and A. Petrin 2003. "Estimating Production Functions Using Inputs to Control for Unobservables." *Review of Economic Studies* 70 (2): 317–41.

Marshall, A. 1920. *Principles of Economics.* London: Macmillan.

Martin, P., and G. I. Ottaviano. 2001. "Growth and Agglomeration." *International Economic Review* 42 (4): 947–68.

Martin, P., T. Mayer, and F. Mayneris. 2011. "Spatial Concentration and Plant-Level Productivity in France." *Journal of Urban Economics* 69 (2): 182–95.

Michaels G., F. Rauch, and S. J. Redding. 2012. "Urbanization and Structural Transformation." *Quarterly Journal of Economics* 127 (2): 535–86.

Mukim, M. 2011. "Industry and the Urge to Cluster: A Study of the Informal Sector in India." Discussion Paper 72, Spatial Economics Research Centre, London.

Olley, G. S., and A. Pakes. 1996. "The Dynamics of Productivity in the Telecommunications Equipment Industry." *Econometrica* 64 (6): 1263–97.

Rai, S. 2015. "Foxconn Could Make India its Next Manufacturing Base, after China,

Investments Suggest." *Forbes*, August 10, 2015. http://www.forbes.com/sites/saritharai/2015/08/10/foxconn-could-make-india-its-next-manufacturing-base-after-china-investments-suggest/#1b3a49753bb9.

Rosenthal, S. S., and W. C. Strange. 2004. "Evidence on the Nature and Sources of Agglomeration Economies." In Vol. 4 of *Handbook of Regional and Urban Economics*, edited by J. Vernon Henderson and Jacques-François Thisse, 2119–71. Amsterdam: Elsevier B.V.

Saleman, Y., and L. Jordan. 2013. "The Implementation of Industrial Parks: Some Lessons Learned from India." World Bank, Washington, DC.

Sturgeon, T., and O. Memedovic. 2011. "Mapping Global Value Chains: Intermediate Goods Trade and Structural Change in the World Economy." UNIDO Development Policy and Strategic Research Branch Working Paper 05/2010, United Nations Industrial Development Organization, Vienna, Austria.

Subramanian, A., and A. Modi. 2015. " 'Make in India' Not by Protecting but by Eliminating Negative Protectionism." *Business Standard*. http://www.business-standard.com/article/opinion/make-in-india-not-by-protecting-but-by-eliminating-negative-protectionism-115050100026_1.html.

Van Beveren, I. 2012. "Total Factor Productivity Estimation: A Practical Review." *Journal of Economic Surveys* 26 (1): 98–128.

World Bank. 2008. *Harnessing Competitiveness for Stronger Inclusive Growth: Bangladesh Investment Climate Assessment*. Washington, DC: World Bank.

———. 2015. *Leveraging Urbanization in South Asia: Managing Spatial Transformation for Prosperity and Livability*. Washington, DC: World Bank.

Limited Success in Linking to Global Value Chains | 5

Part 1 of this report argued that global trade and investment integration are important for productivity growth. In the 21st century, this integration takes place primarily by means of global value chains (GVCs), which divide the production process into stages and distribute these stages across different countries. This process, variously known as "production fragmentation" (Arndt and Kierzkowski 2001), "processing trade" (Görg 2000), "vertical specialization" (Hummels, Rapoport, and Yi 1998), "slicing up the value chain" (Krugman, Cooper, and Srinivasan 1995), or "the second unbundling" (Baldwin 2006), has been made possible by major changes in logistics and managerial organization in the last third of the 20th century.

At the firm level, various aspects of GVC participation, such as imports of parts and components, entry into export markets, and knowledge spillovers from tie-ins with lead firms, have been associated with higher productivity. However, South Asia's participation in GVCs largely remains confined to apparel. And even in this sector, the sophistication of the region's products declined between 2000 and 2010. To take better advantage of the productivity-enhancing opportunities offered by participation in GVCs, South Asia needs to further develop the capabilities that matter for GVCs, including human capital, institutions, logistics, and

removal of trade barriers. The following discussion develops these observations in more detail.

GVC participation supports productivity

GVCs make it possible for firms in developing countries to participate in producing the world's most complex and sophisticated products by specializing in a piece of the production process for which those firms have a comparative advantage and produce at the necessary large scale to be competitive globally (figure 5.1). Lead firms, typically located in advanced economies, perform the higher value-added activities (such as design, branding, and retail), but outsource most or all of the manufacturing to a global network of producers. Beyond their direct contributions, lead firms also have major positive effects through the knowledge and support they provide to suppliers and the competitive pressure they put on all firms in the industry. Foreign firms' subsidiaries in South Asia play a particularly important role in complex, capital- and knowledge-intensive activities such as car assembly (such as Maruti Suzuki in India and Hyundai in Pakistan) and electronics (such as Samsung in India and Tos Lanka, a subsidiary of Toslec from Japan, in Sri Lanka). The relationships between foreign and domestic

FIGURE 5.1 **Structure of the global value chain for apparel**

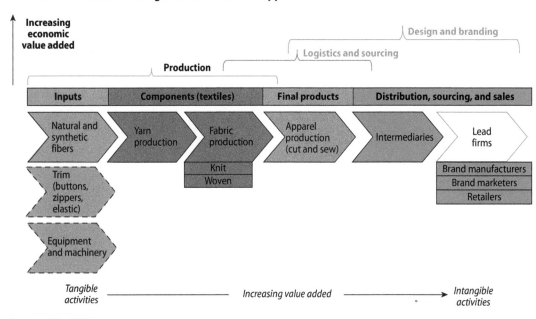

Source: World Bank 2016.
Note: Blue indicates highest-value-added activities and control or power over the supply chain.

firms provide a vital first step toward increasing productivity and producing goods that meet world-market specifications with regard to technological content, quality, and design (Helpman 1984). Nowhere is this more evident than in East Asia, where the transfer of technology and knowledge facilitated through GVCs made it possible for economies at initially low levels of income—such as China; Hong Kong SAR, China; Republic of Korea; Singapore; and Taiwan, China—to move up the ladder of productivity, capital intensity, and quality (Kimura and Ando 2005; Amiti and Konings 2007; Kee and Tang 2015).

An extensive literature documents firm-level productivity benefits from various aspects of GVC participation, such as access to larger markets, learning-by-exporting, and knowledge spillovers from foreign direct investment (FDI), although recent evidence suggests that the contribution of these forces to productivity growth declined in the period 2004–11 compared to 1995–2003, primarily on account of the global trade slowdown (Constantinescu,

Mattoo, and Ruta 2015). Causality is difficult to establish; more-productive firms are more likely to enter export markets than less-productive firms (Melitz 2003; Clerides, Lack, and Tybout 1998; Abraham et al. 2010; Amiti and Konings 2007; Goldberg et al. 2010; Atkin, Khandelwal, and Osman 2016). Empirical studies have used a variety of statistical techniques to control for this selection bias. In a sample of Indonesian firms, Arnold and Javorcik (2009) find evidence of increased labor productivity resulting from capital investment and organizational and management restructuring following acquisition by a foreign affiliate. In South Asia, evidence suggests that firms in Bangladesh that receive FDI are more productive than firms that do not (Kee 2005). In a review of these studies, Havranek and Irsova (2011) conclude that a 10 percent increase in foreign presence is associated with a 9 percent increase in the productivity of local suppliers through their exposure to foreign firms. This evidence suggests that firms often participate in GVCs first and then become more productive, rather than the other way around.

Classifying firms whose share of imported raw materials is greater than 10 percent of the total raw materials used as GVC participants, we find that the total factor productivity (TFP) of GVC participants in Bangladesh and India tends to exceed that of nonparticipants (figure 5.2). The picture remains approximately the same when GVC participants are defined as firms whose share of imported raw materials is greater than 20 percent of the total raw materials used. The same pattern holds for participation in international markets more generally: firms whose trade share (exports plus imports) is greater than 10 percent of value added tend to have, on average, higher levels of TFP in Bangladesh, India, and Sri Lanka. And this picture remains robust to the use of different trade shares to define GVC participant firms. It should therefore come as no surprise that GVC participants, as reflected in evidence from India and Bangladesh, are associated with a higher share of exports in value added.[1]

Various efforts have been made to pinpoint the source of productivity benefits from exporting. Increases in productivity following entry into foreign markets are attributed to greater scale economies in Sub-Saharan Africa (Van Biesebroeck 2005) and Slovenia (De Loecker

2007). Evidence from a randomized trial in the Arab Republic of Egypt documents productivity gains from exporting through knowledge transfers (Atkin, Khandelwal, and Osman 2016). In South Asia, studies have found that learning-through-exporting has boosted the productivity of firms in India that enter export markets (Mukim 2011), in part through scale effects.[2] Similarly, firms in Bangladesh with more export experience exhibit higher productivity (Fernandes 2008). Among domestic producers of apparel inputs in Bangladesh, even those firms that neither export nor supply to exporters can experience productivity spillovers by learning from the experience of firms that are part of a shared supplier network that supports exporters (Kee 2015). On the import side, access to imported intermediate inputs can also boost firm productivity; for example, when India liberalized its tariff regime, access to a greater range of intermediate goods at lower overall prices made manufacturing firms more productive (Goldberg et al. 2010). Case studies document the important productivity benefits from interactions with foreign firms in the context of GVCs. For example, the Desh-Daewoo joint venture, which included the intense technical and managerial training of 130 Bangladeshis in Daewoo's Pusan plant in 1979, established the foundation for the next generation of Bangladeshi entrepreneurs.

FIGURE 5.2   Firms that participate in GVCs also have higher productivity

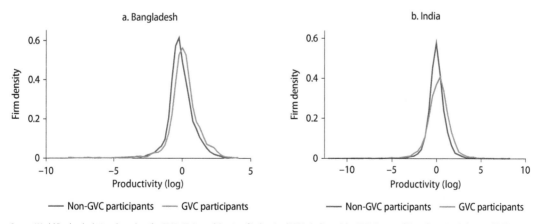

Source: World Bank calculations based on the 2012–13 Annual Survey of Industries (ASI) in India and the 2012 Survey of Manufacturing Industries (SMI) in Bangladesh.
Note: Productivity (TFP) estimates normalized to zero mean. GVC = global value chain.

South Asia's success in global and regional GVCs is limited to apparel

South Asia has the second-highest level of GVC exports out of total exports among developing regions, almost entirely on the strength of its large share of final and intermediate apparel products (reinforcing the findings on global market shares in part 1 of this report). Approximately half of GVC exports from South Asia are in final apparel, whereas East Asia specializes in electronics, and Europe, North America, and Latin America in autos (figure 5.3). In imports, South Asia is relatively less integrated in GVCs: firms making final products tend to obtain inputs from domestic sources (or themselves), indicating a lower level of GVC integration than implied in the export data.[3] In the case of apparel, however, local sourcing of intermediates combined with the predominance of final apparel exports is consistent with FDI-led GVC activity in South Asia; that is, global lead firms set up factories and use local materials to manufacture and export final apparel.

Within the region countries vary greatly in the extent to which they are integrated into GVCs (box 5.1). In 2013, the share of total merchandise exports in major GVC products (apparel, autos, electronics, and footwear) was approximately 80 percent for Bangladesh, 45 percent for Sri Lanka, 40 percent for Pakistan, and 15 percent for India, while the participation of the remaining countries is negligible (table 5.1). By this metric, Bangladesh has one of the highest GVC participation rates in the world, although it reflects the fact that Bangladesh exports little besides final apparel (figure 5.4). India's participation in GVCs, by the same token, is low precisely because it has a more diversified export basket, some of which may also have some of the characteristics of GVC production but are not included in this analysis.[4]

With regard to products, each of the four South Asian countries has a significant export position in final apparel, covering nearly the full range of garment products, while intermediate apparel—dominated by cotton textiles—is particularly important in India and Pakistan. Bangladesh's exports of final apparel in 2013, which have nearly tripled since 2007, amounted to over $26 billion, making it the second-largest

FIGURE 5.3   South Asia's strength in apparel explains the region's high GVC integration

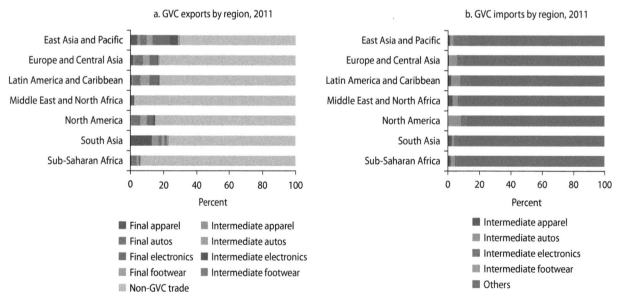

a. GVC exports by region, 2011

b. GVC imports by region, 2011

Final apparel   Intermediate apparel
Final autos   Intermediate autos
Final electronics   Intermediate electronics
Final footwear   Intermediate footwear
Non-GVC trade

Intermediate apparel
Intermediate autos
Intermediate electronics
Intermediate footwear
Others

Source: World Bank calculations based on UN COMTRADE database.

BOX 5.1   Measuring GVC participation

There are a number of ways to measure participation in GVCs. Some analyses, especially those
that focus on tracking global flows of value added
through input-output methods, essentially view
all trade as part of a GVC (Mattoo, Wang, and
Wei 2013). A country that exports only crude oil
or metallic ores may have a high degree of GVC
participation under this definition because these
crude materials are eventually transformed into
sophisticated goods or parts of other goods in
another country.[a] However, links with lead firms
that lead to technology transfer and deeper interactions with final markets are more likely to take
place when countries are engaged in the middle
or later stages of the production process.

GVCs in vehicles, electronics, and apparel and
footwear are characterized by a lead-firm network structure and have been much studied. The
share of total global merchandise exports
accounted for by these three GVCs has fluctuated
between approximately 14 percent and 28 percent
since 1990. Studying the similarities and differences in the organization of these three GVCs can
improve our understanding of GVCs or, as they
are sometimes called, global supply chains (USITC
2011). These three sectors differ in the methods
used to coordinate activity over long distances
and the extent to which they are coordinated by
traditional manufacturers (autos), owners of
brand names with strong research capabilities

(electronics), or buyers of final products working
with global middlemen (apparel and footwear).

This report uses a modified version of the
definition of the three classic GVCs in Sturgeon
and Memedovic (2011). Products are classified
as belonging to one of the three GVCs based on
a combination of expert opinion and their position in the U.N. Statistical Division's Broad
Economic Categories, which help to distinguish
between intermediate and final goods. This leads
to a list of over 400 traded goods, identified in
the United Nations Standard International Trade
Classification (revision 3) classification at the
four-digit or five-digit level. Each of the GVCs is
then divided into two subsectors to reflect intermediate and final goods (such as intermediate
electronics and final electronics), making six
GVC sectors in all. For the purposes of this analysis of South Asia, the Sturgeon and Memedovic
(2011) categories are modified in two ways.
First, the footwear sector, both intermediate and
final, is separated from apparel, making eight
categories instead of six. Second, the definition
of the "autos" sector, which originally included
only passenger motor vehicles and motorcycles,
is broadened to encompass other road vehicles,
such as trucks, buses, and trailers.

a. Following the terminology of the input-output approach to measuring GVC
participation, exporters of primary products participate in GVCs through "forward
linkages" while countries that export final goods requiring large amounts of
imported intermediate goods participate in GVCs through "backward linkages."

TABLE 5.1   Outside of apparel, GVC exports from South Asia lag well behind East Asia
US$ per capita

	Afghanistan 2013	Bangladesh 2013	Bhutan 2012	India 2013	Nepal 2013	Pakistan 2013	Sri Lanka 2013	China 2013	Vietnam 2013
Final apparel	0.0	170.1	0.0	13.1	2.7	24.7	210.3	125.4	189.1
Final autos	0.0	0.0	0.0	6.5	0.0	0.1	1.9	23.6	4.7
Final electronics	2.0	0.0	0.5	3.7	0.2	0.6	6.9	252.8	274.1
Final footwear	0.0	3.2	0.0	1.8	0.0	0.6	1.1	35.5	93.6
Intermediate apparel	0.0	0.5	0.9	6.1	2.3	30.4	6.2	42.3	29.9
Intermediate autos	0.0	0.1	0.1	5.0	0.0	0.3	2.6	39.5	40.3
Intermediate electronics	0.0	0.1	0.0	1.0	0.0	0.0	1.1	67.5	16.2
Intermediate footwear	0.0	0.1	0.0	0.3	0.0	0.0	0.4	1.9	3.6
Total	2.0	174.1	1.5	37.5	5.2	56.1	230.5	588.5	651.5

Note: Data for Bangladesh 2013 are mirror data.

FIGURE 5.4   Apparel accounts for the lion's share of South Asia's GVC exports

Percent of total exports, 2013

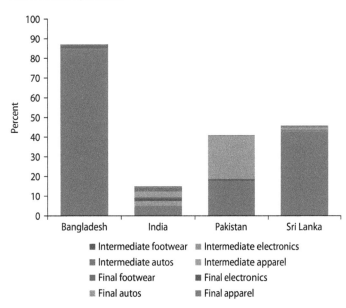

Intermediate footwear • Intermediate electronics
Intermediate autos • Intermediate apparel
Final footwear • Final electronics
Final autos • Final apparel

Source: World Bank calculations based on UN COMTRADE database.

exporter of final apparel in the world after China. Sri Lanka and Bangladesh, in particular because of effective import facilities for exporters, perform at East Asia's level in terms of exports per capita ($216 and $147, respectively), while India and Pakistan are at an order of magnitude lower ($10 and $23, respectively). Annual growth rates of exports over 2003–13 in India (9.6 percent) and Sri Lanka (5.3 percent) were modest, and in Pakistan were sluggish (2.7 percent). These rates of growth, however, may not necessarily reflect productivity improvements because the region benefitted from the 2005 elimination of the Multi-Fiber Agreement (MFA), which had restricted textile imports from developing countries to developed countries.

Most South Asian countries have negligible exports of GVC products other than apparel, with India accounting for almost all of the region's exports of autos and electronics. India has a large auto parts industry, whose growth has been supported by increased exposure to international competition since the lowering of trade barriers in the early 2000s. India's auto parts exports

doubled in the last ten years to $6.4 billion in 2013, reaching sophisticated markets such as the United States, the United Kingdom, Italy, and Germany.[5] India already exports more auto parts than Indonesia, Morocco, or Vietnam, but only about one-tenth as much as China. India is also one of the largest and most rapidly growing developing country exporters of final autos: it exports to middle-income countries (such as Algeria, Mexico, and South Africa) as well as developed countries (such as Australia and the United Kingdom), and, at current growth rates, its exports of final autos may exceed those of China by 2020. In final electronics, India's exports have quadrupled in the six years ended 2013, but growth has come from a small base, and China's exports dwarf those of India by a factor of 20.

India's rapid export growth has come largely from using lower-priced products to penetrate developing country markets (figure 5.5).[6] Seventy-one percent of India's exports of passenger motor vehicles go to the Middle East and North Africa, Latin America and the Caribbean, the rest of South Asia, and Sub-Saharan Africa. Similarly, the largest destinations for Indian cell phone exports are Argentina, the Russian Federation, South Africa, and the United Arab Emirates. On average, therefore, India's exports of GVC products are skewed more toward more middle-income countries than are the exports of Germany or Japan, which are geared more toward developed country markets.

Trade data do not provide a full picture of GVC integration, because many GVC-related sales take place within national borders. Measures of foreign value added in exports that draw on multiregional input-output tables are useful indicators of the extent to which countries are engaging fully in the international division of labor that GVCs make possible.[7] The Organisation for Economic Co-operation and Development (OECD)–World Trade Organization (WTO) Trade in Value Added (TiVA) data, for example, show that the share of foreign value added in India's exports rose from 9.4 percent in 1995 to 24.1 percent in 2011, exceeding Indonesia's share but continuing to lag behind the Republic of Korea, China,

FIGURE 5.5 **India's auto and electronics exports have focused on the lower end of the market**

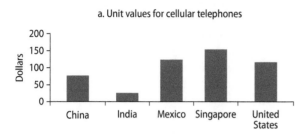

a. Unit values for cellular telephones

b. Unit values for small passenger vehicles

Source: World Bank calculations based on UN COMTRADE database.
Note: Product identification code for telephones = HS851712.

Note: Product identification code for small passenger vehicles = HS870322.

FIGURE 5.6 **India relies less on foreign inputs than its comparators**

a. Foreign value added in total exports

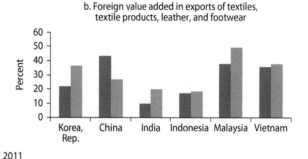

b. Foreign value added in exports of textiles, textile products, leather, and footwear

■ 1995   ■ 2011

Source: World Bank calculations based on UN COMTRADE database.

Malaysia and Vietnam (figure 5.6). This suggests that India is less integrated in GVCs than comparator countries in East Asia when domestic value added is taken into account. Focusing on textiles and apparel as a unified sector, the pattern is similar: India relies less on foreign inputs than its comparators, but that reliance has increased in recent years. By contrast, China's foreign value added in textiles and apparel has declined, perhaps indicating the country's growing position in upstream activities.

Countries in South Asia vary in the extent to which they are upstream (specializing in intermediate goods) or downstream (specializing in final goods) GVC participants. Pakistan is the furthest upstream (with 54 percent of its GVC exports coming from intermediate goods), followed by India (37 percent). By contrast, Sri Lanka is much further downstream (with 4.6 percent of its GVC exports coming from intermediate goods), and

Bangladesh is even further downstream (0.4 percent). These characterizations have been rather stable over time and may be related to the market structure of GVC sectors. In apparel, Bangladesh and Sri Lanka are dominated by large, formal firms geared toward the global market. India and Pakistan, however, have a sizeable informal apparel sector with many firms employing fewer than 10 workers. Yet none of the four countries is fully specialized. For example, Bangladesh imports large amounts of cotton yarn from India but does not export very much fabric because, to a significant extent, the fabric made from the imported yarn is absorbed by the domestic apparel industry. Furthermore, both Pakistan and India have significant exports of both intermediate and final goods, making them upstream in some product lines and downstream in others.

The sophistication of South Asia's exports has improved in some respects.

One way to assess sophistication is by measuring the typical income level associated with countries that export a basket of goods similar to that of the country in question (analogous to PRODY).[8] In the decade between 1999 and 2011, product sophistication of final apparel increased in Bangladesh, India, and Sri Lanka but declined in Pakistan (figure 5.7). However, product sophistication for cloth, yarn, and other apparel inputs converged over the same decade, with sophistication increasing in India and Pakistan and declining in Bangladesh and Sri Lanka.

Indicators of market sophistication, measured by the average income level of the destination market, are more varied across countries in South Asia than are the indicators of product sophistication. Although final apparel in Sri Lanka and Pakistan is directed at higher-income markets than is apparel from Bangladesh and India, market sophistication declined between 2000 and 2010 in all four countries (figure 5.7). This may reflect either increased sales to middle-income markets or more intense competition in high-income markets, or both. In the case of intermediate apparel market sophistication, Pakistan and Bangladesh showed gains between 1999 and 2001 and between 2009 and 2011, indicating an increasing ability to penetrate high-income

FIGURE 5.7 Although product sophistication has increased in some instances, market sophistication of South Asia's textile and apparel exports has gone down

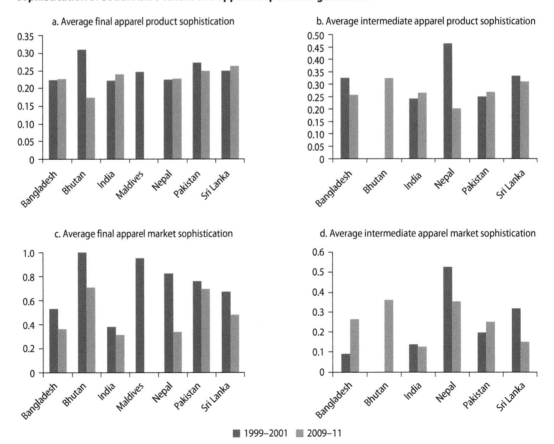

Source: World Bank calculations based on UN COMTRADE database and World Development Indicators data.
Note: Both product and market sophistication measures are normalized with the United States = 1. The relative income levels for South Asian countries are as follows: Bangladesh = 0.04, Bhutan = 0.11, India = 0.07, Maldives = 0.16, Nepal = 0.03, Pakistan = 0.06, and Sri Lanka = 0.11.

markets. India and Sri Lanka, on the other hand, have shifted exports toward lower-income markets.

Even though it is more feasible than ever to produce complex goods on a "made-in-the-world" basis, considerations of transport and other transaction costs, as well as timely delivery, often cause value chains to cluster on a regional basis. The best-known of these clusters are the East Asian regional value chains in electronics and the U.S.-Germany-Japan automotive regional value chains. In South Asia, a regional value chain is emerging in intermediate apparel: intra–South Asian apparel trade amounted to $2.5 billion in 2013, up sharply from $400 million in

2003, and in 2013 24 percent of imported intermediate apparel inputs came from within the region, up from 18 percent in 2003. In the region, Bangladesh and Sri Lanka have the highest share of final apparel goods (at 86 percent and 44 percent of total exports, respectively) and source many apparel inputs from Pakistan and India, which focus relatively less on final products (at 18 percent and 6 percent of total exports, respectively). In 2013, two-thirds of India's exports of knit and crochet fabric were destined for Sri Lanka and Bangladesh, while nearly half of Pakistan's exports of woven cotton denim were destined for Bangladesh and Sri Lanka (figure 5.8).

FIGURE 5.8 **South Asia is developing a regional GVC in apparel**

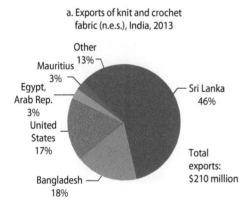

a. Exports of knit and crochet fabric (n.e.s.), India, 2013

Note: SITC 65529.

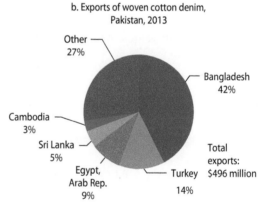

b. Exports of woven cotton denim, Pakistan, 2013

Note: SITC 65243.

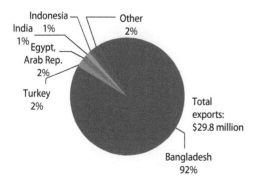

c. Exports of dyed woven cotton, Sri Lanka , 2013

Note: SITC 65242.

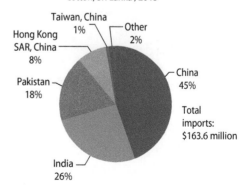

d. Imports of dyed woven cotton, Sri Lanka , 2013

Note: SITC 65242.

Source: World Bank calculations based on UN COMTRADE database.

There also is evidence of an East Asia–South Asia regional value chain. Seventy percent of South Asia's imported apparel inputs come from East Asia, with a growth rate about the same as that of intra–South Asian trade. Overall, South Asia sends 26 percent of its exports of GVC intermediates to East Asia and purchases 68 percent of its extraregional inputs from East Asia (figure 5.9). This level of orientation of South Asia's exports of intermediates to East Asia is well above global averages in apparel, autos, and electronics.

Most policy determinants of GVC participation are lacking

Although a number of studies have looked at the determinants of production fragmentation (for example, Hillberry 2011) and supply chain trade (for example, Rahman and Zhao 2013), the literature is yet to give a clear picture of the drivers of GVC participation and competitiveness. At the level of the firm, local businesses need reasonably high productivity, a capacity to absorb new technologies (skill and capital intensity), and, ideally, experience with trading across borders to be qualified suppliers (Corcos et al. 2013; Defever and Toubal 2013; and Jabbour 2012). The lack of these firm-level capabilities can inhibit the extension of GVCs to certain countries (see Farole and Winkler (2014) for the case of Africa). Other studies have tested the importance of specific drivers of GVCs, including trade policy (Orefice and Rocha 2014), transport (Hummels and Schaur 2013), trade logistics (Saslavsky and Shepherd 2012), and time zones (Dettmer 2014). Although these and other studies give us a sense of what factors are likely to be important in determining GVC dynamics, the question of which specific drivers matter most for country-level participation in GVCs remains open.

In a recent study, Pathikonda and Farole (2015) find a greater intensity of GVC products compared to non-GVC products

FIGURE 5.9   South Asia is highly integrated with East Asia in GVC products

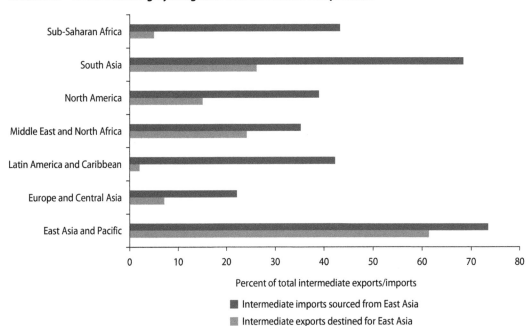

Percent of total intermediate exports/imports

■ Intermediate imports sourced from East Asia
■ Intermediate exports destined for East Asia

Source: World Bank calculations using UN COMTRADE database.

(as defined by combining lists generated by Athukorala [2010] and Sturgeon and Memedovic [2011]) across a sample of over 100 countries for a range of capabilities that are most common in the theoretical, policy, and empirical literature on GVC trade. (The sample comprised 102 countries, which together represented 81 percent of world trade in 2012.) They divide capabilities into three categories: (1) fixed capabilities; (2) long-term policy variables; and (3) short-term policy variables. Fixed capabilities include proximity to markets and natural (resource) capital. Long-term policy variables, which can be changed gradually over a relatively long period, include human capital, physical capital, and institutional capital. Short-term policy variables, which can be changed directly through a policy shift or negotiations in the short to medium term, include logistics

and connectivity, wage competitiveness, market access, and access to inputs.

South Asian countries vary on these capabilities (table 5.2). Sri Lanka scores highest on the level of human capital as measured by average years of schooling. India's total natural capital far outpaces that of other countries, with Pakistan a distant second. Bhutan's institutions are rated ahead of those of the other countries, followed by India, with Pakistan and Bangladesh lagging behind considerably. Geographically, Afghanistan and Pakistan in the region's northwest appear the most disadvantaged, whereas Sri Lanka is closest to markets. India is a much more sophisticated logistical hub, whereas some countries—such as Afghanistan, Bhutan, and Nepal—are in some of the most challenging logistics environments in the world. The minimum wage is not very different across Bangladesh, India,

TABLE 5.2 Many GVC capabilities and endowments in South Asia are limited

Category	Capability	Indicator	Afghanistan	Bangladesh	Bhutan	India	Sri Lanka	Maldives	Nepal	Pakistan
Fixed	Proximity to markets	Proximity to markets (GDP-weighted distance index; 0 to 1)	0.59	0.43	0.47	0.51	0.33	0.32	0.48	0.57
	Natural capital	Total value of natural capital	—	197.74	8.92	2,959.7	40.71	0.33	66.83	522.55
Long-term	Human capital	Average years of schooling (16 years and older)	3.85	5.91	—	6.24	10.06	6.02	4.23	5.02
	Physical capital	Capital stock ($ per capita)	—	—	—	2,764.3	—	—	—	—
	Institutional capital	Rule of law (rating from −2.5 to 2.5)	−1.90	−0.79	0.12	−0.04	−0.08	−0.33	−1.01	−0.74
Short-term	Logistics and connectivity	Logistics Performance Index (rating; 1 to 5)	2.24	2.74	2.38	3.12	2.29	2.40	2.20	2.53
	Wage competitiveness	Minimum wage for a 19-year-old worker or an apprentice ($ per month)	—	38.57	—	28.37	38.55	—	75.90	41.59
	Market access	Overall Trade Restrictiveness Index of trading partners (MAOTRI)	23.49	16.87	1.68	8.37	18.47	34.23	1.68	14.73
	Access to inputs	Overall Trade Restrictiveness Index (OTRI)	—	—	—	14.90	7.42	20.20	12.63	7.37

Source: World Bank calculations.
Note: The values for natural capital, wage competitiveness, and the two access indexes correspond to 2005, 2014, and 2009, respectively. In the indexes measuring market and input access, a higher number indicates lower access. — = not available.

Pakistan, and Sri Lanka. For access to foreign markets, India faces fewer trade barriers than Bangladesh, Pakistan, and Sri Lanka. For trade barriers on imported inputs, however, India appears to be more restrictive. To put these figures in context, figure 5.10 shows the standardized capability levels in South Asia compared to two regional blocs: the Association of Southeast Asian Nations (ASEAN), which is already of major importance in GVCs, and the Southern African Customs Union (SACU), which is a potential competitor of South Asia. Data on India are shown separately from the rest of South Asia because of its size and level of industrialization.

India has several advantages relative to ASEAN and SACU: natural capital, wage competitiveness, and proximity to markets. Yet it lags behind the two other blocs in physical capital, human capital, institutions, and logistics. India erects barriers to imported inputs that are higher than those of both ASEAN and SACU. At the same time, on the export side, India faces barriers lower than those of ASEAN but higher than those of SACU. Similarly, Bangladesh, Bhutan, Maldives, Nepal, Pakistan, and Sri Lanka are on average more wage competitive than ASEAN and SACU and are closer to markets. Their level of natural capital is higher than SACU's, but lower than ASEAN's. This group of South Asian countries (excluding India), on average, fares worse than SACU and ASEAN countries on other capabilities, including logistics, institutions, human capital, and access to markets overseas. Last, on average, they have better access to imports of intermediate inputs than ASEAN, but worse access than SACU.[9]

FIGURE 5.10   GVC capability gaps compared to ASEAN and SACU are concentrated in areas amenable to policy intervention

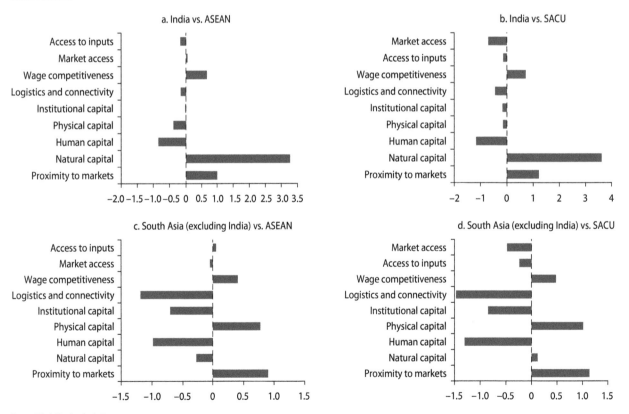

Source: World Bank calculations.
Note: A positive number indicates an advantage for South Asia compared to the other regions. ASEAN = Association of Southeast Asian Nations; SACU = Southern African Customs Union.

INDUSTRY CASE STUDY C

The effect of trade barriers on the apparel sector

This case study is based on *Stitches to Riches?: Apparel Employment, Trade, and Economic Development in South Asia* (World Bank 2016).

With rising labor costs in East Asia, South Asia has an historic opportunity to capture its fair share of the global apparel market (currently 12 percent compared to 41 percent for China alone), in the process pulling millions out of poverty, especially women.

However, taking advantage of lower labor costs will not be sufficient as global buyers have ever more stringent conditions for quality, lead time, reliability, and social and environmental compliance. Lead firms from across South Asia show that it can be done. A key reason for their success was their ability to connect to GVCs—both to source world-class fabrics and to serve demanding customers, which pushed them to ever greater heights.

Trade barriers are the main constraints to South Asia's realizing its great potential in apparel. In particular, problematic duty drawback schemes in India and Pakistan make it difficult for exporters to import textiles, imposing delays that are unacceptable to global buyers and cutting them off from the increasingly important manmade fiber segment. These issues have been resolved in Sri Lanka (which has no import duties on textiles) and Bangladesh (which has a very effective system of bonded warehouses to facilitate duty-free import of textiles). As a result, Sri Lanka and Bangladesh export ten times more apparel than India and Pakistan (adjusted for population size).

South Asia's historic apparel opportunity

The apparel sector is one of the most important employers in developing countries. Export-oriented apparel production has the potential to generate "good" jobs that contribute to rising living standards and poverty reduction. In particular, increased apparel exports tend to boost female employment in the formal sector and provide workers with wages higher than those they can earn in agriculture or other informal sectors (Frederick and Staritz 2012). Women employed in the formal sector tend to have fewer children, which reduces population growth and improves children's health, and women are more likely than men to dedicate their income to the health and education of children (World Bank 2012).

Rising wages in China may improve South Asia's competitive position in the global apparel market. China accounted for 41 percent of global apparel exports in 2012 (up from 25 percent in 2000), compared to only 12 percent for South Asia. A 2013 survey of leading global buyers in the sector found that 72 percent of respondents planned to decrease their share of sourcing from China over the next five years.

The challenge: Meeting ever more stringent demands from global buyers on factors other than cost

To seize this opportunity, South Asia will need to compete not only on cost but also on quality and lead time as well as on social and environmental compliance, which are increasingly important to buyers.

Surveys of global buyers show that East Asian apparel manufacturers rank well above South Asian firms along these increasingly important dimensions (table 5.3).

Quality. Besides being cost competitive, suppliers must also be able to consistently offer quality products. Quality is influenced by the raw materials used, the skill level of the sewing machine operator, and the thoroughness of the quality control team. On the basis of combined results from buyer surveys and interviews, countries can be placed in three groups according to the quality of apparel production, in order of strongest to weakest: (1) China, Vietnam, and Sri Lanka; (2) Indonesia, Cambodia, and Bangladesh; and (3) India and Pakistan.

Lead time and reliability. Lead time and reliability are greatly affected by the efficiency

TABLE 5.3 South Asia is less competitive than Southeast Asia in noncost areas

Country comparison: non-cost-related factors impacting performance

Country	Buyers' perceptions of		
	Quality	Lead time and reliability	Social compliance and sustainability
China	● 1	● 1	▲ 3
Bangladesh	● 5	● 5	● 6
India	● 6	● 6	● 5
Vietnam	● 2	● 2	● 2
Cambodia	▲ 4	▲ 4	▲ 4
Indonesia	▲ 3	▲ 3	● 1

Note: Based on data from (Birnbaum (2013) and stakeholder surveys conducted for this study. Countries were ranked from 1 to 6 on each factor, with 1 being the best and 6 being the worst. Blue indicates the factor is not a constraint; Yellow indicates some problems; Red shows an important constraint.

and availability of transportation networks and customs procedures. On the basis of survey and interview results (Birnbaum 2013), the countries can be placed in three groups, in order of strongest to weakest: (1) China, Vietnam, and Indonesia; (2) Sri Lanka and Cambodia; and (3) Bangladesh, India, and Pakistan. China has consistently had the shortest lead times throughout the last decade (Muzzini and Aparicio 2013; World Bank 2005; World Bank 2013).

Social compliance and sustainability. These criteria have become central to buyers' sourcing decisions in response to pressure from corporate social responsibility (CSR) campaigns by nongovernmental organizations (NGOs) and compliance-conscious consumers following safety incidents in apparel factories. Noncompliant countries risk damaging their country's brand. To that end, Bangladesh, in partnership with global buyers, is taking steps to boost compliance.

The key to the success of lead firms: Connectivity to GVCs

Lead apparel firms in South Asia (such as Pacific Jeans in Bangladesh, MAS in Sri Lanka, Orient Craft in India, and US Apparel in Pakistan) show that world-class performance can be achieved in the region. Their success was based not only on high labor productivity, but also on their capacity to source high-quality fabrics and to learn from suppliers and demanding global customers.

High labor productivity was achieved through training and performance incentives, such as incentives to reduce absenteeism. Computerized cutting machines are essential to reducing material waste and also are used for grading and marking by, for example, Pacific Jeans of Bangladesh. Technology is also used to increase compliance with environmental standards (a must for selling to leading brands). For example, Pacific Jeans recycles its waste water through a very efficient effluent treatment plant. Orient Craft of India, like most Chinese apparel manufacturers, helped reduce costs and motivate workers by setting up housing close to the factory, which reduced the time and cost of commuting and facilitated the employment of migrant workers, including female workers.

Companies relied on foreign experts (Bangladesh, for example, benefitted from Sri Lankan expertise) to develop technical and managerial skills or benefitted from training abroad (a generation of Bangladeshi entrepreneurs was trained in Korea by Daewoo in the 1980s). Skills were also acquired through the machine suppliers, for example, by Orient Craft.

Innovation often arose as a result of interaction with leading global buyers and suppliers. For example, Pacific Jeans and MAS developed new products in partnership with leading brands from the United States, the European Union, and Japan. MAS of Sri Lanka has been developing innovative, high-performance sports apparel by investing heavily in research and development (R&D), as well as by importing world-class textiles from around the world. On the other hand, leading firms from India and Pakistan (such as US Apparel and Orient Craft), which had difficulty in importing high-performing textiles, either were limited to sourcing fabric locally (mostly cotton-based fabrics) or had to develop their own textile production. When asked to name his main constraint, the senior executive from Orient Craft said, "The difficulty to import manmade fiber in India."

Trade barriers hold back the growth of the sector, especially in India and Pakistan[10]

Raw materials and other inputs to production, over which each apparel supplier has limited influence, make up two-thirds of total cost. Fabrics are the most expensive input in apparel production, and the quality of textiles is directly related to the quality of the final product. Furthermore, the global apparel industry is quickly diversifying across a broad range of textiles (manmade fibers in particular) for which the most efficient producers are located overseas. Thus, efficient import regimes, characterized by rapid clearance through customs and low duties (or effective duty drawback systems) are critical for export competitiveness. Bangladesh and Sri Lanka have achieved considerable progress in improving their import regimes, while India and Pakistan have yet to do so.

High import tariffs on cotton and manmade fibers (table 5.4) combined with ineffective duty drawback mechanisms, have been the main constraint to the growth of the apparel sector in India and Pakistan.

In India, manmade fiber imports are subject to a customs duty of 10 percent, which increases to the mid-teens for imports from Korea, China, and other principal producers because of antidumping measures. Furthermore, excise duties on the production of manmade fibers are 12 percent, while natural fibers are exempt. Total duty and tax rates for some fabrics, such as polyester staple plain weave and polyester filament, reach nearly 30 percent (Birnbaum 2013). Exporters can be competitive in global markets only if they are exempt from these taxes on inputs. However, providing exemptions is fraught with difficulty. The categorization of different inputs is subject to interpretation and negotiation, creating risks for firms importing critical inputs for the production of garments with tight production schedules. For example, duties are paid up-front and exporters apply for a drawback, which is calculated on the cost of materials less the amount of duty paid—but no drawback on trim items is permitted. Administrative procedures are quite rigid. For example, one firm reported that, if it obtained preclearance to import synthetic fabric listed at a certain weight but—because fabric production is inherently unpredictable—the actual consignment contained a few items at a slightly different weight, customs officers, rather than accepting minor differences from the original application, might hold up the consignment to apply a different tariff rate or on suspicion of a tariff violation (which carries very heavy fines). In the meantime, the firm would be unable to complete production, even if these fabrics were only a small share of inputs (Jordan and Kamphuis 2014). Similarly, in the advance license scheme no duty is paid on imports used in export products (Birnbaum 2013), but stakeholders contend that compliance with procedures is extremely difficult and any error results in heavy fines.

TABLE 5.4   Import tariffs in South Asia and East Asia, 2014
Percent

Product category	Bangladesh	India	Pakistan	Sri Lanka	Cambodia	China	Indonesia	Vietnam
Yarn								
Cotton (5203–5207)	5–10	10	5–25	0	0	5–6	5	5
MMF (5401–5406/ 5501–5511)	5–25	10	0–10	0	0	5	0–5	0–5
Woven fabric								
Cotton (5208–5212)	25	10	15–25	0	7	10–14	10–15	12
MMF (5407–5408/5512–5516)	25	10–12.5	15	0–15	7	10–18	10–15	12
Knit fabric (60)	25	10	20–25	0	7	10–12	10	12
MFN average Applied Duties	19.4	12.2	16.6	3.5	5.5	9.6	9.2	9.6
Textiles		12.9				8.5		

Source: ITA-OTEXA 2014; WTO, UNCTAD and ITC 2014.
Note: MMF = manmade fiber. MFN = most favored nation.

Import barriers also affect the textiles industry. In India, purified terephthalic acid, which is essential to the production of polyester or synthetic fibers, can be purchased only from two Indian firms, one of which owns 79 percent of the production capacity (Jordan, Kamphuis, and Setia 2014).

The duty and tax remission for export program (DTRE) in Pakistan is also problematic (box 5.2). Remission can take two to four months for textile imports, which is not acceptable to global buyers (Nabi and Hamid 2013). As a result, the Pakistani apparel industry is dominated by the production of low-value, cotton-based garments, using poor-quality textiles sourced domestically.

The apparel export associations of India and Pakistan have put the reform of the import regime for textiles at the top of their "wish lists" to their governments. The first proposal submitted by India's Apparel Export Promotion Council (AEPC) during an interministerial workshop held in April 2013 reads as follows:

Enlargement of the garment export basket by manufacturing garments (knitted and woven) from fabrics which are not widely available in India—Issuance of duty credit scrip (offsetting custom duties) on import of specialty fabrics at the rate of 5 percent for the export performance in the year 2012–13 and in the entire 12th five year plan.

In contrast, Sri Lanka eliminated all import tariffs on textiles, and Bangladesh established 2,000 bonded warehouses that enable rapid, duty-free import of textiles for exporters, including small and medium enterprises (SMEs). When asked to name the keys to its success, the founder of Pacific Jeans in Bangladesh answered: "The system of bonded warehouses put in place by the government together with back to back letters of credit."[11]

As a result of these constraints on the import of manmade fiber in India and Pakistan, the industry in the region is excessively concentrated in cotton fiber (figure 5.11), which is problematic because cotton-based apparel has been losing global market share to manmade fiber–based apparel. It also limits the capacity of firms to

---

BOX 5.2   Expert evaluation of the duty drawback system in Pakistan

"The present system of suspension of duties and taxes is governed by several Statutory Rule Orders (SROs) issued under Customs Rules 2001 for 'DTRE and Manufacturing Bond Licensing' and 'DTRE Approval.' The approval process involves multiple, parallel and overlapping regimes; plethora of steps at each stage of which concerned officials have wide discretions; the system itself is not clear and with no standard operating procedures; intermediaries falsify the supporting documentation which maximizes the economic rent. The system involves physical verifications of business premises; calculation of 'input wastages' through physical checking by the Input Output Co-efficient Organization (IOCO); drawing of samples of imported input goods and output goods meant for exports at the time of import and export—an archaic procedure; suspension or cancellation of DTRE by the Regulatory Collector as he may deem fit; extensive documentation requirements, and centralization of authority and approvals.

The system complexities have led to extensive delays in processing of applications for DTRE, Manufacturing Bonds Licensing, and payment of DTRE claims resulting in the firms being unable to timely import the quality inputs and meet their export orders; receive their blocked funds as well as pay the economic rent to the concerned officials rendering these enterprises (and the export sector as a whole) non-competitive—hence, there is need for fundamental changes in the present DTRE system."

Source: Ahmad Khan 2014.

FIGURE 5.11   SAR, unlike its competitors, focuses heavily on cotton

Composition of apparel exports by region and fiber type, 2012

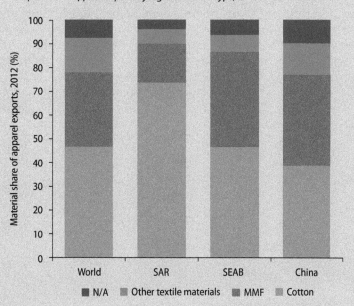

Source: UNSD 2014.
Note: Exports represented by world imports; classifications created by author. MMF = Manmade fiber; SAR = South Asian sample countries (Bangladesh, India, Pakistan, and Sri Lanka); SEAB = Southeast Asian benchmark countries (Cambodia, Indonesia, and Vietnam). N/A indicates the material is not available in trade data classification definition.

FIGURE 5.12   India and Pakistan are far behind in apparel exports, 2005–12

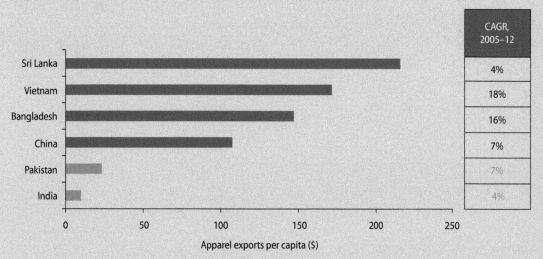

Source: Export data from UN COMTRADE database. Population figures from World Bank 2014.
Note: Total Apparel Exports are a sum of HS 61 and 62. Exports are based on world imports from partner countries; data retrieved March 6, 2014.
CAGR = compound annual growth rate.

diversify their offerings and innovate. Finally, cotton-based apparel is sold mostly in the global spring and summer seasons while manmade fiber–based apparel is sold mostly during the fall and winter seasons. Thus, absence from the manmade fiber market reduces capacity use—apparel factories in India operate only 6.5 months annually, while the global average is 9 months (Jordan, Kamphuis, and Setia 2014).

Thus, the much greater ease at which firms in Bangladesh and Sri Lanka can import fabrics goes a long way in explaining why they export so much more apparel than do firms in India and Pakistan and are at levels comparable to East Asian countries on a per capita basis (figure 5.12).

The extended version of this case study is available online at www.worldbank.org/SouthAsiaCompetes.

Notes

1. In India, the share of exports in value added is, on average, 12.9 percent for GVC participant firms and 2.4 percent for nonparticipant firms. The corresponding figures for Bangladesh are 47.6 percent and 17.4 percent, respectively.
2. A recent study based on a panel of 10,685 Indian manufacturing firms between 1990 and 2011 found, however, that firms experience productivity growth a year prior to entering export markets rather than after entering—pointing to potential reverse causality (Gupta, Patnaik, and Shah 2013).
3. Bangladesh, India, Pakistan, and Sri Lanka (the South Asian 4) run a substantial trade surplus in final GVC goods ($68.0 billion of exports versus $23.8 billion of imports) and have approximately balanced trade in intermediate goods ($24.3 billion of exports versus $25.1 billion of imports). They are significant net importers of electronics intermediates, modest net importers of automotive intermediates, and net exporters of apparel and footwear intermediates.
4. India's largest exports are refined petroleum, diamonds, jewelry (including gold jewelry), pharmaceuticals for retail sale, and processed rice. All of these lie outside the scope of this analysis.
5. India exports chassis and engines, including spark-ignition auto engines, diesel engines, and aircraft engines, as well as a variety of smaller parts.
6. It is a stylized fact of international trade that rich countries import goods with higher unit values than do poorer countries, presumably because their consumers can afford higher-quality varieties of products (Ferrantino, Feinberg, and Deason 2012; Manova and Zhang 2009; Bastos and Silva 2010).
7. In the archetypal case of China, foreign value added is highest in those sectors with the highest degree of foreign investment and in more technologically progressive sectors such as computers and telecommunication equipment (Koopman, Wang, and Wei 2012). In contrast, products like steel and ceramics tend to have higher domestic value added in exports. Similarly, in international comparisons, the share of foreign value added is higher for East Asian countries and Mexico, which are deeply imbedded in GVCs, and

lowest for primary-product exporters such as Brazil, Russia, and Saudi Arabia (Koopman et al. 2010).
8. PRODY (as well as EXPY, described in an earlier section) is an index that measures the quality of export baskets. The index, proposed by Hausmann, Hwang, and Rodrik (2007), is an average of per capita incomes of countries producing a given product, weighted by global export share. A higher PRODY means that a product is associated with a higher level of per capita income (that is, the product is more likely to be exported by a richer country). For South Asia, this means that the product sophistication of each South Asian country's bundle corresponds to a level of income significantly higher than today's levels.
9. These comparisons remain unchanged when South Asia is defined by the country group formed by Bangladesh, Pakistan, and Sri Lanka.
10. Other, less important, barriers also hold back the sector. They are discussed in the extended version of the case study available at www.worldbank.org/SouthAsiaCompetitiveness.
11. The system of bonded warehouses in Bangladesh caters mostly to the apparel industry. Other high-potential industries would greatly benefit from it, such as footwear, which has great difficulty importing leather (World Bank 2013).

References

Abraham, F., J. Konings, and V. Slootmaekers. 2010. "FDI Spillovers in the Chinese Manufacturing Sector: Evidence of Firm Heterogeneity." *Economies of Transition* 18 (1): 143–82.

Amiti, M., and J. Konings. 2007. "Trade Liberalization, Intermediate Inputs, and Productivity: Evidence from Indonesia." *American Economic Review* 97 (5): 1611–38.

Arndt, S.W., and H. Kierzkowski, eds. 2001. *Fragmentation: New Production Patterns in the World Economy*. Oxford: Oxford University Press.

Arnold, J. M., and B. S. Javorcik. 2009. "Gifted Kids or Pushy Parents? Foreign Direct Investment and Plant Productivity in Indonesia." *Journal of International Economics* 79 (1): 42–53.

Athukorala, P. C. 2010. "Production Networks and Trade Patterns in East Asia: Regionalization or Globalization?" ADB Working Paper Series on Regional Economic Integration, No. 56.

Atkin, D., A. Khandelwal, and A. Osman. 2016. "Exporting and Firm Performance: Evidence from a Randomized Experiment," NBER Working Paper 20690, National Bureau of Economic Research, Cambridge, MA.

Bastos, P., and J. Silva. 2010. "The Quality of a Firm's Exports: Where You Export to Matters." *Journal of International Economics* 82 (2): 99–111.

Baldwin, Richard. 2006. "Managing the Noodle Bowl: The Fragility of East Asian Regionalism," CEPR Discussion Paper 5561, CEPR, London.

Birnbaum, D. 2013. "Competitiveness of India's Apparel Export." Apparel Export Promotion Council (AEPC).

Birnbaum, D. 2014. Comment: Bangladesh Industry Development Moving Backwards. *Just-style.com*, April 16. http://www.just-style.com/comment/bangladesh-industry-development-moving-backwards_id121251.aspx.

Clerides, S. K., S. Lack, and J. R. Tybout. 1998. "Is Learning by Exporting Important? Microdynamic Evidence from Colombia, Mexico, and Morroco," *Quarterly Journal of Economics* 113: 903–47.

Constantinescu, C., A. Mattoo, and M. Ruta. 2015. "The Global Trade Slowdown: Cyclical or Structural?" Policy Research Working Paper 7158, World Bank, Washington, DC.

Corcos, G., D.M. Irac, G. Mion, and T. Verdier. 2013. "The Determinants of Intra-Firm Trade." *Review of Economics and Statistics* 95 (3): 825–838.

Defever, F., and F. Toubal. 2013. "Productivity, Relationship-Specific Inputs and the Sourcing Modes of Multinationals." *Journal of Economic Behavior and Organization* 94 (October): 345–57.

De Loecker, J. 2007. "Do Exports Generate Higher Productivity? Evidence from Slovenia." *Journal of International Economics* 73 (1): 69–98.

Dettmer, B. 2014. "International Service Transactions: Is Time a Trade Barrier in a Connected World?" *International Economic Journal* 28 (2): 225–54.

Fernandes, A. M. 2008. "Firm Productivity in Bangladesh Manufacturing Industries." *World Development* 36 (10): 1725–44.

Farole, T., and D. Winkler, eds. 2014. *Making Foreign Direct Investment Work for Sub-Saharan Africa: Local Spillovers and Competitiveness in Global Value Chains.* Washington, DC: World Bank.

Ferrantino, M. J., R. M. Feinberg, and L. Deason. 2012. "Quality Competition and Pricing-to-Market: A Unified Framework for the Analysis of Bilateral Unit Values." *Southern Economic Journal* 78 (3): 860–77.

Frederick, S., and C. Staritz. 2012. "Developments in the Global Apparel Industry after the MFA Phaseout." In *Sewing Success? Employment, Wages and Poverty Following the End of the Multi-fibre Arrangement*, edited by G. Lopez-Acevedo and R. Robertson, 41–86. Washington, DC: World Bank.

Goldberg, P., A. Khandelwal, N. Pavcnik, and P. Topalova. 2010. "Imported Intermediate Inputs and Domestic Product Growth: Evidence from India." *Quarterly Journal of Economics* 125 (4): 1727–67.

Görg, H. 2000. "Fragmentation and Trade: U.S. Inward Processing Trade in the EU." *Review of World Economics* 136 (3): 403–22.

Gupta, A., I. Patnaik, and A. Shah. 2013. "Learning by Exporting: Evidence from India." Working Paper Series on Regional Economic Integration No. 119, Asian Development Bank, Manila.

Hausmann, R., J. Hwang, and D. Rodrik. 2007. "What You Export Matters." *Journal of Economic Growth* 12 (1): 1–25.

Havranek, T., and Z. Irsova. 2011. "Estimating Vertical Spillovers from FDI: Why Results Vary and What the True Effect Is." *Journal of International Economics* 85 (2): 234–44.

Helpman, E. 1984. "A Simple Theory of International Trade with Multinational Corporations." *Journal of Political Economy* 92 (3): 451–71.

Hillberry, R. 2011. "Causes of International Production Fragmentation: Some Evidence." In *Global Value Chains: Impacts and Implications.* Canadian Department of Foreign Affairs and International Trade.

Hummels, D. L., D. Rapoport, and K.-M. Yi. 1998. "Vertical Specialization and the Changing Nature of World Trade." *Federal Reserve Bank of New York Economic Policy Review* 4 (2): 79–99.

Hummels, D.L., and G. Schaur. 2013. "Time as a Trade Barrier." *American Economic Review* 103 (7): 2935–59.

ITA-OTEXA (U.S. International Trade Administration, Office of Textiles and Apparel).

2014. *Market Reports/Tariffs: Textiles, Apparel, Footwear and Travel Goods.* Washington, DC: ITA-OTEXA.

Jabbour, L. 2012. "Slicing the Value Chain Internationally: Empirical Evidence on the Off-Shoring Strategy by French Firms. *The World Economy* 35 (11): 1417–47.

Jordan, L.S., and B. Kamphuis. 2014. *Supply Chain Delays and Uncertainty in India: The Hidden Constraint on Manufacturing Growth.* Washington DC: World Bank.

Jordan, L.S., B. Kamphuis, and S.P. Setia. 2014. *A New Agenda: Improving the Competitiveness of the Textiles and Apparel Value Chain in India.* Washington DC: World Bank.

Kee, H. L. 2005. "Foreign Ownership and Firm Productivity in Bangladesh Garment Sector." World Bank, Washington, DC.

———. 2015. "Local Intermediate Inputs and the Shared Supplier Spillovers of Foreign Direct Investment." *Journal of Development Economics* 112 (January): 56–71.

Kee, H. L., and H. Tang. 2015. "Domestic Value Added in Exports: Theory and Firm Evidence from China." Policy Research Working Paper 7491, World Bank, Washington DC.

Kimura, Fukunari, and Mitsuyo Ando. 2005. "The Formation of International Production and Distribution Networks in East Asia." In *International Trade in East Asia*, edited by T. Ito and A. K. Rose 177–216. Chicago: University of Chicago Press.

Koopman, R., W. Powers, Z. Wang, and S.-J. Wei. 2010. "Give Credit Where Credit Is Due: Tracing Value Added in Global Production Chains." NBER Working Paper No. 16426, National Bureau of Economic Research, Cambridge, MA.

Koopman, R., Z. Wang, and S.-J. Wei. 2012. "Estimating Domestic Content in Exports When Processing Trade is Pervasive." *Journal of Development Economics* 99 (1): 178–89.

Krugman, P., R. N. Cooper, and T. N. Srinivasan. 1995. "Growing World Trade: Causes and Consequences." *Brookings Papers on Economic Activity* 26 (1): 327–77.

Manova, K., and Z. Zhang. 2009. "Export Prices Across Firms and Destinations." NBER Working Paper No. 15342, National Bureau of Economic Research, Cambridge, MA.

Mattoo, A., Z. Wang, and S. J. Wei. 2013. *Trade in Value-Added: Developing New Measures of Cross-Border Trade.* Washington, DC: World Bank.

Melitz, M. J. 2003. "The Impact of Trade on Intra-industry Reallocations and Aggregate Industry Productivity." *Econometrica* 71: 1695–1725.

Mukim, M. 2011. "Industry and the Urge to Cluster: A Study of the Informal Sector in India." Discussion Paper 72, Spatial Economics Research Centre, London.

Muzzini, E., and G. Aparicio. 2013. *Bangladesh: The Path to Middle-Income Status from an Urban Perspective.* http://elibrary.worldbank.org/doi/book/10.1596/978-0-8213-9859-3.

Nabi, I., and N. Hamid. 2013. *Garments as a Driver of Economic Growth: Insights from Pakistan Case Studies.* Lahore, Pakistan: International Growth Centre.

Orefice, G., and N. Rocha. 2014. "Deep Integration and Production Networks: An Empirical Analysis." *The World Economy* 37 (1): 106–36.

Pathikonda, V.G., and T. Farole. 2015. *A Capability-Based Assessment of GVC Competitiveness for the SACU Region.* Washington, DC: World Bank.

Rahman, J., and T. Zhao. 2013. "Export Performance in Europe; What Do We Know from Supply Links?" IMF Working Papers 13/62, Washington DC, International Monetary Fund.

Saslavsky, D., and B. Shepherd. 2012. "Facilitating International Production Networks : The Role of Trade Logistics." Policy Research Working Paper 6224, World Bank, Washington, DC.

Staritz, C., and S. Frederick. 2014. "Sector Case Study—Apparel." In *Making Foreign Direct Investment Work for Sub-Saharan Africa: Local Spillovers and Competitiveness in Global Value Chains*, edited by T. Farole and D. Winkler, 209–44. Washington, DC: World Bank.

Sturgeon, T., and O. Memedovic. 2011. *Mapping Global Value Chains: Intermediate Goods Trade and Structural Change in the World Economy.* Vienna: UNIDO.

USITC (U.S. International Trade Commission). 2011. *The Economic Effects of Significant U.S. Import Restraints: Seventh Update 2011. Special Topic: Global Supply Chains.* USITC Publication 4253. Washington, DC: USITC.

Van Biesebroeck, J. 2005. "Exporting Raises Productivity in Sub-Saharan African

Manufacturing Firms." *Journal of International Economics* 67 (2): 373–91.

UNSD (United Nations Statistics Division). 2014. World Apparel Imports (2000, 2005, 2009, 2012).

World Bank. 2005. "End of MFA Quotas: Key Issues and Strategic Options for Bangladesh Readymade Garment Industry." Bangladesh Development Series Paper 2, World Bank, Washington, DC.

———. 2012. *More and Better Jobs in South Asia.* Washington, DC: World Bank.

———. 2013. "Value Chain Analysis for Polo Shirts." In *Bangladesh Diagnostic Trade Integration Study*, Vol. 3, 107–59. Washington, DC: World Bank.

———. 2014. *World Development Indicators 2013.* Washington DC: World Bank.

———. 2015. *Leveraging Urbanization in South Asia: Managing Spatial Transformation for Prosperity and Livability.* Washington, DC: World Bank.

———. 2016. *Stitches to Riches?: Apparel Employment, Trade, and Economic Development in South Asia.* Washington, DC: World Bank.

WTO (World Trade Organization), UNCTAD (United Nations Conference on Trade and Development), and ITC (International Trade Centre). 2014. World Tariff Profiles 2014 Geneva: WTO, UNCTAD and ITC.

Firm Capabilities Are Constrained | 6

An average firm in South Asia does not operate at optimum efficiency. Counterintuitively, the region's firms overemploy relatively scarce capital and underemploy labor, South Asia's abundant resource. Performance varies widely with regard to knowledge inputs—ranging from extensive technology use in India to limited information and communication technology (ICT) adoption in Bangladesh and Nepal—but even among leaders, the use of e-commerce and other productivity-enhancing online business tools is relatively low. With respect to innovation, the region again has both leaders and laggards, but innovation is generally concentrated in a few, mature firms and, even then, is more likely to be of the imitation, catching-up-to-the-frontier variety. However, innovation of all types—to a large extent enabled through ICT adoption—is an important driver of productivity at the firm level. This suggests that further investment in firm capabilities, including better resource management, improving skills, deepening technology adoption, and nurturing innovation, could raise productivity in South Asia. The following discussion develops these observations in more detail.

Firms lack managerial quality and do not use resources efficiently

Differences in management practices can account for as much as 30 percent of cross-country differences in total factor productivity (TFP) (Bloom, Sadun, and Van Reenen 2016). In South Asia, organizational factors such as skills and management practices hold back firm productivity (Bloom et al. 2010). For example, management practices in India are weaker than those in the United States, Brazil, and China (Bloom and Van Reenen 2010), as well as in many other developing countries (figure 6.1), because Indian firms generally do not collect and analyze data, set and monitor clear performance targets, or explicitly link pay or promotion with performance. Conversely, improved management practices in South Asia have led to increased profitability and productivity. Bloom et al. (2013) performed an experiment that provided management consulting to large textile firms in Maharashtra, India, and found that the intervention led to an 11 percent improvement in firm productivity. McKenzie and Woodruff (2015) show that business practices matter as much for microenterprises as for larger firms—boosting productivity,

FIGURE 6.1 **Management capabilities in South Asia are relatively weak**

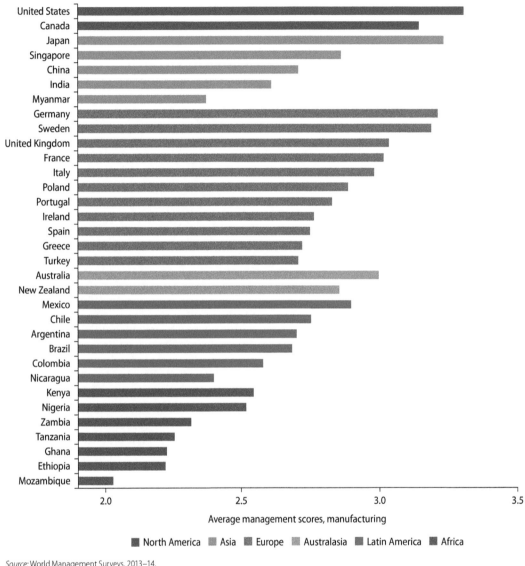

Average management scores, manufacturing

■ North America ▨ Asia ▨ Europe ▨ Australasia ■ Latin America ■ Africa

Source: World Management Surveys, 2013–14.
Note: Management scores range from 1 (worst practice) to 5 (best practice).

profits, survival rates, and sales growth—and the positive effects of improved practices are robust to numerous measures of owners' human capital.

Managerial capabilities can be assessed indirectly by looking at how firms use the resources available to them. For example, profit maximization requires that firms employ resources such as labor and capital until the additional contribution of these factors to firm revenue (the marginal revenue product) equals the going wage or rental rate. Of course, firms often do not observe marginal product directly; however, in the absence of major distortions (physical, regulatory, or information asymmetries), an average firm should employ something close to an optimal factor mix—otherwise, a firm could gain by hiring relatively cheaper resources, and factor owners could gain by commanding returns above their productivity levels, until marginal products and costs were equalized.

In South Asia, many firms do not use the available resources efficiently. Case studies reveal low capacity utilization in India and Pakistan among apparel makers (which operate 6.5 months annually versus the global average of 9 months) and automakers (which operate at 66 percent and 44 percent capacity, respectively, versus more than 75 percent in China). Only 4 of the 18 original equipment manufacturers (OEMs) in the auto sector in India and Pakistan operate at the industry standard for efficiency of 100,000 units per model.

Previous research on India and Sri Lanka has attributed weak performance of the manufacturing sector to firms' consistently underemploying relatively abundant labor and overemploying relatively scarce capital (Fernandes and Pakes 2008; Dougherty, Herd, and Chalaux 2009; Hasan, Mitra, and Sundaram 2013).[1] In India, these results suggest that the optimal level of employment was 6 times the actual level in 2001 and 3 times the actual level in 2004, whereas in Sri Lanka, the optimal level of labor was 1.1 times the manufacturing employment in 2003.[2] Repeating this analysis with the most recent data available for Bangladesh, India, Nepal, Pakistan, and Sri Lanka reveals that underutilization of labor remains a persistent feature of the operating environment for firms in most of South Asia.[3] The optimal level of employment of firms in India and Sri Lanka is 1.7 and 2.2 times current employment levels, respectively, while estimates for Nepal and Pakistan suggest underutilization on the order of 14 to 16 times the existing workforce. Bangladeshi firms, on the other hand, appear to overutilize labor: firms hire approximately 18 percent more workers than would be optimal at the prevailing wage rate.[4]

Although the data include businesses as small as five employees, larger firms make up the majority of the sample. However, this makes the findings of even greater concern, because larger firms could be expected to have a greater capacity to manage resource use, leverage economies of scale, and be closer to the knowledge frontier. Instead, most large firms in South Asia do not operate close to what would be considered optimum efficiency levels given the prevailing factor prices, costing themselves lost profits and bringing down aggregate productivity.

Adoption of knowledge and technology is low

Firms rely on technology to enhance the efficiency of production processes and to connect more effectively with customers and suppliers. In particular, ICT is a major potential driver of productivity growth, especially in countries and locations further from the technological frontier. In this report, ICT is defined as the use of computers and other electronic equipment and systems to collect, store, use, and send data electronically. Therefore, ICT includes any communication device or application, such as cellular telephones, computer and network hardware and software, as well as the various services and applications associated with them, such as Internet and videoconferencing.

In developed countries, penetration of ICT is by now nearly universal: 97.9 percent of businesses with ten or more employees in the countries of the Organisation for Economic Co-operation and Development (OECD) have an Internet connection (OECD 2012). Many developing countries also have high levels of ICT penetration: for example, over 90 percent of Turkish and Mexican firms use the Internet (OECD 2012). However, based on data collected by the World Bank in the latest round of Enterprise Surveys, adoption of ICT in South Asia is uneven (box 6.1). Only half of Nepalese and Bangladeshi firms use computers in their businesses, lower than the average in Africa (figure 6.2).[5] On the other hand, nearly all Indian firms use computers, at a level similar to that in the European Union. Twice as many Indian firms use computers and software as firms in Bangladesh and Nepal, and 30 percent more firms use computers and software in India than in Pakistan. Pakistani firms lie between India, on the one hand, and Bangladesh and

FIGURE 6.2   **ICT adoption varies substantially across countries in South Asia**

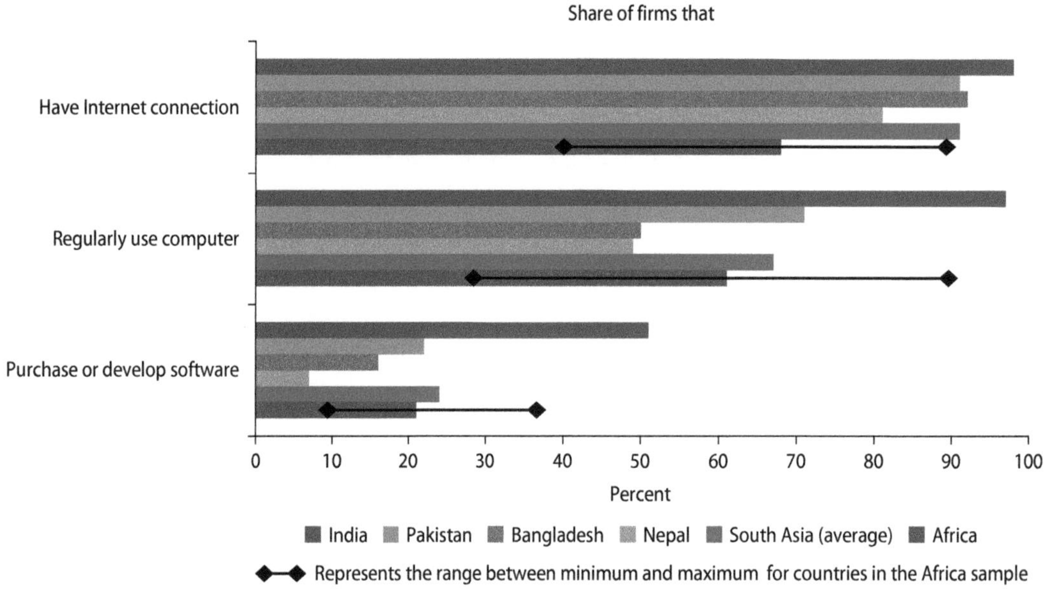

Share of firms that

Legend
India   Pakistan   Bangladesh   Nepal   South Asia (average)   Africa
◆——◆ Represents the range between minimum and maximum for countries in the Africa sample

Source: World Bank calculations based on 2013 Enterprise Surveys for Bangladesh, Nepal, and Pakistan, and 2014 Enterprise Survey for India.
Note: Calculations for Africa based on data from the Democratic Republic of Congo, Ghana, Kenya, Namibia, Nigeria, South Sudan, Sudan, Tanzania, Uganda, and Zambia.

BOX 6.1   Data for analysis of ICT adoption in South Asia

The analysis of ICT and innovation practices is based on the data collected by the World Bank Enterprise Surveys, which were implemented in Bangladesh, Nepal, and Pakistan in 2013 and in India in 2014. Overall, the dataset has approximately 5,500 observations unevenly distributed among Bangladesh, India, Nepal, and Pakistan (with the number of firms surveyed in India exceeding the total number surveyed in the other three countries). More than 4,000 manufacturing firms and 1,266 service firms were surveyed. The survey is representative of mostly medium, and to a lesser extent larger, firms, although a few firms in the survey would have been characterized as micro when surveyed because they had fewer than five employees.

The innovation module from the World Bank Enterprise Survey includes questions on ICT use, although the survey does not report how much firms invest in ICT. Specifically, the ICT section of the innovation module provides information on two aggregate dimensions of ICT use: (1) computer and software use and (2) different types of Internet use. Computer and software use is a critical channel for the improvement of the production process, and Internet use can be a critical tool for improving performance by reducing information costs, enabling e-commerce, and facilitating communication. Table B6.1.1 provides an overview of the questions in the module.

In order to obtain a meaningful measure of ICT use, and given the lack of information on what specific subdimensions of ICT use are more important for performance, this report calculates a synthetic index for each ICT use using the average of the normalized subcomponents in each country. For computer use, the two continuous variables (percentage of workers using a

(continues next page)

BOX 6.1   Data for analysis of ICT adoption in South Asia (continued)

TABLE B6.1.1   ICT questions from the Innovation Module

Computer and software use	Percentage of workers using a computer regularly
	Whether a firm has purchased or developed any software in-house
	Whether a firm has information technology (IT) staff
	Total cost of hiring an external computer or software consultant
Internet use	Communication: whether a firms uses the Internet for internal communication among its employees or for communication with clients and suppliers
	E-commerce: whether a firm uses the Internet for online purchases or sales
	Information: whether a firm uses the Internet for managing inventory, marketing products, or researching or developing ideas for new products and services

computer regularly and total cost of ICT consultants) are normalized by subtracting the sample mean and dividing by the standard deviation.

Seven indicators are available for Internet use: two for communication (whether a firm uses Internet for internal or external communication), two for e-commerce (buying or selling online), and three for information (online management of inventory, marketing, and research), which are then normalized and averaged to form an Internet use index. Finally, an aggregate ICT total index (figure B6.1.1) is calculated as the average of the computer and Internet indexes.

FIGURE B6.1.1   Components of the ICT Index

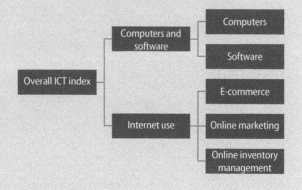

Nepal, on the other, with approximately 71 percent of firms having at least one worker using a computer. ICT adoption rates also vary considerably by sector within and across countries. In most South Asian countries, the use of ICT is much higher in electronics than in apparel, and ICT use is higher in sectors more exposed to international competition, such as apparel and some automotive sectors, than in sectors that are less exposed to competition, such as agribusiness.

As expected, almost every firm using a computer also uses the Internet (figure 6.2). Similar to computer use, Internet use is higher in larger and more foreign-exposed firms. Although the difference in the share of Internet use in large and small firms in India is

around 6.5 percentage points (at 99.6 percent and 93.1 percent, respectively), it increases to 23.4 percentage points in Nepal and 18.1 percentage points in Bangladesh. In Nepal, Internet use appears to increase with age—only half of firms less than 5 years old use the Internet, while 88 percent of those older than 20 years do. The picture in Pakistan is, however, the opposite—younger firms are more likely to use the Internet. In all countries, service sector firms are more connected to the Internet than are firms in manufacturing, although the difference is not large.

Firms appear to use the Internet more often to reach customers than to connect with suppliers (figure 6.3). Given the high rates of connectivity in South Asia (and particularly in India),

FIGURE 6.3   **Firms use the Internet to reach customers more than to connect with suppliers**

Share of Internet-connected firms that:

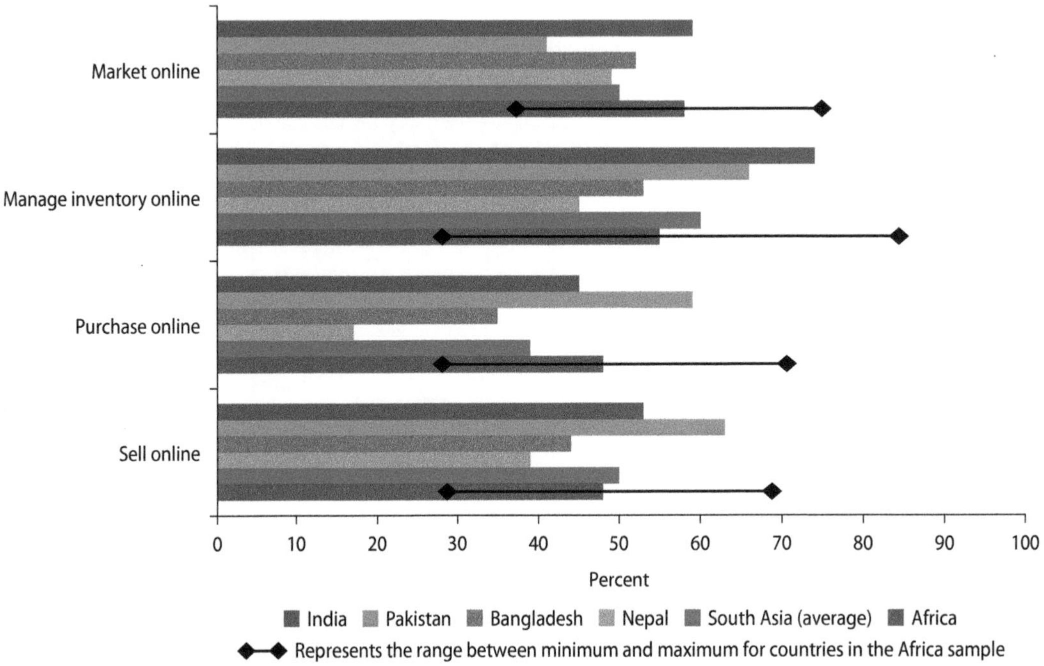

Source: World Bank calculations based on 2013 Enterprise Surveys for Bangladesh, Nepal, and Pakistan, and 2014 Enterprise Survey for India.
Note: Calculations for Africa based on data from the Democratic Republic of Congo, Ghana, Kenya, Namibia, Nigeria, South Sudan, Sudan, Tanzania, Uganda, and Zambia.

it is striking that South Asian firms are doing less e-commerce than firms in a number of African countries. In all four countries, the share of firms selling goods on the Internet is higher than the share of firms purchasing online, a pattern different from that observed in Africa. South Asian firms generally do less marketing on the Internet than do African countries; 58 percent of firms in African countries market online, but only Indian firms (the highest share in the region) advertise on the web at the same rate. Although Internet use for marketing increases with size, large firms in Bangladesh, India, and Pakistan do less marketing online than large firms in African countries. Overall, and despite greater Internet access in South Asia than in Africa, the use of important Internet management strategies, such as e-commerce and marketing, is still much lower than it has the potential to be.

Overall, the data reveal three important patterns for ICT use in South Asia. First, ICT

adoption varies significantly across countries: India scores highly on multiple dimensions of technology use and Pakistan is in line with global peers, but ICT adoption in Bangladesh and Nepal is very low and lower than that in African countries. Second, India is a regional leader in computer and software use among firms, suggesting that there are potential spillovers from the country's strong software industry. Third, despite prevalent Internet use, the adoption of Internet commercialization practices for marketing products (e-commerce) is relatively low, with the difference particularly stark in India.

What determines these different rates of ICT adoption? The literature identifies four sets of factors: firm characteristics, market structure, demand-side variables, and complementary factors such as skills, other technologies, and agglomeration economies that may facilitate diffusion (box 6.2). Econometric analysis shows that all are

---

BOX 6.2   Determinants of ICT adoption

The literature has identified a number of firm characteristics that are important for adoption of ICT at the firm level. (Some of these parallel the observations from the World Bank Enterprise Surveys discussed in the preceding section.) A number of studies find a positive correlation between firm size and the adoption of ICT (Teo and Tan 1998; Thong 1999; Fabiani et al. 2005; Giunta and Triveri 2007; and Haller and Siedschlag 2011). Walczuch, Van Braven, and Lundgren (2000) point out that small firms in the Netherlands are not adopting Internet use at the same speed as larger firms.[a] Beyond size, some studies suggest that adoption and use of ICT is higher in younger firms (Commander et al. 2006; Haller and Siedschlag 2011). Some studies have examined the role of education or skills (human capital) in the adoption of new technologies (Bartel and Lichtenberg 1987; Chun 2003), while others have shown that the demand for educated workers rises with the use of the new technology (Berman, Bound, and Machin 1994; Doms, Dunne, and Troske 1997; Haskel and Heden 1999; and Bugamelli and Pagano 2004).

The environment in which the firm operates also matters for ICT adoption. Firms facing stronger competition are more inclined to innovate and adopt new technologies, such as ICT, in order to improve their performance and chances of survival. Some studies show that competitive pressure is positively associated with ICT adoption (Dasgupta et al. 1999; Kowtha and Choon 2001; Hollenstein 2004; and Kretschmer, Miravete, and Pernías 2012). Firms exposed to international competition in export markets may be more inclined to adopt new technologies (Hollenstein 2004; Lucchetti and Sterlacchini 2004; Bayo-Moriones and Lera-López 2007; Giunta and Trivieri 2007; and Haller and Siedschlag 2011). Similarly, foreign-owned firms are more likely to be early adopters of new technology as well as potentially important channels of new technology diffusion (Keller 2004; Narula and Zanfei 2005).

a. Other studies find a weak or insignificant relationship (Teo, Lim, and Lai 1998; Lefebvre et al. 2005; and Love et al. 2005). Hollenstein (2004) argues that the relationship between ICT adoption and firm size might be nonlinear, which would partially explain the weak or insignificant relationship.

---

important in South Asia. Larger firms and exporters are more likely to adopt ICT practices, with the size of each coefficient inversely related to the country's economic development, suggesting larger effects in poorer countries in the region (see table 6A.1 for detailed regression results).[6] Younger firms are more likely to adopt ICT practices only in India, which contrasts with the results of Commander et al. (2011), and foreign-owned firms are not more ICT intensive. The link between importing and ICT adoption, suggested in Hollenstein (2004) and Haller and Siedschlag (2011), is statistically significant only for India and Bangladesh.

Consistent with the complementarity between technology and skills observed in OECD countries (Berman, Bound, and Machin 1994; Doms, Dunne, and Troske 1997; Haskel and Heden 1999; and Bugamelli and Pagano 2004), skills matter critically for technology adoption in South Asia. The share of high school graduates among firm employees is positively and significantly associated with ICT adoption in the region pooled sample and in all the country estimations except Pakistan. In Bangladesh and Nepal, access to finance also matters, while in India, access to foreign technology through licensing is an important channel for ITC adoption. Agglomeration matters for ICT diffusion only partially: in India (but not in other countries) firms in the main business cities are more likely to adopt ICT, while in Nepal city size matters a great deal. Results for individual components of ICT adoption largely parallel those for the aggregate index.

These findings suggest different policy priorities for countries within the region. Nepal and Bangladesh could concentrate on supporting the adoption of the Internet and the use of computers in the private sector. The public sector can play a role by investing in infrastructure (especially in Nepal where diffusion is higher in larger cities), by helping to train skilled workers, and by supporting the diffusion of technology. Once basic ICT adoption is mainstreamed across all firms in these countries, the focus should shift toward greater integration of ICT practices that improve management and performance, represented in our indexes by the use of software and the use of the Internet for the commercialization of products. In India, where the use of ICT is pervasive in the private sector, the focus could be on the use of the Internet

for the commercialization of products, facilitated by improved access to finance. Given the large number of firms in software development and the availability of IT engineers, it is likely that improving access to finance and the establishment of broad-based online financial transactions platforms could help broaden e-commerce use.

Innovation is widespread but novelty is limited

As with ICT use, adoption of innovation practices (box 6.3) differs significantly across South Asian countries. Bangladesh and India have a larger percentage of firms conducting research and development (R&D) than the average in Eastern Europe and Central Asia and in Africa, while Nepal and Pakistan

---

BOX 6.3   Innovation activities and outputs in the Enterprise Surveys

Innovation can be measured by looking at innovation inputs, innovation outputs, or both. However, the subjective nature of many of the questions used in innovation surveys presents a challenge. The Oslo manual, which is the main reference for this type of survey, defines innovation as "the implementation of a new or significantly improved product (good or service), or process, a new marketing method, or a new organizational method in business practices, workplace organization or external relations" (OECD/Eurostat 2005). Most surveys use this definition to identify innovations by directly asking firm managers and owners whether they have implemented "new" or "significant" changes or improvements in the last three years. This is problematic because "significant" is a highly subjective term and any implementation is self-reported. In general, any sound analysis of innovation activity should combine a focus on

both knowledge-capital inputs and innovation outputs. The World Bank Enterprise Surveys provide the following information on various sources of knowledge capital and innovation outputs.[a]

Innovation or knowledge inputs include:

- *Research and development.* Source and expenditures on R&D (internal versus external)
- *Capacity building.* Training, including expenditures, provided as a result of new innovations
- *Purchase or licensing of inventions or other knowledge forms.* Expenditures on inventions or intellectual property that helped firms innovate
- *Acquisition of business intelligence.* Key sources of information and ideas for their innovative activities
- *Intellectual property.* Patents, utility models, trademarks, or copyright designs, or registered industrial designs

(continues next page)

BOX 6.3   Innovation activities and outputs in the Enterprise Surveys (continued)

With respect to innovation outputs, the Enterprise Survey innovation module differentiates between two types of technological innovations (product and process) and two types of nontechnological innovations (organization and marketing):

- *Product innovations.* New, redesigned, or substantially improved goods or services:
  - Products new to the firm
  - Significantly improved products
  - Products new to the market
- *Process innovations.* Implementation of new or significantly improved production or delivery methods (including significant changes in techniques, equipment, or software):
  - Innovation methods for manufacturing products or offering services
  - Innovative logistics, delivery, or distribution methods for inputs, products, or services
  - Innovative supporting activity for processes, such as maintenance systems or operations for purchasing, accounting, or computing

The following are not considered to be innovations: minor changes or improvements; an increase in production or service capabilities through the addition of manufacturing or logistical systems that are very similar to those already in use; ceasing to use a process; simple capital replacement or extension; changes resulting purely from changes in factor prices, customization, regular seasonal, and other cyclical changes; and the trading of new or significantly improved products.

- *Organizational innovations.* These are new organizational methods in business practices, workplace organization, or external relations. Organizational innovations are grouped into one of two categories. *Structural innovations* affect responsibilities, accountability, command lines, and information flows, as well as the number of hierarchical levels, the divisional structure of functions (such as R&D, production, human resources, and financing), or the separation between line and support functions. *Procedural innovations* consist of changes to the routines, processes, and operations of a company. Procedural innovations change or implement new procedures and processes within the company, such as simultaneous engineering or zero buffer rules.
- *Marketing innovations.* These include changes to incorporate advances in marketing science, technology, or engineering to increase the effectiveness and efficiency of marketing for a competitive advantage.

a. The distinction between types of innovations, although clear in theory, can be a matter of some confusion for survey respondents. For example, new marketing processes (such as discounts), new packaging, and new client segments are sometimes confused with process or product innovations. Interviewees provide a recorded description of product and process innovations, which allows the user to verify the identified innovations, reclassify wrongly attributed cases to the proper category, and invalidate cases that do not constitute an innovation. This exercise has been conducted by Cirera et al. (2015), who kindly provided us with "clean innovation data." For the overall sample of South Asia firms, the "cleaning" exercise decreased the rate of product innovation from 53 percent to 51 percent and the rate of process innovation from 64 percent to 58 percent. Although the cleaning exercise reduced innovation rates for most countries, in Nepal the rate of product innovation increased from 10 to 12 percent as the result of the reclassification of some innovations originally designated as process innovations.

display a lower percentage (table 6.1). With respect to R&D expenditures per employee, however, South Asia's performance across the region is below both Eastern Europe and Central Asia and Africa. Thus, even though many firms invest in R&D, the average

intensity of R&D is low. There are some exceptions, of course. Bangalore, India, is home to one of Bosch's global R&D centers (where it employs 15,000 personnel) and to a recently opened IBM enterprise mobility platform for developing iOS applications.

TABLE 6.1 Knowledge capital intensity in South Asia is lower than in other regions

Type	Indicator	Bangladesh	Pakistan	India	Nepal	South Asia	Europe and Central Asia	Africa
R&D	Percent of firms	19	6	56	4	21	9	19
	$ per worker (median)	8	—	14	6.5	14	498	18
Equipment	Percent of firms	75	17	68	23	46	—	29
	$ per worker (median)	92	197	227	130	179	—	180
Licensing	Percent of firms	5	3	4	1	3	—	8
	$ per worker (median)	6	82	25	234	27	—	21
Training	Percent of firms	19	6	56	4	21	9	19
	$ per worker (median)	12	107	21	73	21	—	47

Source: World Bank calculations based on 2013 Enterprise Surveys for Bangladesh, Nepal, and Pakistan, and 2014 Enterprise Survey for India.
Note: Intensity is calculated only for firms engaged in research and development (R&D). Only 23 firms reported this information in Pakistan. — = not available.

Investment in innovation differs significantly across firms. Small, nonexporting, national, and very young firms are more R&D–intensive in India, while in Bangladesh, large, exporting, foreign, and old firms are significantly more R&D–intensive. In Pakistan, there is a very large concentration of R&D activity in a very small number of firms. Investment in innovation in the global value chain (GVC) sectors discussed earlier in the report is greater in large firms. In the automotive sector, for example, field interviews show that large firms spend more on innovation and R&D than do smaller firms. And in agribusiness, 65 percent of large firms reported expenditures on innovation, compared to only 49 percent of small and medium enterprises (SMEs). Innovation expenditures in electronics are relatively low at only 1.1 percent of sales in firms employing more than 100 workers and 4.7 percent in smaller firms.

Studies show that training and R&D are complementary in supporting productivity outcomes.[7] Firms across South Asia, however, spend relatively little on training. Lead firms do substantially more training than laggards, although it is challenging to compare training levels because so few firms in the laggard group extend training to their employees.

Turning to innovation outputs, Bangladesh and India exhibit overall innovation rates of approximately 80 percent, well above the average of Europe and Central Asia and Africa, while Pakistan and Nepal have innovation rates of 15 percent and 21 percent, respectively (figure 6.4). Process innovation is more prevalent in Bangladesh and India, while product innovation is more common in Nepal and Pakistan. Consistent with the earlier discussion of firm capabilities, firms in all countries are more likely to innovate in marketing than in organization.

As suggested by the literature (Hall and Lerner 2009; and Kerr and Nanda 2014), technological and nontechnological innovation rates are significantly higher for larger firms, consistent with evidence from Europe and Central Asia and Africa.[8] On the other hand, the evidence for the relationship between innovation and firm age is mixed: in India, younger firms display significantly higher rates of organizational innovation and marketing while the opposite is true in the rest of the region. Trader firms (exporters, importers, or both) have higher rates of technological and nontechnological innovation, again consistent with the literature (Lileeva and Trefler 2010), although the differences are statistically significant in few cases. In all countries except Pakistan, exporters are more innovative than importers in creating new products; but importers and two-way traders are more innovative than exporters in process and organizational innovation (except in Nepal). With the exception of Pakistan, foreign-owned firms are also more innovative (Brambilla 2009; Aghion et al. 2013), although the differences are relatively minor.[9]

FIGURE 6.4   Innovation rates vary significantly across South Asia

Share of firms engaged in innovation activities

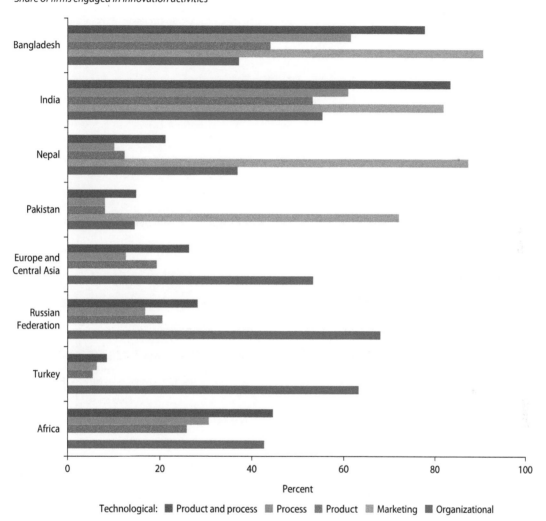

Percent

Technological: ■ Product and process ■ Process ■ Product ■ Marketing ■ Organizational

Source: World Bank calculations based on 2013 Enterprise Surveys for Bangladesh, Nepal, and Pakistan, and 2014 Enterprise Survey for India.
Note: Calculations for Africa based on data from the Democratic Republic of Congo, Ghana, Kenya, Namibia, Nigeria, South Sudan, Sudan, Tanzania, Uganda, and Zambia.

Few firms engage in disruptive innovative activities, such as introducing new products to the country or to the world; the majority of firms conduct incremental innovations or pure imitation—either by upgrading the quality of existing goods or introducing products new to the firm (Cirera et al. 2015). This pattern, observed in Europe and Central Asia and in Africa, also holds in South Asia: despite high average innovation rates in the region, there is only a low degree of novelty in innovation (table 6.2). Even in Bangladesh and India, the region's innovation leaders, most innovation involves the imitation of existing products or processes. In these countries, firms that introduce radical innovations are young, middle- or larger-sized, exporters, and domestically owned. At the opposite end, Nepal and Pakistan show very low innovation rates in general, including imitation activities. In these countries, innovating firms tend to be older, larger, nonexporters, and

TABLE 6.2   Imitation is the most common form of innovation in South Asia

Percent of firms that have introduced an innovation

	Bangladesh	Pakistan	India	Nepal	South Asia (average)	Europe and Central Asia	Africa
New to firm	44	8	54	12.3	30	18	25
Of which, new product	20	38	56	0	29	74	68
Of which, product upgrade	80	62	44	100	72	26	32
New to firm or local market	37	6	47	12	26	10	20
New to national market	4	2	4	0.3	3	6	3
New to international market	3	0.5	2	0.03	1	2	2

Source: World Bank calculations based on 2013 Enterprise Surveys for Bangladesh, Nepal, and Pakistan, and 2014 Enterprise Survey for India.
Note: Calculations for Africa based on data from the Democratic Republic of Congo, Ghana, Kenya, Namibia, Nigeria, South Sudan, Sudan, Tanzania, Uganda, and Zambia.

FIGURE 6.5   The majority of innovation takes place in-house rather than collaboratively

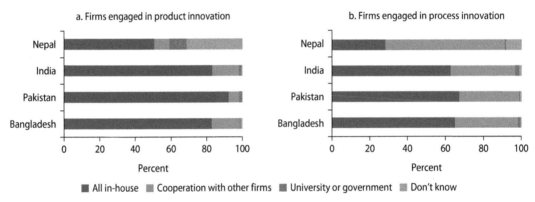

Source: World Bank calculations based on 2013 Enterprise Surveys for Bangladesh, Nepal, and Pakistan, and 2014 Enterprise Survey for India.

more likely foreign. In general, firms that have a higher level of R&D intensity introduce more radical innovations.

Most of the product and process innovations in the region are developed in-house (figure 6.5). External cooperation is, in most cases, linked to other firms, although cooperation with the private sector plays a more important role for process innovation than for product innovation. Successful firms report that in-house R&D capability has been an important driver of competitiveness, enabling them to compete on quality as well as cost. Nevertheless, this high reliance on in-house innovation development—larger than in Africa and much larger than in Europe and Central Asia—implies a limited scope to introduce more novel products and likely

underpins the large imitation rates in India and Bangladesh.

Innovation activity is also spatially concentrated, but only with respect to the novelty of the innovation. Although in general, R&D investments and innovation are more concentrated than employment (Carlino and Kerr 2014), with patents originating mostly in few and large cities (Fornahl and Brenner 2009; Bairoch 1988), innovation activities in South Asia are less concentrated than employment except in Pakistan (table 6.3). However, higher degrees of novelty, such as products that are new to the national or international market, are more concentrated than employment. Thus, agglomeration in South Asia may matter more for radical innovation than for imitation.

TABLE 6.3   Agglomeration in South Asia matters most for radical innovation

Concentration of economic and innovative activities per Hirschman-Herfindahl Index

	Employment share	Firm share	Innovators (product or process)	Innovators (product)	Radical (national-international)	R&D
Bangladesh	0.390	0.280	0.280	0.280	0.400	0.240
India	0.017	0.006	0.006	0.009	0.040	0.007
Nepal	0.510	0.310	0.270	0.220	0.630	0.700
Pakistan	0.260	0.170	0.440	0.550	0.420	0.290

Source: World Bank calculations based on 2013 Enterprise Surveys for Bangladesh, Nepal, and Pakistan, and 2014 Enterprise Survey for India.
Note: R&D = research and development.

Returns to innovation are high

Innovation is a key determinant of firm-level productivity. Process innovation increases firm productivity through more efficient use of intermediate inputs and factors of production, while organizational innovation encourages the reallocation of inputs and factors of production across activities within firms. Product innovation facilitates learning-by-doing and helps firms offer new and upgraded products, while marketing innovation and innovative branding strategies allow firms to differentiate their products from those of their competitors and gain market share. Precise estimation of the impact is clouded by complementarities across different innovation concepts and issues of causality and endogeneity. However, once these are addressed convincingly, the estimated impact of innovation on productivity can be substantial. In a survey of evidence, Mohnen and Hall (2013) show that the most common value of the elasticity of firm-level productivity with respect to the intensity of product innovation—measured as the contribution of new products developed in the last three years to total sales—is 0.25, suggesting that a 10 percent increase in intensity raises productivity by 2.5 percent. This relationship is stronger in manufacturing than in services (Criscuolo 2009).

The approach pioneered by Crepon, Duguet, and Mairesse (1998), which links knowledge inputs (such as R&D and ICT adoption) to innovation outputs (such as better machines or more efficient managerial practices) and innovation outputs to productivity, generates several insights concerning the sources and effects of innovation in South Asia (box 6.4). With respect to knowledge inputs, the most important determinant of R&D adoption for all countries in South Asia is firm size, with larger firms more likely to engage in R&D. Having a license to use foreign technology increases R&D in all countries except Bangladesh. Exporters in India and older firms in Pakistan are also more likely to engage in R&D than nonexporters and young firms, respectively. Further, financial constraints are associated with lower investment in R&D for all countries except Bangladesh. Market structure appears to affect R&D only through informal sector competition in India. Other variables related to market structure are not significant, perhaps because less than 9 percent of the sample firms compete in an oligopolistic or monopolistic market.

Moving on to the determinants of innovation outputs, R&D drives the intensity of innovation (that is, the share of a company's sales that can be attributed to the introduction of product or process innovation), but does not affect the probability of adopting a technological innovation (table 6A.2). ICT is significantly related to innovation intensity only for India and the adoption of technological innovations in Nepal, but not in Pakistan or Bangladesh. Lack of complementary factors, such as skilled labor, reduces innovation intensity, although marginally, in all countries except Bangladesh. Other constraints, however, such as access to external sources of funding, do not appear to play a significant role. Knowledge spillovers have a positive effect on innovation-induced turnover for leading firms, but they are insignificant for laggards.

BOX 6.4   The Crepon-Duguet-Mairesse model

The Crepon-Duguet-Mairesse (CDM) model explores the relationships between the basic determinants of firms' investment in knowledge and productivity. Firms invest in knowledge inputs that can be transformed into innovation outputs. At a later stage, these outputs have an effect on firm-level productivity, depending on the capacity of firms to transform innovation outputs into improvements in product quality and efficiency (Crepon, Duguet, and Mairesse 1998). The CDM model requires the estimation of three main components: (1) the knowledge function, which involves estimating the determinants of R&D and ICT adoption; (2) the innovation equation; and (3) the productivity equation. The model is a recursive system of four blocks of equations, in which each endogenous variable is determined sequentially. Firms first decide the intensity of two input choices—R&D and ICT. These input choices and other factors feed into different types of innovation outcomes (product or process, or innovation sales). Finally, innovation drives productivity (measured as output per worker) at the firm level through an augmented Cobb-Douglas production function, which includes innovation outcomes as inputs.

The determinants of the adoption of knowledge inputs include firm characteristics, market conditions and structure, and technology push factors. The first set includes variables capturing firm size, age, and financial constraints (measured by the share of internal sources used to finance working capital). With regard to market structure, early empirical evidence provided by Porter (1990), Geroski (1990), Baily and Gersbach (1995), Nickell (1996), and Blundell, Griffith, and Van Reenen (1995) supports the view that competitive pressures encourage innovation, while more recent evidence by Aghion et al. (2005) shows that the relation is shaped like an inverted U. With regard to composition, Cusolito (2009) shows that competition induces firms to specialize vertically by upgrading the quality of existing goods. To account for these effects, the model includes variables measuring whether competition from informal firms is an obstacle for the firm, if the sector in which the firm operates has a duopoly structure, and the extent of integration into international markets through trade. With regard to technology, the model considers whether the firm recently upgraded some of its working capital and whether the firm has a license to use foreign technology because these variables can make investments in knowledge capital more attractive.

Further, agglomeration or urbanization effects do not appear to be an important determinant of innovation, while in Nepal most of the innovation activity occurs outside main business cities. Demand-pull factors, which reflect consumers' willingness to pay a higher price for a given quantity, are important in explaining innovation-induced sales gains in Bangladesh, India, and Pakistan.

Results from the final stage of the analysis, which links innovation outputs to labor productivity, show that the impact of innovation on productivity in Nepal and Bangladesh is positive, statistically significant, and larger than that in OECD countries (table 6.4). In India, the large number of observations allows for separate estimation of product and process innovation, with both coefficients positive and statistically significant. The degree of novelty does not introduce any additional effect on productivity, and the returns are the same as for imitation. Thus, the evidence suggests that there are positive returns to imitation in South Asia, mostly coming from very incremental innovations in Bangladesh and India, but radical innovations do not increase firm performance above and beyond the gains from imitation.[10]

TABLE 6.4   Innovation helps increase firm productivity

	Bangladesh		India		Nepal	
Log(L)	0.1429***	0.1416***	0.0886***	0.0901***	0.3769***	0.3586***
Log(K/L)	0.2827***	0.3006***	0.1567***	0.1567***	0.2369***	0.2421***
Product or process	0.5544*	0.6902**			1.3959***	1.5707***
Product innovation			1.2050***	1.2146***		
Process innovation			0.9759***	0.9739***		
Product or process (national)		0.0094				0.2742
Product or process (international)		−0.0103				0.4718
Product (national)				0.0233		
Product (international)				−0.0972		
Process (national)				−0.0273		
Process (international)				−0.1172		
Observations	990	990	3,481	3,481	470	470

Source: World Bank calculations based on 2013 Enterprise Surveys for Bangladesh, Nepal, and Pakistan, and 2014 Enterprise Survey for India.
Note: Constant and sector dummies included but not shown.
***$p < 0.01$ **$p < 0.05$ *$p < 0.1$.

Annex 6A

TABLE 6A.1   Determinants of overall ICT adoption

	South Asia (average)	Nepal	Bangladesh	India	Pakistan
Firm size (log)	0.1807***	0.3598***	0.1654***	0.1198***	0.1908***
	(0.0072)	(0.0529)	(0.0244)	(0.0170)	(0.0412)
Firm age (log)	−0.0033	−0.0055	0.0021	−0.0759***	−0.0106
	(0.0108)	(0.0602)	(0.0308)	(0.0276)	(0.0812)
Exporter	0.1603***	0.2770**	0.4836***	0.1230***	0.2857**
	(0.0223)	(0.1368)	(0.1275)	(0.0426)	(0.1132)
Importer	0.2058***	−0.1158	0.1757*	0.3120***	0.0431
	(0.0273)	(0.1121)	(0.0937)	(0.0655)	(0.1278)
Foreign	0.1074	−0.0688	−0.0127	−0.1115	−0.5897*
	(0.0799)	(0.3687)	(0.1162)	(0.1373)	(0.3173)
New capital t−1	0.0174	0.2311**	0.1194**	−0.0138	−0.1777
	(0.0166)	(0.0910)	(0.0607)	(0.0342)	(0.1101)
Informal sector obstacle	−0.0146	0.0013	−0.1220**	0.0417	0.2723**
	(0.0240)	(0.0885)	(0.0537)	(0.0575)	(0.1088)
License for foreign technology	0.0528*	−0.0136	0.0291	0.1753**	0.1072
	(0.0288)	(0.1703)	(0.0775)	(0.0880)	(0.1210)
Share used for working capital	−0.0004*	−0.0012	−0.0004	−0.0001	−0.0041**
	(0.0002)	(0.0011)	(0.0006)	(0.0006)	(0.0021)
Duopoly or monopoly	0.0499*	0.4256**	0.2233**	0.0540	−0.1430
	(0.0274)	(0.1867)	(0.1117)	(0.0508)	(0.1164)
Business city	0.0163	0.1664	0.0562	0.0990**	0.0633
	(0.0209)	(0.1018)	(0.0689)	(0.0498)	(0.1344)
City over 1 million	0.1332***	0.4064***	−0.1652*	0.1399	−0.4271
	(0.0510)	(0.1483)	(0.0943)	(0.1051)	(0.3941)
City 250,000 to 1 million	0.1050**	0.4660***	−0.0674	0.0888	−0.5418
	(0.0503)	(0.1548)	(0.0939)	(0.1083)	(0.4103)
City 50,000 to 250,000	0.0583	0.3629***	−0.1528	0.1335	−0.1968
	(0.0506)	(0.1234)	(0.1034)	(0.1092)	(0.4049)
High school workers	0.0017***	0.0045***	0.0058***	0.0009*	0.0013
	(0.0003)	(0.0013)	(0.0013)	(0.0006)	(0.0014)
Observations	5116	470	967	3318	361

Source: World Bank calculations based on 2013 Enterprise Surveys for Bangladesh, Nepal, and Pakistan, and 2014 Enterprise Survey for India.
Note: Robust standard errors in parentheses. Estimates use sampling weights, and country dummies are included in regional pooled estimates. Constant term not shown.
***$p < 0.01$ **$p < 0.05$ *$p < 0.1$.

TABLE 6A.2   **Determinants of innovation**

	Nepal		Bangladesh		India		Pakistan	
	Technological innovation	Innovation sales	Technological innovation	Innovation sales	Technological innovation	Innovation sales	Technological innovation	Innovation sales
Firm size (log)	−0.5037***	−0.0190	0.2318	0.0055	0.2800***	−0.0504***	0.3496***	0.0124
	(0.118)	(0.035)	(0.228)	(0.054)	(0.028)	(0.016)	(0.048)	(0.010)
Invests in R&D	0.2946	0.1817***	−1.1062***	0.4595***	−1.8674***	0.1978**	0.1914	0.0924***
	(0.375)	(0.025)	(0.339)	(0.033)	(0.066)	(0.096)	(0.451)	(0.035)
ICT Index	1.9345***	0.0497	−0.5478	−0.1465	0.2354	0.1908***	−1.5988***	−0.0468
	(0.197)	(0.096)	(0.911)	(0.203)	(0.239)	(0.062)	(0.122)	(0.043)
Firm age (log)	−0.1699*	−0.0126	0.0246	−0.0085	−0.0697	−0.0088	0.2090**	0.0152
	(0.089)	(0.010)	(0.063)	(0.015)	(0.043)	(0.006)	(0.085)	(0.011)
Education as obstacle	−0.0404	−0.0280*	0.2207*	−0.0045	−0.0412	−0.0218*	−0.1052	−0.0310**
	(0.117)	(0.016)	(0.124)	(0.022)	(0.041)	(0.013)	(0.109)	(0.015)
Exporter	−0.4398***	−0.0475*	0.3432	−0.0309	0.1827***	0.0290*	0.4155***	−0.0076
	(0.151)	(0.027)	(0.288)	(0.076)	(0.053)	(0.016)	(0.159)	(0.021)
Demand-pull effect	−0.0611	−0.0173	0.1592*	−0.0526***	0.0376	0.0220**	0.0413	0.0264**
	(0.098)	(0.015)	(0.095)	(0.019)	(0.037)	(0.010)	(0.061)	(0.013)
Share used for working capital	−0.0005	−0.0001	−0.0017	0.0008**	−0.0005	−0.0001	−0.0059*	−0.0001
	(0.002)	(0.000)	(0.001)	(0.000)	(0.001)	(0.000)	(0.003)	(0.000)
Duopoly or monopoly	−0.1417	0.0355	−0.2531	0.0467	0.0796	0.0133	−0.0351	0.0061
	(0.226)	(0.030)	(0.350)	(0.069)	(0.065)	(0.015)	(0.140)	(0.017)
Business city	−0.2419**	−0.0294*	−0.0306	0.0253	0.0177	0.0020	0.1533	0.0204
	(0.118)	(0.017)	(0.097)	(0.020)	(0.023)	(0.010)	(0.154)	(0.022)
Spillover	−2.8679	−0.1570	2.4450*	−0.7407***	8.4422	3.1811**	1.5389	0.3170
	(1.877)	(0.274)	(1.482)	(0.284)	(7.763)	(1.536)	(1.258)	(0.205)
Constant	2.2236***	0.1590	−0.3917	−0.0933	−0.8571***	0.2784***	−1.7833***	−0.0998
	(0.433)	(0.189)	(1.426)	(0.296)	(0.241)	(0.063)	(0.569)	(0.087)
Observations	470	470	990	990	3,481	3,480	499	502
Sector dummies	ISIC-1digit	ISIC-1digit	ISIC-2digit	ISIC-2digit	ISIC-2digit	ISIC-2digit	ISIC-1digit	ISIC-1digit

Source: World Bank calculations based on 2013 Enterprise Surveys for Bangladesh, Nepal, and Pakistan, and 2014 Enterprise Survey for India.
Note: Technological innovation is a dummy variable with the value 1 if any new or significantly improved product, service, or process has been introduced by a firm in the previous three years. Innovation sales is the share of sales that can be attributed to the introduction of a new or upgraded innovation process. ICT = information and communication technology; R&D = research and development.
Standard errors in parentheses.
***$p < 0.01$, **$p < 0.05$, *$p < 0.1$.

INDUSTRY CASE STUDY D

Protection from global good practices limits the spread of world-class firm capabilities in the automotive industry

The automotive sector is one of the most important industries globally and in South Asia, contributing 19 million direct and indirect jobs in India alone. The potential for South Asia to become globally competitive in this sector is shown by the experience of Indian auto-parts manufacturers, who became world leaders by first having acquired technical and managerial skills from leading OEMs in India, followed by a process of serving increasingly discerning customers in competitive export markets. Although the level of investment in R&D remains low, a few leading global manufacturers are moving their R&D centers to India, pointing to the region's potential to be at the heart of the technological revolution taking hold in a critical industry that has important ramifications for others, such as electronics, machining, and tooling.

The challenge for the region is twofold. First is to spread these world-class firm capabilities throughout the industry, from OEMs and tier 1 companies to tier 2 and tier 3 suppliers. In effect, large productivity gaps persist in the sector, with most OEMs and their suppliers having subscale or fragmented operations with low capacity use, quality levels, and investments in skills below international benchmarks. A second—and connected—challenge is that of moving up the GVC through greater innovation, investment in R&D, and commercialization of new products, all of which remain below global averages, with local suppliers relying primarily on build-to-print models.

Policies such as high import tariffs on completely built units (CBUs) of passenger cars, which helped attract market-seeking OEMs in the 1990s and 2000s, are now slowing down the spread of world-class managerial good practices. The situation is worse in Pakistan than in India because only a few OEMs are "competing" behind even higher import tariffs on both CBUs and auto parts. The experience of the Indian auto-parts and commercial vehicle sectors shows that a gradual reduction of import tariffs, far from leading to the debilitation of an industry, could be a powerful catalyst to its global success. Converging toward international environmental and safety standards would further encourage automotive firms in South Asia to adopt and contribute to international good practices.

South Asia's opportunity: Become globally competitive in a major industry

The automotive sector (including the auto-parts industry) is a key contributor to jobs and economic growth in India and Pakistan with significant domestic growth potential. Approximately 19 million and 2.5 million people are employed (directly or indirectly) in the Indian and Pakistani auto industries, respectively. There is much scope for further growth with rising income. At approximately 20 cars per 1,000 inhabitants, the car penetration rate in India is one-sixth the Chinese level, which is one-sixth the level in the United States. Car penetration is 30 percent lower in Pakistan than in India because of higher prices that result from less competition and lower productivity.

The sector has also a lot of room to grow in export markets. Even though India is the world's sixth-largest auto producer by volume, it holds less than 1 percent of the global export market compared with more than 3 percent for China, 4.5 percent for Korea, and 7 percent for Mexico (figure 6.6). In India, exports accounted for only 5 percent of the total sales of the average auto firm, compared to 16 percent in China. Intraregional trade is not significant—Pakistan, the closest largest automaker, remains a relatively closed market and did not feature in the top 40 exporters in 2014.

FIGURE 6.6   **Share of exports in production in the automotive sector, 2014**

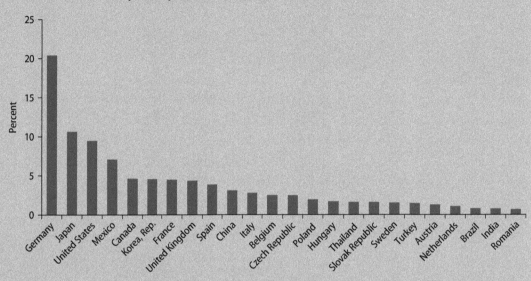

Source: World Integrated Trade Solutions database 2013–14, http://wits.worldbank.org/.

The export performance of the auto-parts industry in India shows the potential of the region. Forty-four percent of auto parts produced in India are exported. Exports of auto components increased by 15 percent per year from 2009 to 2014 (ACMA and McKinsey and Co. 2012).[11] OEMs and tier 1 firms accounted for 80 percent of end customers, with the share of sophisticated end markets rising, indicating high-quality exports. Less than a decade ago, only 35 percent of parts were sold to OEMs, with the rest going to the much less demanding aftermarket. An increasing number of Indian auto-parts manufacturers have become first-class global companies, such as Bharat Forge and Motherson Sumi, which supply most global car companies and have developed world-class capabilities.

In fact, India is showing that leading-edge R&D can be done in South Asia at a fraction of the price. Leading foreign companies such as BMW, Mercedes, Renault-Nissan, Volvo, GM, and Honda are establishing R&D centers in India, emulating Bosch, which is already conducting most of its global R&D in India with 15,000 workers based in

Bangalore. There is a similar trend in the electronics industry, which is increasingly important to the automotive industry; for example, Samsung has one of its three global R&D centers in Noida, India. The region's global preeminence in the ICT industry is no doubt a key explanation for the arrival of these global manufacturing R&D centers—R&D in manufacturing increasingly relies on ICT skills.

This is all very good news for the region, which could position itself as offering a combination of strong R&D and manufacturing capabilities with competitive labor costs together with a very large and fast-growing market.

South Asia's challenges

Spreading strong capabilities evenly to the rest of the industry

Unfortunately, most of the automotive industry in South Asia does not achieve these levels of manufacturing excellence. The average labor productivity of the 500 automotive firms surveyed in India by the World Bank was less than one-third the level in China, with Pakistan further behind (figure 6.7).

FIGURE 6.7   Value added per worker in the automotive sector

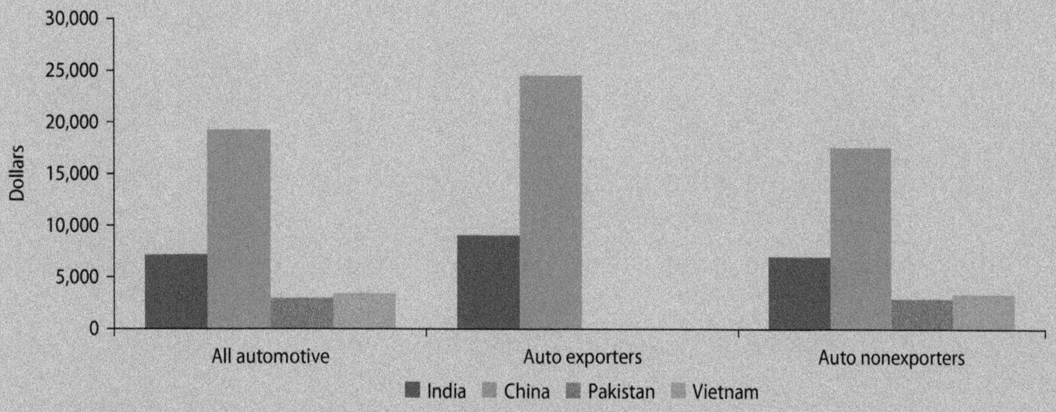

Source: World Bank Enterprise Surveys for India (2014), Pakistan (2013), China (2013), and Vietnam (2009).

Firm size, export orientation, and share of foreign ownership are positively associated with productivity in both India and Pakistan.

The first explanation for low productivity is low scale at the plant level. In India, only 4 of the 18 OEMs operate at the industry standard for efficiency of 100,000 units per model. In contrast, at least three Maruti-Suzuki models achieve more than 200,000 units annually and are profitable.[12] Hyundai, Honda, and Mahindra & Mahindra also have managed to cross the 100,000-unit efficiency mark. Pakistan also suffers from subscale production in all segments except tractors. In China, however, 25 out of 27 OEMs have reached this level. In 2014, 47 models were produced at annual volumes higher than 100,000 units, including 22 models at more than 200,000 units.

Low scale is compounded by low capacity utilization in many OEMs. India produced 4 million cars in 2013 despite a production capacity of 6 million—66 percent capacity utilization compared to 90 percent in China. Capacity utilization among OEMs in Pakistan is below 50 percent. Furthermore, low capacity utilization among OEMs in a vertically integrated industry, such as the automotive sector, is often reflected in low capacity utilization among suppliers.

The next explanation for low productivity is low quality, especially among tier 2 and tier 3 suppliers. External rejection rates are one good measure of quality. External rejection rates are product specific; therefore we use the example of seat makers in India (Sutton 2004). The international best-practice standard for seat makers is between 100 and 500 defects per million produced (ppm). In India, some leading suppliers were nearing 120 ppm, but one-fifth were experiencing rates as high as 2,000 ppm (Sutton 2004).[13] As 40 percent of the value added of a car lies in the tier 2 and tier 3 segments, the competitiveness of the auto industry depends on its ability to improve quality, deliveries, and efficiency in these segments.

Many of these quality issues can be related to large skill gaps, which are prevalent among both production and nonproduction workers, particularly managers. As final products become more complex, manufacturing processes require an increasingly diverse range of problem-solving skills, instead of traditional, linear ones. In China, 90 percent of auto firms provide training to their employees, as opposed to 37 percent of firms in India. Only 43 percent of nonproduction workers in auto firms are formally trained in India, compared to nearly 70 percent in China (figure 6.8). When asked about its main challenge to growth, the chairman of Bharat Forge said, "Talent." Even though there are numerous publicly subsidized training programs, leading

FIGURE 6.8   **Overview of skills in Indian and Chinese automotive firms**

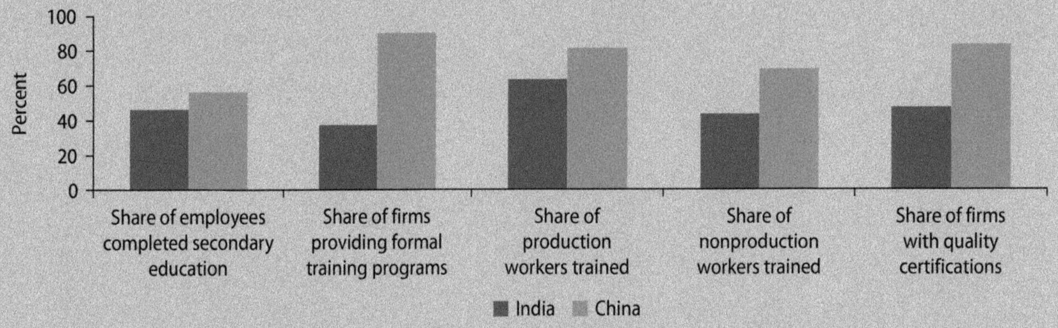

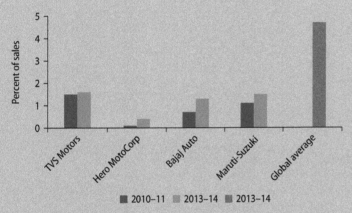

Source: World Bank Enterprise Surveys for India (2014) and China (2013).

FIGURE 6.9   **Expenditures on R&D in India and globally**

Source: Odgers Berndtson India 2014.

firms invest in their own training programs to ensure a constant supply of talented line managers, business managers, and floor-level technical workers.

Moving up the GVC in design and R&D capabilities

Although increasingly important, R&D capabilities are spread thin across the automotive industry in South Asia. Global OEMs now expect design capabilities from firms at all levels of the value chain, because subcontracting makes sense only when the supplier can be held responsible for entire modules of tasks. During interviews, global tier 1 companies mentioned that design capabilities are becoming critical factors in selecting tier 2 subcontractors. With a few exceptions, firms

in India and Pakistan are not demonstrating sufficient and quick use of design capabilities. In most cases, specifications are provided by the customer and the execution is done by the local firm on the basis of build-to-print plans provided by the OEM or tier 1 company. Design abilities are closely linked to a firm's R&D capabilities. The average expenditure on R&D in Indian auto firms ranges between 0 percent and 2 percent of sales, much lower than the global average of 4.7 percent (figure 6.9).

Leading South Asian firms built their capabilities through exposure to global good practices

The world-class Indian auto-parts firms have acquired their capabilities by linking with leading global firms, either as suppliers or through technology agreements. Many started as suppliers to Maruti-Suzuki, which transferred its technical and operational know-how, and above all, according to its past chairman, its management ethic. Co-location in clusters also greatly facilitated these transfers. Subsequent exposure to demanding customers in competitive export markets increased economies of scale and induced quicker adoption of modern, international standards, leading to faster and deeper knowledge transfers and technological spillovers than available in less-advanced and less-competitive South Asian automotive markets (box 6.5).

BOX 6.5   How leading Indian automotive firms acquired their world-class skills

Alliances with OEMs for early capability acquisition

Leading suppliers in India first acquired their technical and managerial capabilities from leading domestic OEMs like Maruti-Suzuki and Hero Honda (now Hero MotoCorp). According to a senior executive at Motherson Sumi Systems Ltd. (MSSL), "We did not have a background in automotive pre-Maruti. Through a technical collaboration . . . with Sumitomo, we set up a wiring harness in India. Within 1–2 years, the [technical collaboration] became a [joint venture] leading to MSSL." At that time, more than 85 percent of MSSL's sales were to Maruti. Similarly, in the 1980s, Maruti was the most important customer of Bharat Forge, which became India's largest auto-part exporter. The story is similar for firms involved in motorcycles. Hi-Tech Gear Ltd. (HTGL) started as a preferred supplier of gear-cutting tools to Hero Honda. After receiving their first order from Hero Honda, HTGL moved into aluminum- and steel-based tubular parts. HTGL chose this product segment because steel of the standard required by Hero Honda was not available in India. HTGL worked with Hero Honda to locate two steel suppliers. They climbed a steep learning curve to meet the high standards demanded by Hero Honda. At the same time, Honda was convincing some of its own suppliers to locate in India and, according to HTGL, the "interactive working relationship between HTGL, Honda's suppliers, and [Hero Honda] helped HTGL learn rapidly."

Rapid absorption and adaptation of technologies

Leading firms became expert at absorbing the technology acquired through technical collaboration and joint ventures and adapting it to expand into production of related products—both forward and backward. For instance, when they were making interior locks and needed zinc parts, Sandhar improved its ability to work with zinc. "If we do a good job with locks, we would suggest we could handle the client's plastic needs," said the senior executive at Sandhar. Once MSSL had acquired new technology and fulfilled its contract with a customer, management would ask their engineers, "What more could we do with it?" MSSL expanded from basic plastic components to building tooling and injection-molding machines to deliver complex plastic products. MSSL initially imported wires for their wire harness products, but then bought copper to manufacture wires. This allowed them to increase sales to existing customers and enter new product markets. Bharat Forge has managed to break into design, engineering, testing, and other higher-value-added services through such approaches and in-house R&D.

Co-location to facilitate learning and business development

Physical proximity to the customer helped upgrade products and processes, co-location allowed MSSL to hold frequent meetings with Hero Honda, and new requirements would sometimes emerge during the course of these discussions. "We make the decision to co-locate based on several factors. Is the job big enough in size to justify co-location? Is the OEM reputed enough to learn from? Is there potential to increase share of wallet? Is there potential to learn something new completely?" asked the MSSL senior executive. Similarly, proximity to the customer helped Sandhar become a designer as well as a supplier of locks and mirrors. As reported by the Sandhar senior executive, "A leading OEM was having trouble with one of its Indian suppliers which wasn't meeting delivery or quality standards. During a lunch with the client I proposed myself even though we had never

(continues next page)

BOX 6.5   How leading Indian automotive firms acquired their world-class skills (continued)

made locks before." One thing led to another, and, pleased with Sandhar's performance in metal sheets, Hero Honda helped it set up a technical collaboration with one of their lock suppliers in Japan. Sandhar became their single-source supplier of locks. Bharat Forge bought plants in Germany to be physically closer to its leading customers.

Diversifying to more sophisticated and demanding export markets

Many auto-parts suppliers increased production and productivity by serving sophisticated and competitive export markets. "Many players at that time went into aftermarkets because barriers to entry were low and there was promise of high margins, but we avoided this route like the plague," said the MSSL senior executive. Working for a demanding customer meant that the firm was forced to be efficient, adopt international standards, and keep costs down. For Bharat Forge, exports started as early as 1995. "Exports challenged us to design, develop, manufacture, and supply products to discerning customers in global markets. This in turn motivated us to scale up the value chain and adopt new technologies," said the Bharat Forge senior executive. An HTGL senior executive noted that, "I wanted to find the most discerning customers, whether in India or abroad. I would bend over backwards to work with them because I found we learnt the most when we worked with OEMs who held very high standards."

Source: World Bank interviews in India.

The spread of world-class capabilities, including in design and R&D, is limited by protection from global good practices

High levels of import tariffs for final cars in India and Pakistan contributed to attracting foreign OEMs, but now these protections are reducing their incentives to export and slowing down the diffusion of good practices. The situation is worse in Pakistan than in India, where only three OEMs "compete" domestically behind higher import tariffs (76 percent and 60 percent, respectively). The experience of the Indian auto-parts and commercial vehicle sectors shows that a gradual reduction of import tariffs, far from debilitating an industry, could be a powerful catalyst for its global success and support the adoption and spread of world-class capabilities. Tariffs on auto parts and commercial vehicles in India have gradually fallen since the 1990s with a concomitant sharp rise in production and exports (figure 6.10). Competition exposed the auto-parts sector to global good practices and pushed it to improve productivity and build design skills to compete in world markets. Exports now constitute more than 40 percent of production. Millions of local jobs were created. Similarly, the decline in import duties on commercial vehicles led to increases in production and employment, and the subsector currently shows a trade surplus (figure 6.11).

International experience shows the positive impact of trade liberalization. A large and globally competitive automotive industry developed rapidly in Mexico following the implementation of the North American Free Trade Agreement (NAFTA). More recently, between 2002 and 2005, China reduced import tariffs from 90 percent to 25 percent. Subsequent competitive pressure was felt throughout the automotive value chains. Net trade in cars rose from $672 million to $5.3 billion, and output among suppliers increased by 25 percent per year.

Obsolete and unpredictable safety and environmental standards have also shielded

FIGURE 6.10   Domestic production of auto parts and nominal tariff reduction in India

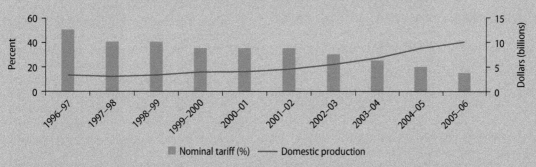

Source: World Integrated Trade Solutions database, http://wits.worldbank.org/; ACMA and McKinsey and Co. 2012; Narayan and Vashisht 2008.
Note: Domestic production is stated in current prices.

FIGURE 6.11   Exports of commercial vehicles and nominal tariff reduction in India

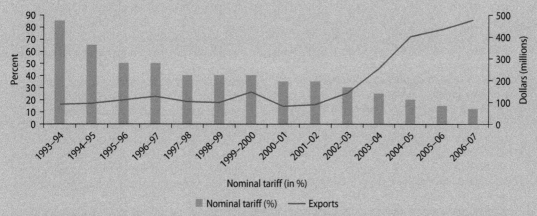

Source: World Integrated Trade Solutions database, http://wits.worldbank.org/; ACMA and McKinsey and Co. 2012; Narayan and Vashisht 2008.

the South Asian automotive industries from global good practices and have reduced the incentives for firms to invest and export. The Euro I emissions standards, introduced in the European Union in 1983, came into force in India in 1996. Although the Euro II standards were introduced in the European Union in 1997, they were not applied throughout India until 2005. Europe has now moved to Euro III. To complicate matters, India's automotive sector suffered from frequent changes and backtracking in regulations for fuel taxes and emission standards. The situation is worse in Pakistan, which has not yet adopted Euro II norms.

The extended version of this case study is available online at www.worldbank.org /SouthAsiaCompetes.

Notes

1. The analysis in Fernandes and Pakes (2008) is based on the 2002 and 2005 rounds of the Investment Climate Survey (now the Investment Enterprise Survey) in India, and the 2005 round of the Investment Climate Survey in Sri Lanka. The authors measure factor under- and overutilization by estimating a Cobb-Douglas production function to calculate the marginal products of labor and capital and comparing these marginal products with factor costs (wages for labor and interest and depreciation rates for capital). The estimation approach followed Olley and Pakes (1996) to correct for entry and exit (selection) and the endogeneity of input use (that inputs may be selected at the same time as output).

2. The reported underutilization rates do not imply that employment would rise by the indicated factor if firms were able to use factors optimally—as firms hired more labor, wages would rise, putting downward pressure on optimal employment levels.

3. These estimates are based on the World Bank Enterprise Survey for each country for the year indicated: Pakistan (2010), Sri Lanka (2011), Bangladesh and Nepal (2013), and India (2014).

4. To obtain these estimates, using an approach similar to that of Fernandes and Pakes (2008), marginal products of labor and capital are estimated using country-specific Cobb-Douglas production functions with sector dummies and then compared with the prevailing wage and rental rates for each country. However, because of the absence of panel data, the estimation approach does not explicitly account for firm selection and endogeneity of input choices. Although the extent of the implied basis is difficult to judge, results reported by Fernandes and Pakes (2008) for India show that coefficient estimates obtained by ordinary least squares (OLS) lie within two standard errors of results obtained with the Olley-Pakes estimator when firms are allowed to optimize labor volumes in every period, even when controlling for firm exit.

5. In the discussion that follows, South Asia's performance is benchmarked against the average in the Africa region, which includes the following 10 countries in which the innovation module from the Enterprise Survey was used: the Democratic Republic of Congo, Ghana, Kenya, Namibia, Nigeria, South Sudan, Sudan, Tanzania, Uganda, and Zambia. Although South Asia and Africa are very different in many respects, levels of gross domestic product (GDP) per capita are similar among the sampled countries.

6. All equations control for sector effects using 2-digit International Standard Industrial Classification (ISIC) dummies. Country models are estimated individually, and a pooled sample with country fixed effects is estimated for the South Asia region. The regional pooled estimates are dominated by India because of its large number of observations. All individual country estimates use sampling weights.

7. In a study for Mexico, Lopez-Acevedo and Tan (2003) found that training produced large and statistically significant wage and productivity outcomes, that joint training and R&D yielded larger returns than investments in one or the other, and that both training and technology investments enabled firms to improve their relative position in the wage and productivity distribution.

8. These differences are significantly different for almost all types of innovation in India and Nepal, for product and marketing innovation in Bangladesh, and for organizational innovation in Pakistan.

9. Foreign-owned firms are defined as those with more than 25 percent ownership by private foreign individuals, companies, or organizations. The differences are statistically significant for product and process innovation in Bangladesh and India, marketing in Nepal, and process innovation and marketing in Pakistan.

10. The estimates are robust to alternative methodologies. Because the generalized structural equation model (GSEM) methodology is more robust with large samples and well-specified models, we also estimate the same models using three-stage least squares (3sls). The disadvantage of this methodology is that it uses the sample of the stage with lower number of estimates and does not allow for a mixed process, because all the stages have to be estimated linearly. On the other hand, it is computationally less demanding than full information maximum likelihood and still addresses the issue of

endogeneity instrumenting at each stage. The results for the returns to innovation, although larger than those under GSEM, are identical in statistical significance.

11. World Bank and UNCTAD (2015) estimates auto-parts exports at $2 billion in 2009 and $6 billion in 2014.

12. Maruti-Suzuki Annual Reports.

13. These data were confirmed by World Bank site visits to Indian auto clusters in December 2014.

References

Aghion, P., U. Akcigit, and P. Howitt. 2013. "What Do We Learn from Schumpeterian Growth Theory?" NBER Working Paper 18824. National Bureau of Economic Research, Cambridge, MA.

Aghion, P., N. Bloom, R. Blundell, R. Griffith, and P. Howitt. 2005. "Competition and Innovation: An Inverted-U Relationship." *Quarterly Journal of Economics* 120 (2): 701–28.

ACMA (Automotive Component Manufacturers Association of India) and McKinsey and Co. 2012. *Auto Component Industry—Ready for the Transition*. New Delhi: ACMA.

Baily, M. and Gersbach, H. 1995. "Efficiency in Manufacturing and the Need for Global Competition." In *Brookings Papers on Economic Activity: Microeconomics*. Washington, DC: The Brookings Institution.

Bairoch, P. 1988. "Cities and Economic Development from the Dawn of History to the Present." University of Chicago Press, Chicago.

Bartel, A. P., and F. R. Lichtenberg. 1987. "The Comparative Advantage of Educated Workers in Implementing New Technology." *The Review of Economics and Statistics* 69 (1): 1–11.

Bayo-Moriones, A., and F. Lera-López. 2007. "A Firm Level Analysis of Determinants of ICT Adoption in Spain." *Technovation* 27 (6/7): 352–66.

Berman, E., J. Bound, and S. Machin. 1994. "Changes in the Demand for Skilled Labor within U.S. Manufacturing: Evidence from the Annual Survey of Manufactures." *Quarterly Journal of Economics* 109 (2): 367–97.

Bloom, N., B. Eifert, A. Mahajan, D. McKenzie, and J. Roberts. 2013. "Does Management Matter? Evidence from India." *Quarterly Journal of Economics* 128 (1): 1–51.

Bloom, N., A. Mahajan, D. McKenzie, and J. Roberts. 2010. "Why Do Firms in Developing Countries Have Low Productivity?" *American Economic Review: Papers & Proceedings 2010* 100 (2): 619–23.

Bloom, N., R. Sadun, and J. Van Reenen. 2016. "Management as Technology?," Harvard Business School Working Paper 16-133, Harvard University: Cambridge, MA.

Bloom, N., and J. Van Reenen. 2007. "Measuring and Explaining Management Practices Across Firms and Countries." *Quarterly Journal of Economics* 122 (4): 1341–1408.

———. 2010. "Why Do Management Practices Differ across Firms and Countries?" *Journal of Economic Perspectives*, American Economic Association 24 (1): 203–24.

Blundell, R., R. Griffith, and J. Van Reenen. 1995. "Dynamic Count Data Models of Technological Innovation." *The Economic Journal* 105 (429): 333–44.

Brambilla, I. 2009. "Multinationals, Technology, and the Introduction of Varieties of Goods." *Journal of International Economics* 79 (1): 89–101.

Bugamelli, M., and P. Pagano. 2004. "Barriers to Investment in ICT." *Applied Economics* 36 (20): 2275–86.

Carlino, G., and W. R. Kerr. 2014. "Agglomeration and Innovation." NBER Working Paper 20367, National Bureau of Economic Research, Cambridge, MA.

Chun, H. 2003. "Information Technology and the Demand for Educated Workers: Disentangling the Impacts of Adoption versus Use." *Review of Economics and Statistics* 85 (1): 1–8.

Cirera, X., D. Lederman, J. A. Máñez, M. E. Rochina, and J. A. Sanchis. 2015. "The Export Productivity Link for Brazilian Manufacturing Firms." Economics Discussion Papers 2015-26. Kiel Institute for the World Economy. http://www.economics-ejournal.org/economics/discussionpapers/2015-26.

Commander, S., R. Harrison, and N. Menezes-Filho. 2011. "ICT and Productivity in Developing Countries: New Firm-Level Evidence from Brazil and India." *Review of Economics and Statistics* 93 (2): 528–41.

Crepon, B., E. Duguet, and J. Mairesse. 1998. "Research, Innovation and Productivity: An Econometric Analysis at the Firm Level." *Economics of Innovation and New Technology* 7 (2): 115–58.

Criscuolo, P. 2009. "Inter-firm Reverse Technology Transfer: The Home Country

Effect of R&D Internationalization." *Industrial and Corporate Change* 18 (5): 869–99.

Cusolito, Ana. 2009. "Competition, Imitation, and Technical Change: Quality vs. Variety." Policy Research Working Paper 4997, World Bank, Washington, DC.

Dasgupta, S., D. Agarwal, A. Ioannidis, and S. Gopalakrishnan. 1999. "Determinants of Information Technology Adoption: An Extension of Existing Models to Firms in a Developing Country." *Journal of Global Information Management* 7 (3): 30–40.

Doms, M., T. Dunne, and K. R. Troske. 1997. "Workers, Wages, and Technology." *Quarterly Journal of Economics* 112 (1): 253–90.

Dougherty, S., R. Herd, and T. Chalaux. 2009. "What Is Holding Back Productivity Growth in India? Recent Microevidence." *OECD Journal: Economic Studies* 2009 (1): 1–22.

Fabiani, S., F. Schivardi, and S. Trento. 2005. "ICT Adoption in Italian Manufacturing: Firm-Level Evidence." *Industrial and Corporate Change* 14 (2): 225–49.

Fabiani, S., F. Schivardi, and S. Trento. 2005. "ICT Adoption in Italian Manufacturing: Firm-Level Evidence." *Industrial and Corporate Change* 14 (2): 225–49.

Fernandes, A., and A. Pakes. 2008. "Factor Utilization in Indian Manufacturing: A Look at the World Bank Investment Climate Surveys Data." NBER Working Paper 14178, National Bureau of Economic Research, Cambridge, MA.

Forman, C., A. Goldfarb, and S. Greenstein. 2005. "Geographic Location and the Diffusion of Internet Technology." *Electronic Commerce Research and Applications* 4 (1): 1–13.

Fornahl, D., and T. Brenner. 2009. "Geographic Concentration of Innovative Activities in Germany." *Structural Change and Economic Dynamics* 20 (3): 163–82.

Geroski, P. A. 1990. "Innovation, Technological Opportunity, and Market Structure." *Oxford Economic Papers* 42 (3): 586–602.

Giunta, A., and F. Trivieri. 2007. "Understanding the Determinants of Information Technology Adoption: Evidence from Italian Manufacturing Firms." *Applied Economics* 39 (10): 1325–34.

Hall, B. H., J. Lerner. 2009. "The Financing of R&D and Innovation." NBER Working Paper w15325. National Bureau of Economic Research, Cambridge, MA.

Haller, S., and I. Siedschlag. 2011. "Determinants of ICT Adoption: Evidence from Firm-Level Data." *Applied Economics* 43 (26): 3775–88.

Hasan, R., D. Mitra, and A. Sundaram. 2013. "What Explains the High Capital Intensity of Indian Manufacturing?" *Indian Growth and Development Review* 6 (2): 212–41.

Haskel, J., and Y. Heden. 1999. "Computers and the Demand for Skilled Labour: Industry- and Establishment-Level Panel Evidence for the UK." *Economic Journal* 109 (454): 68–79.

Hollenstein, H. 2004. "Determinants of the Adoption of Information and Communication Technologies (ICT): An Empirical Analysis Based on Firm-Level Data for the Swiss Business Sector." *Structural Change and Economic Dynamics* 15 (3): 315–42.

Keller, W. 2004. "International Technology Diffusion." *Journal of Economic Literature* 42 (September): 752–82.

Kerr, W. R., and R. Nanda. 2014. "Financing Innovation." NBER Working Paper 20676, National Bureau of Economic Research, Cambridge, MA.

Kowtha, N. R., and T. W. I. Choon. 2001. "Determinants of Website Development: A Study of Electronic Commerce in Singapore." *Information and Management* 39 (3): 227–42.

Kretschmer, T., E. J. Miravete, and J. C. Pernías. 2012. "Competitive Pressure and the Adoption of Complementary Innovations." *American Economic Review* 102 (4): 1540–70.

Lefebvre, L. A., É. Lefebvre, E. Elia, and H. Boeck. 2005. "Exploring B-to-B E-Commerce Adoption Trajectories in Manufacturing SMEs." *Technovation* 25 (12): 1443–56.

Lileeva, A., and D. Trefler. 2010. "Improved Access to Foreign Markets Raises Plant-Level Productivity… for Some Plants." *Quarterly Journal of Economics* 125 (3): 1051–99. http://ideas.repec.org/a/tpr/qjecon/v125y2010i3p1051-1099.html.

Lopez-Acevedo, G., and H. Tan. 2003. "Mexico: In-Firm Training for the Knowledge Economy." Policy Research Working Paper 2957, World Bank, Washington, DC.

Love, P. E., Z. Irani, C. Standing, C. Lin, and J. M. Burn. 2005. "The Enigma of Evaluation: Benefits, Costs and Risks of IT in Australian Small–Medium-Sized Enterprises." *Information & Management* 42 (7): 947–64.

Lucchetti, R., and A. Sterlacchini. 2004. "The Adoption of ICT among SMEs: Evidence from an Italian Survey." *Small Business Economics* 23 (2): 151–68.

McKenzie, D., and C. Woodruff. 2015. "Business Practices in Small Firms in Developing

Countries." NBER Working Paper 21505, National Bureau of Economic Research, Cambridge, MA.

Mohnen, P., and B. H. Hall. 2013. "Innovation and Productivity: An Update." *Eurasian Business Review* 3 (1): 47–65.

Narayan, B. G., and P. Vashisht. 2008. "Determinants of Competitiveness of the Indian Auto Industry." Working Paper 201, Indian Council for Research on International Economic Relations, New Delhi.

Narula, R., and A. Zanfei. 2005. "Globalisation of Innovation: The Role of Multinational Enterprises." In *Oxford Handbook of Innovation*, edited by J. Fagerberg, D. Mowery, and R. Nelson 318–45. New York: Oxford University Press.

Nickell, S. 1996. "Competition and Corporate Performance." *Journal of Political Economy* 104 (4): 724–46.

Odgers Berndtson India. 2014. "Indian Automotive Sector Gearing Up to Accelerate." Search Intelligence Automotive Business Leaders Survey.

OECD (Organisation for Economic Co-operation and Development). 2012. "Community Survey on ICT Usage in Enterprises." OECD.

OECD/Eurostat. 2005. *Oslo Manual: Guidelines for Collecting and Interpreting Innovation Data*. 3rd Edition. Paris: OECD Publishing.

Olley, G. S., and A. Pakes. 1996. "The Dynamics of Productivity in the Telecommunications Equipment Industry." *Econometrica* 64 (6): 1263–97.

Porter, M. 1990. "The Competitive Advantage of Nations." *Harvard Business Review* 68 (2): 73–93.

Sutton, J. 2004. "The Auto-Component Supply Chain in China and India—A Benchmark Study." Research Paper No. EI34, London School of Economics, London, England.

Teo, T. S. H., V. K. G. Lim, and R. Y. C. Lai. 1998. Intrinsic and Extrinsic Motivation in Internet Usage. *Omega* 27 (1): 25–37.

Teo, T. S. H., and M. Tan. 1998. "An Empirical Study of Adoptors and Non-adopters of the Internet in Singapore." *Information and Management* 34 (6): 339–45.

Thong, J. Y. L. 1999. "An Integrated Model of Information Systems Adoption in Small Business." *Journal of Management Information Systems* 15 (4): 187–214.

Walczuch, R., G. Van Braven, and H. Lundgren. 2000. "Internet Adoption Barriers for Small Firms in the Netherlands." *European Management Journal* 18 (5): 561–72.

World Bank. 2013. World Bank Enterprise Survey, China. Washington, DC: World Bank. http://www.enterprisesurveys.org/.

———. 2014. World Bank Enterprise Survey, India. Washington, DC: World Bank. http://www.enterprisesurveys.org/.

World Bank and UNCTAD (United Nations Conference on Trade and Development). 2015. World Integrated Trade Solutions.

The Way Forward

Potential for Increased Growth through Policy Reforms | 7

The potential benefits of becoming more productive and, therefore, more competitive are discussed below at the macro, sectoral, and firm levels. The policy actions underlying these scenarios are discussed in the next chapter.

Macro benefits: Faster export growth through higher productivity

South Asia has tremendous potential to raise incomes through policies that enhance productivity and increase exports. The economy-wide implications of these policies can be assessed using a global computable general equilibrium model, which is used here to consider how a reduction in both international and domestic trade costs could increase income growth in South Asia through 2030. The model uses the latest Global Trade Analysis Project (GTAP) dataset with a 2011 base year, and its key assumptions are calibrated to the *Middle of the Road* scenario of the Integrated Assessment Modeling Consortium (IAMC).[1] (Annex 7A provides a brief introduction to the model.) Most important, productivity in South Asia is calibrated to contribute an average of 2 percentage points to total gross domestic product (GDP) growth through 2030, consistent with what the region was able to achieve during its best recent decade of growth in the 2000s, but well above the experience thus far in the current decade (about 0.9 percentage points per year).

In the baseline scenario, South Asia's relatively young population and strong productivity growth underpin a substantial increase in per capita income through 2030. Unlike China, where total population is projected to decline after 2025, South Asia's population is expected to continue growing. In particular, India will become the world's most populous country shortly after 2020. The number of skilled workers—those with a secondary school degree or higher—is expected to rise by an average of 84 percent by 2030, ranging from 42 percent to 125 percent across the countries in the region. The shift from agriculture to industry and services is expected to accelerate, driven by rising incomes and much lower wages in agricultural versus nonagricultural activities. The agricultural workforce is projected to increase only 10 percent, but the labor force in nonagricultural activities is projected to rise by approximately 60 percent (adding up to an average increase in the overall labor force of 30 percent). Consequently, the share of the region's workers employed in nonagricultural activities is projected to increase from 40 percent to 50 percent.

Real GDP in the region is projected to rise by 6 percent per year (tripling by 2030), giving South Asia one of the highest GDP growth rates in the world and mirroring the growth in East Asia. Per capita income would rise from about $1,400 in 2011 to about $3,400 in 2030 (in 2011 prices and market exchange rates), but remain well below the average of $55,000 in high-income countries. Despite rapid gains in productivity, increases in the number of workers and especially in the volume of capital represent the most important source of growth, as has been true in the past.

Under these assumptions, South Asia becomes the world's fastest-growing region for exports. Merchandise exports (in constant U.S. dollars) rise by 264 percent between 2011 and 2030, compared with a 138 percent increase for all developing countries and 83 percent for the world. The majority of this growth comes from manufacturing and service exports, whereas exports of agricultural goods (excluding processed food) rise by a much more moderate 27 percent. This reflects a limited increase in the agricultural labor force and availability of land, some deceleration in yield growth, and relatively high income growth, which shifts demand toward more highly valued agricultural goods (such as fruits, vegetables, and dairy products) and nonagricultural goods. On the other hand, services exports would more than triple and manufacturing exports rise by nearly 300 percent, as South Asia's rapid labor force growth, rising skill endowments, and rapid productivity growth (implicit in the baseline growth scenario) capture a growing share of the global market in higher-value-added products (figure 7.1). Overall, the region would more than double its global export share in manufacturing and increase its global share of services exports by 75 percent.

Within manufacturing, more skill-intensive sectors account for a larger portion of the overall growth: export growth rates range from 193 percent for textiles to 220 percent

FIGURE 7.1   Continued productivity growth could lead to substantial gains in South Asia's global market share

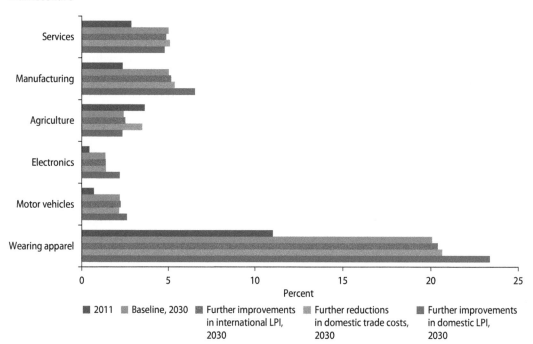

Source: World Bank calculations.
Note: See annex 7A for a detailed description of the scenarios. LPI is the Logistics Performance Index.

for wearing apparel to 400 percent for motor vehicles to 435 percent for electronics. Starting from a relatively low base, by 2030 South Asia more than triples its share of global exports of electronics and motor vehicles, and comes close to doubling its already significant market share of wearing apparel (excluding textiles and leather). In electronics and motor vehicles, nearly all the growth comes from India while other countries—despite rapidly increasing their exports—remain small players in global markets. Even though India's exports in these sectors increase more rapidly than China's, by 2030 India's exports of motor vehicles only just approach China's levels in 2011, and its 2030 electronics exports remain an order of magnitude below what China exported in 2011. In wearing apparel, performance is more equal across the region.

If productivity growth is instead closer to what the region has achieved in the current decade, the growth of exports and incomes will be significantly slower. Exports would rise by 5.7 percent per year, compared to 6.9 percent in the baseline, and gains in global market share of manufacturing and services would be significantly lower. However, even with lower productivity growth, real GDP in the region would still expand by 5 percent per year, on a par with the developing country average and well above the 2 percent GDP growth in high-income countries. The region still increases its share of global export markets, although its performance suffers compared to China and the rest of East Asia. Slower productivity growth reduces South Asia's share of the global apparel market by nearly 4 percentage points, and its shares of automobiles and electronics by 0.5 percentage points each, compared to the baseline scenario.

On the other hand, productivity-enhancing improvements in trade facilitation and the functioning of domestic markets could generate additional gains in exports. Improvements in port infrastructure and warehousing and a reduction in burdensome customs regulations that would lower the region's high logistics costs (comparable, for example, to improved

performance on the domestic component of the Logistics Performance Index (LPI)), could raise total export growth over the forecast period from 256 percent in the baseline to nearly 340 percent and increase the trade-to-GDP elasticity from 1.1 to 1.5. An alternative scenario that targets the international component of the LPI through more rapid implementation of ongoing improvements in port-to-port trade and transportation costs would generate smaller effects, because, according to the GTAP database, the margins between free on board (FOB) and cost, insurance, and freight (CIF) prices are already low (4 percent to 8 percent on average). Exports would increase by 11 percent in 2030 relative to the baseline, or roughly half the increase generated by the first scenario.

Improved economic performance under these scenarios gives rise to increased labor demand in manufacturing. Employment rises relative to the baseline in agribusiness and falls in sectors such as agricultural crops; fossil fuels; and trade, transport, and business services—the last because of increased efficiency in providing trade and transport services. As the aggregate supply of labor is the same across simulations, rising demand for labor because of lower trade costs leads to higher wages.[2] Reductions in logistics costs and in domestic trade costs raise the average wage by approximately 12 percent, while the drop in international trade costs increases the average wage by only 1 percent. The average wage of unskilled and skilled workers rises by 17 percent and 8 percent, respectively, compared to the baseline.

The efforts required to achieve the cost reductions differ across the three scenarios. Thus, while the scenarios indicate the magnitude of the effect of policy improvements, decisions on what policies to undertake would also require identifying the needed measures and quantifying their costs.

Sectoral benefits: More jobs, higher earnings, greater inclusion

An additional perspective on how productivity improvements could affect the domestic economy can be gained by estimating an elasticity of substitution for South Asia's exports—that is, an expected increase in the region's exports given a change in relative prices compared to South Asia's competitors. (See annex 7A for the methodology used.) The advantage of this partial equilibrium approach, compared to the general equilibrium approach in the previous section, is that estimates can be obtained at a detailed product level and with much higher precision. To keep the exercise manageable, the analysis focuses on apparel, which accounts for 12 percent of the region's merchandise exports and employs 3 percent of the region's workers, and only on exports to the United States and the 15 countries of the European Union (EU-15).[3]

South Asian exports could increase sharply if prices were to rise more rapidly in China than in South Asia. (Table 7.1 combines the coefficients estimated by the procedure outlined in annex 7A with the import shares of each country to generate the elasticity of substitution.) A 10 percent increase in Chinese prices would reduce U.S. imports from China by 7.9 percent (almost $700 million), while exports from Bangladesh, India, and Pakistan would increase by 13.6 percent ($519 million), 14.6 percent ($414 million), and 25.3 percent ($336 million), respectively.[4] South Asia's emerging competitors could benefit even more: Vietnam's exports could increase by 37.7 percent ($2.2 billion) and Cambodia's by 51.3 percent ($1.1 billion). The same relative price increase in the European Union

markets would have little effect on exports from Bangladesh and Pakistan, but would raise exports from India and Sri Lanka by 19.0 percent and 22.5 percent, respectively, consistent with the current production relationships between these countries and the European Union. These results suggest that competition in the apparel markets is intense, with buyers highly sensitive to price changes. Thus, policies that increase productivity in apparel may be effective in generating large export gains.

Increases in exports in the apparel and textile sector would be particularly beneficial to employment in South Asia, because the textile and apparel sectors are relatively labor intensive. (The procedure used to estimate labor demand is explained in annex 7A.) These jobs are also more likely to be formal. Evidence from Bangladesh suggests that permanent employment is more sensitive to increases in output than is informal employment—formal workers are more expensive, but they are also more productive (Diaz-Mayans and Sanchez 2004).[5]

Increased employment and wages also would particularly benefit women (box 7.1). The demand for female labor in Bangladesh's garment sector is more elastic than the demand for male labor—a 1 percent increase in foreign sales is associated with a 0.04 percent increase in female labor demand and 0.02 percent increase in male labor demand. In 2012, a 1 percent increase in expected wages was associated with an increase in the probability of female labor

TABLE 7.1   Southeast Asia benefits more than South Asia from a rise in Chinese apparel prices

Elasticity of Substitution, U.S. and EU Imports

	Bangladesh	Cambodia	India	Pakistan	Sri Lanka	Vietnam
U.S.	1.358[a]	5.125[a]	1.462[a]	2.531[a]	0.024	3.770[a]
	(0.039)	(0.093)	(0.027)	(0.086)	(0.058)	(0.029)
EU	−0.238	2.525	1.895[a]	−0.060	2.249[a]	1.644[a]
	(0.534)	(2.031)	(0.455)	(1.068)	(0.745)	(0.960)

Source: World Bank calculations using data from the U.S. Department of Commerce's Office of Textiles and Apparel (OTEXA).
Note: Seemingly unrelated regression (SUR) estimates with homogeneity and symmetry and fixed effects and weights. The numbers in this table are elasticities for a 1 percent increase in prices of Chinese apparel. Standard errors are in parentheses. The change in the exports of a given country heading the columns would be the elasticity times a given percent change in China. A negative value means a decline.
a = statistically significant at 1 percent.

force participation of 89 percent in Sri Lanka, 31 percent in Bangladesh, 19 in India, and 16 in Pakistan, although the importance of this channel seems to have declined over time.[6] (See annex 7A for the estimation procedure and table 7.2 for results.) This is particularly important for South Asia, which has a large pool of potential female workers: its female labor participation rate is only 32 percent, compared to 58 percent in Latin America and the Caribbean, 62 percent in Europe and Central Asia, and 67 percent in East Asia (World Bank 2014). Because apparel is a relatively low-skilled industry, employment opportunities in apparel that pay more than agriculture could potentially draw South Asia's nonparticipating women into the labor force.

BOX 7.1   Why focus on women?

There is growing evidence that gender gaps in the labor market and low female labor force participation rates have a major impact on incomes. Lower employment and wage rates for women are estimated to reduce GDP per capita by as much as 27 percent in some regions (Cuberes and Teignier 2012). Another study estimates that raising the female labor force participation rate to equal the male rate would raise the GDP in the United States by 5 percent, in Japan by 9 percent, in the United Arab Emirates by 12 percent, and in the Arab Republic of Egypt by 34 percent (Aguirre et al. 2012). A third study finds that countries with a comparative advantage in female-labor-intensive goods are characterized by lower fertility, likely indicating that women delay marriage and childbearing, which can result in better pregnancy outcomes and better health (Do, Levchenko, and Raddatz 2014).

At the microeconomic level, some studies show that female labor force participation and employment are beneficial for a number of household indicators, including children's health and education and decision making about fertility and marriage.

- In India, a randomized experiment finds that an increase in labor market opportunities for women raised their labor force participation and their probability of going to school instead of getting married or having children, along with better nutrition and health investments for school-aged girls (Jensen 2012).
- Also in India, a recent study on women employed in the textile industry finds that those with a longer history of employment tended to delay marriage and had a lower desired fertility rate. Moreover, these effects had spillovers within the family—the younger sisters of women who worked in textiles also married later, and their younger brothers were less likely to drop out of school (Sivasankaran 2014).
- In Bangladesh, a study shows that the growth of the garment sector was associated with a 0.27 percentage point increase in girls' school enrollment over 1983–2000—a more sizeable effect than a simultaneous supply-side intervention of providing a subsidy for girls to remain in school (Heath and Mobarak 2012). Girls who live near a garment factory are 28 percent less likely to be married and 29 percent less likely to have given birth than those living in villages farther away from a factory.
- Also in Bangladesh, a recent study finds that formally employed women had fewer children and possessed greater decision-making power over their own health expenses and formal savings (either through insurance or a bank account) (Kabeer et al. 2013).

(continues next page)

BOX 7.1   Why focus on women? (continued)

FIGURE B7.1.1   Working in garments with fewer children
Number of children ages 5 years and younger in a household by female sector of employment

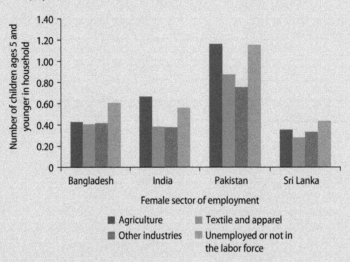

Source: World Bank estimation from household data.

The estimates in this report confirm that South Asian households with working women, especially in the textile and apparel sectors in India and Pakistan, have fewer young children on average than those with women working in agriculture or those with women who are not in the labor force or unemployed (figure B7.1.1). Estimates from the Sri Lanka 2008 household survey show that households with women working in textiles or apparel spend almost twice as much per month on education per student (SL Rs 1,112) than households with women working in agriculture (SL Rs 657).

TABLE 7.2   Higher wages increase women's labor force participation
Marginal effects of female labor participation with respect to log expected wage

	1995	2000	2005	2012
Bangladesh	—	1.646***	0.141***	0.306***
India	0.551***	0.426***	0.410***	0.189***
Pakistan	0.085***	0.194***	0.188***	0.163***
Sri Lanka	1.011***	0.939***	0.696***	0.892***

Source: World Bank calculations using household and labor force surveys of various years.
Note: Bangladesh—the last column is 2010; India—the first column is 1994, second is 2001, last is 2010; Pakistan—the first column is 1996, second is 2001; Sri Lanka—first column is 1996, third is 2006. — = not available.

Combining the empirical evidence presented so far in this section—the price sensitivity of South Asian apparel exports to high-income markets and the responsiveness of employment to apparel output—provides an estimate of the potential number of jobs that South Asia could generate through greater apparel exports. For the U.S. market, a 10 percent increase in Chinese apparel prices would increase apparel employment in Pakistan for males by 8.93 percent—by far the largest increase among South Asian economies—followed by Bangladesh and India. The gains for

Sri Lanka are less than 1 percent, but it is important to keep in mind that these estimates are for exports to the United States only. For the European Union market, a 10 percent increase in Chinese apparel prices would increase apparel employment for males by 8.55 percent in Sri Lanka and 4.30 percent in India, but Bangladesh and Pakistan would experience small decreases because their products are not close substitutes for Chinese apparel in the European Union. All of the results are qualitatively similar for females (table 7.3).

Firm benefits: Greater density of successful firms

At the firm level, the region's potential is shown by the achievements of its leading firms, which have risen to standards of global excellence. These firms have flourished because they operate in countries and sectors (for example, apparel in Bangladesh and Sri Lanka) or subsectors (for example, auto parts in India) in which the policy environment is conducive to success or because they were able to internalize some of the constraints in

TABLE 7.3   Increased apparel price competitiveness vis-à-vis China can create many jobs in South Asia

Panel a: Male employment responses for exports to United States

Country	Elasticity of exports to prices (ε_{xp})	Elasticity of jobs to exports (ε_{Ex})	Elasticity of jobs to prices $\left(\dfrac{\%\Delta Employment}{\%\Delta Prices}\right)$
Bangladesh	1.358*	0.311***	**0.422**
India	1.462*	0.176***	0.332
Pakistan	2.531*	0.353***	**0.893**
Sri Lanka	0.024	0.380***	0.009

Panel b: Female employment responses for exports to United States

Country	ε_{xp}	ε_{Ex}	$\dfrac{\%\Delta Employment}{\%\Delta Prices}$
Bangladesh	1.358*	0.323***	**0.439**
India	1.462*	0.172***	0.251
Pakistan	2.531*	0.336***	**0.850**
Sri Lanka	0.024	0.350***	0.008

Panel c: Male employment responses for exports to the EU

Country	ε_{xp}	ε_{Ex}	$\dfrac{\%\Delta Employment}{\%\Delta Prices}$
Bangladesh	−0.238	0.311***	−0.074
India	1.895*	0.176***	**0.430**
Pakistan	−0.060	0.353***	−0.021
Sri Lanka	2.249*	0.380***	**0.855**

Panel d: Female employment responses for exports to the EU

Country	ε_{xp}	ε_{Ex}	$\dfrac{\%\Delta Employment}{\%\Delta Prices}$
Bangladesh	−0.238	0.323***	−0.077
India	1.895*	0.172***	**0.326**
Pakistan	−0.060	0.336***	−0.020
Sri Lanka	2.249*	0.350***	**0.787**

Source: Lopez-Acevedo and Robertson 2016.
Note: The elasticities reported here are for a 1 percent increase in prices of Chinese apparel. The ratios denoted in bold highlight high values of the elasticity of jobs to prices.
***$p < .01$, **$p < .05$, *$p < .1$.

their external environment (for example, through vertical integration in agribusiness and apparel in both Pakistan and India). These examples show the potential of more conducive and supportive policies to increase the number of successful firms.

Leading firms play a critical development role by providing major sources of productive employment, exports, and innovation; helping improve the performance of suppliers by providing them with access to high-value markets, technology, skills, and financing; increasing competitive pressure on other firms; and, through example, providing a source of inspiration for local businesses and sending a strong message to potential international investors. This section summarizes the experience of more than 100 leading firms in South Asia interviewed for the industry case studies—apparel, automotive, electronics, and agribusiness.

The case studies reveal that many of South Asia's top firms are indigenous. These include most of the leading firms in apparel (such as US Apparel in Pakistan, Orient Craft in India, Pacific Jeans in Bangladesh, and MAS in Sri Lanka) and a growing number of auto-parts suppliers (such as Bharat Forge and Hi-Tech Gears Ltd. [HTGL] in India). Notable leading South Asian firms in agribusiness include Fauji Foundation (a food conglomerate in Pakistan), Dilmah (producing high-value tea in Sri Lanka), and KRBL Ltd. (processing basmati rice in India). Even in the electronics sector, which is relatively new to the region, there are examples of emerging world-class South Asian firms, such as Dixon Technologies and Micromax in India. Most of these firms started from modest beginnings but expanded substantially over time; Dilmah, for example, started with 18 staff in 1974 and has grown to 35,000 employees.

The experience of these leading firms demonstrates that world-class levels of operational excellence, efficiency, and innovation can be achieved with the right management, scale and technology, and worker training. For example, the Samsung plant in Noida, India (outside New Delhi) ranks second in efficiency out of 30 comparable Samsung plants around the world, Dilmah and KRBL are recognized as premium tea and rice brands globally, and MAS has developed a range of high-performance sportswear based on its innovative synthetic fabric. Some of these firms are extending their global reach by acquiring leading firms abroad. Bharat Forge—a company that has broken into design, engineering, R&D, testing, calibration, and other higher-value-added services and integrated these with their existing manufacturing product lines—has acquired automotive companies in Germany.

In order to acquire these capabilities, South Asia's leading firms pursued international integration, reaped the productivity gains generated by locating close to suppliers and clients, invested in skills and improved management practices, and benefitted from public investment in trade logistics and innovation. For example:

- *Global links.* Many of South Asia's leading firms actively sought to connect with global leaders through links to suppliers. Examples include Bharat Forge and Motherson Sumi Systems Ltd. (MSSL) with Maruti-Suzuki, HTGL with Hero Honda (now Hero MotoCorp), and MAS with Victoria's Secret. Over time, these companies challenged themselves further through exposure to export markets and very competitive domestic markets (in auto parts, for example, following the reduction in import tariffs and in electronics).

- *Agglomeration economies.* Geographic proximity to customers appears to have aided efforts to upgrade products, process, and functions for these firms. Their close location enabled MSSL to hold frequent meetings with original equipment manufacturers (OEMs) on existing products. At times during the course of these discussions, a new need would reveal itself, leading to subsequent meetings to identify OEMs' requirements.

- *Skills.* To compete in global markets, these firms made significant investments in acquiring skilled manpower at all levels and meeting international standards. For example, workers at Tos Lanka undergo training in Japan for a period ranging from three months to one year. The chairman of Bharat Forge said, "We have leveraged our tie-ups with leading academic institutions to create a strong talent pipeline. Our efforts have resulted in creation of an over 7,000-strong global pool of skilled engineers and technicians." According to a senior executive from HTGL, "We train workers and lose them to OEMs. But we still train because the ones who stay are crucial for our productivity. Unskilled workers are cheaper but costs match up when their mistakes are financially accounted for."

- *Innovation.* When MSSL successfully acquired a new technology and delivered the product to the customer, management would ask its engineers, "How can we leverage this technology for adjacent products? What more could we do with it? What would that take?" In several instances MSSL upgraded products or began to produce the inputs for their existing products. It expanded from producing basic plastic components to building tooling and injection-molding machines to deliver a range of complex plastic products. As a result, MSSL was able to deepen its relationships with and increase sales to existing customers, enter new product categories, and expand its participation in global value chains (GVCs).

- *Public investment.* Public investment in trade logistics and innovation capacity has also been important to these firms' successes. Pacific Jeans in Bangladesh said that the system of bonded warehouses and back-to-back letters of credit provided by the government in the 1970s supported the industry by providing access to critical imported inputs. In the case of KRBL, the Indian government played a critical role in the development of the Pusa-1121 variety of basmati rice.

Annex 7A

Estimating changes in market share: the global computable general equilibrium model

The forward-looking analysis in this report is based on a global recursive dynamic computable general equilibrium (CGE) model. The CGE approach has several key advantages that can be used to complement other forms of analysis. First, it is deeply structural with multiple sectors and globally integrated markets that determine bilateral flows of goods and services. Second, it is both country- and globally consistent. Third, its richness allows productivity growth to be introduced in several ways.

The model is calibrated in the base year (2011) to Version 9 of the Global Trade Analysis Project (GTAP) database—the latest available version. The database has been configured for 15 regions—including all of those available for South Asia: Bangladesh, India, Nepal, Pakistan, Sri Lanka, and rest of South Asia aggregate region—and 32 economic activities: 12 in agriculture and food, 4 in fossil fuels and other mining, 10 manufacturing sectors (including wearing apparel, electronic equipment, and motor vehicles, which are the subject of in-depth case studies carried out for this report), and 6 service sectors

The model is constructed as a time sequence of comparative static equilibria with dynamic equations linking the periods. In each static equilibrium, the model is a relatively standard CGE model. Production is modeled as a nested series of constant elasticity of substitution (CES) functions, with a different nesting for crops, livestock, and other sectors. Energy is treated as a special input—a complement to capital in the short run, but a substitute in the long run. One additional feature of the production structure is its vintage structure. Substitutability is assumed to be lower with installed capital, and there is a degree of capital mobility friction with installed capital. Thus a negative shock to a sector leads to only a partial adjustment to the capital stock in that sector.

Household demand is based on the constant-differences-in-elasticity (CDE) utility function that is nonhomothetic.[7] The government sector purchases goods and services, and collects taxes on sales, imports, exports, factors, and household income. The government deficit is assumed to be held constant—and the direct tax on households adjusts to meet the fiscal target. Investment is savings driven and is equal to the sum of household, public, and foreign savings. The baseline assumes a targeted path for investment as a share of GDP; given that government and foreign savings are assumed to be fixed at base year levels, household savings are allowed to adjust to meet the investment target.

Trade is modeled using the ubiquitous Armington assumption (Armington 1969), whereby goods are differentiated by region of origin. In the current version of the baseline, preferences between domestic and foreign consumption are held constant, and thus trade shares, in the absence of changes in relative prices, move in rough proportion to GDP (with adjustments largely due to compositional effects). With a fixed capital account balance, the real exchange rate adjusts to ex ante movements in the trade balance. Bilateral trade is identified with four different prices and three wedges. The first wedge is between the producer price and the exporter's border (or FOB) price—this is an export tax (or subsidy). The second wedge reflects the costs of international trade and transport and converts the FOB price to the CIF price at the border of the importer. The importer adds to this a tariff, the third and final wedge.

Factor markets are assumed to clear. The model also allows for a segmented labor market between agriculture and nonagriculture using a Harris-Todaro specification (Harris and Todaro 1970). In the case of a segmented market, migration reflects changes in the relative return to labor across the two labor markets. Capital markets clear at the national level. However, installed capital is only partially mobile in sectors with deficient growth. Finally, land is only partially mobile across agricultural activities.

Dynamics is composed of three broad elements. The aggregate supply of labor is assumed to grow at the rate of growth of the working-age population—defined as the population aged between 15 and 64. The growth of skilled labor is aligned with the growth rate of higher education (those with a secondary degree or higher) as projected by the International Institute for Applied Systems Analysis (IIASA) for the shared socioeconomic pathways, with unskilled labor measured as the difference between aggregate and skilled labor. Capital is equated to the previous period's capital stock, less depreciation, plus the previous period's investment—the standard motion equation for capital. Productivity is labor-augmenting: it is uniform between skilled and unskilled labor, but the model allows it to be differentiated across sectors. In the current baseline, it is assumed to be uniform across all sectors and is calibrated to target a given growth path for real income per capita.

In the baseline scenario, real GDP in South Asia rises by 6 percent per year (tripling by 2030), supported by rapid population growth, an increasing share of skilled workers, and the relatively optimistic productivity growth assumptions embedded in the OECD GDP projections for South Asia. The sources of growth are projected to change somewhat from recent experience. The share of GDP growth accounted for by increases in labor and capital falls from 70 percent in 2011–15 to a little over 60 percent in 2026–30 (figure 7A.1). Increases in labor productivity make a greater contribution to GDP growth in the later period, averaging a contribution of 2 percentage points to total GDP growth through 2030 (figure 7A.1). Still, as in the past, increases in the number of workers and in the volume of capital (particularly the latter) represent the most important source of growth.

Because the baseline scenario holds the policy environment constant, three alternative scenarios model improvements in trade facilitation and the functioning of domestic markets in order to quantify the possible effects of policy interventions aimed at enhancing productivity:

- The first scenario lowers the "iceberg" cost of trade. Iceberg costs refer to logistic difficulties, for example weak port infrastructure, burdensome customs regulations, or inefficient behind-the-border services (such as warehousing and transportation) that raise the costs of trade. In the model, iceberg costs are measured by a lower quantity of imports arriving at a destination than what was exported at origin. In this simulation, the iceberg parameter is modified to produce a 10 percent increase in the quantity of exports arriving at destination (compared to the baseline), but only for bilateral trade between South Asian countries and the rest of the world. The magnitude of this change is consistent with the potential for improving logistics in the region, given its poor performance on the domestic component of the LPI.

- The second scenario assumes a more rapid implementation of ongoing improvements in the port-to-port trade and transportation costs in the region, as measured by a decline in the trading margin between the FOB and CIF prices. In the baseline scenario, the margin is assumed to fall by 1 percent per year across all trade relationships; in this simulation the margin declines by 2 percent per year for all trade relationships involving the South Asian countries—for both their exports and their imports. This would be consistent, for example, with South Asia taking advantage of improved international transportation networks (for example, a denser network), enhanced competition, and some technological upgrading of ports to handle larger, more sophisticated vessels—consistent with improvements in the international component of the region's LPI.

- In the third scenario, a similar assumption is used to lower the domestic cost of trade. We assume that the cost of moving goods from the farm or factory gate to local markets or the border for export is reduced from an average of 10 percent of the total value of goods to as little as 5 percent.[8] This scenario would be consistent with

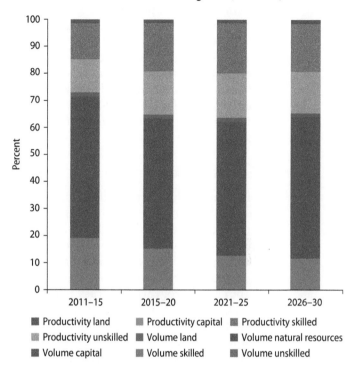

FIGURE 7A.1 **South Asia's sources of growth, baseline, 2011–30**

Legend:
- Productivity land
- Productivity capital
- Productivity skilled
- Productivity unskilled
- Volume land
- Volume natural resources
- Volume capital
- Volume skilled
- Volume unskilled

Source: World Bank calculations.

improved functioning of domestic markets through better product market regulation and reduced distortions in the movement of goods within countries.

Estimating the elasticity of substitution for exports

The empirical approach employed here is similar to Feenstra (1994), adapted to be used with panel data rather than his cross-sectional approach. The methodology therefore combines elements from a standard gravity model, direct estimation of elasticities, and Feenstra's model. As in any typical demand equation, the quantity of apparel that buyers want to purchase from each country depends on the price P_i that country offers, the prices P_j that other countries offer, and the total income Y of the buyer. For tractability, the analysis focuses on two major destinations (the United States and the EU-15, which are the two top import markets for apparel with 63 percent of global imports in 2012), two market leaders in apparel exports (China and Latin America), and two emerging competitors of South Asia (Cambodia and Vietnam). The system is estimated with three equations: U.S. or EU-15 imports from focus countries (Bangladesh, Cambodia, India, Pakistan, Sri Lanka, and Vietnam), U.S. imports from China, and U.S. imports from Latin America.

Estimating labor demand

This approach modifies the classic labor demand model (Hamermesh 1993) by controlling for structural differences in labor productivity related to the size of firms, macro-global changes over time, and imposing symmetrical cross-wage elasticities.[9] Labor is heterogeneous across males and females, all factor prices including wages and rental rates are exogenous to the firm, and output serves as a proxy for exports because most apparel firms in the region are export-oriented. The model is similar in spirit to Grossman (1986), who proposes that intersectoral labor mobility is responsible for how import competition affects jobs.[10] Along the same lines, Revenga (1997) studies the impact of trade liberalization on wages and employment in Mexico's manufacturing sector, and Currie and Harrison (1997) conduct a similar study for Morocco.

Estimates of labor demand are based on a two-step procedure. First, standard Mincer-type equations are used to establish whether working in apparel carries a wage premium over agriculture (a labor-intensive, low-skilled alternative), especially for women. Individual wages are estimated as a function of age, education, and a set of industry and occupation dummies, controlling for self-selection as in Heckman (1978). Second, building on Becker (1965, 1973, 1974), whose seminal work developed a framework for the analysis and the classic labor supply model (Hausman 1980; Blundell and MaCurdy 1999), we explore whether expected higher wages—which could be induced by a greater availability of jobs in apparel in response to an increase in apparel exports—would attract more women into the labor force. Here, female labor supply is a function of the expected wage as well as marital status, education, household size, education of household head, number of children between birth and age 5 and between the ages of 6 and 18, and the rural-urban location dummy. Although Klasen and Pieters (2012) use India data to estimate the female labor supply, this is the first study to do this exercise for the region.

Notes

1. The IAMC community has developed five distinct scenarios (referred to as social economic pathways) with different storylines, such as equitable and environmentally sustainable growth or a fragmented world with poor global governance, low growth, and persistent high poverty levels. All projections are available at the website of the International Institute for Applied Systems Analysis, http://www.iiasa.ac.at/. The *Middle of the Road* scenario used here is based on Organisation for Economic Co-operation and Development (OECD) projections for gross domestic product (GDP) and the medium variant of the 2010 revision of the United Nations population projections. The growth projections have been modified to gap fill for the missing countries, re-base to a different base year (holding the growth rates constant), and annualize the projections that were made available at five-year intervals.

2. By design, there is no change in the aggregate level of employment across scenarios. More plausibly, the changes induced by each scenario would lead to changes in labor force participation rates, in the aggregate as real wages increase, and perhaps across gender lines if sectors such as wearing apparel, with a higher concentration of female employment, expand.

3. The European Union countries used in the analysis are Austria, Belgium, Denmark, Finland, France, Germany, Greece, Ireland, Italy, Luxembourg, the Netherlands, Portugal, Spain, Sweden, and the United Kingdom.

4. Sri Lanka would experience an increase in exports of less than 1 percent in this scenario.

5. Results for India—the only other country for which the data distinguish between permanent and temporary employees—suggest that the elasticities for the two types of labor are about the same.

6. There are a number of potential explanations for the decline, most involving a U-shaped relationship between female labor force participation and economic development (Goldin 1995; Verik 2014). For example, female participation rates may be high in the poorest countries, where many women are engaged in subsistence activities, and lower in countries with somewhat higher incomes because of the rising importance of industrial jobs. At some point in the development process, however, higher female education levels, lower fertility, and a larger share of services in output, which opens up opportunities for women, result in higher female participation rates. There is also evidence in India that labor market outcomes depend in part on differences in the level of urbanization, with relatively few employment opportunities for women in growing areas that are more urbanized than villages but less urbanized than large cities (Chatterjee, Murgai, and Rama 2015). Other factors might be limited availability of transportation to work, bad working conditions, and a lack of institutions for early childhood education.

7. The CDE utility function allows for much greater richness in cross-price substitutability than the ubiquitous linear expenditure system (LES). But nonetheless, both systems suffer from relatively poor dynamic behavior. In the case of the CDE, income elasticities are relatively stable relative to income growth.

8. The current version of the GTAP database incorporates the domestic trade margins in the input-output table. The decline in the domestic trade margin is achieved by reducing the input-output coefficient of selected service sectors (if there are not enough services to justify a domestic margin of 10 percent, service requirements are halved). Note that this scenario has no direct impact on the cost of imports because it does not directly affect the end-user price of imports. This is somewhat contrary to reality, as one would anticipate that improvements in domestic margins would also lead to a reduction in the end-user price of imports.

9. Cross-wage elasticity is modeled as elasticity of male (female) employment with respect to change in female (male) wage.

10. Seddon and Wacziarg (2001) and Levinsohn (1999) provide further reading on the intersectoral reallocation of labor.

References

Aguirre, D., L. Hoteit, C. Rupp, and K. Sabbagh. 2012. *Empowering the Third Billion: Women and the World of Work in 2012*. New York: Booz & Co.

Armington, Paul. 1969. "A Theory of Demand for Products Distinguished by Place of Production." Staff Paper 16, International Monetary Fund, Washington DC.

Becker, G. S. 1965. "A Theory of the Allocation of Time." *Economic Journal* 75 (299): 493–517.

———. 1973. "A Theory of Marriage: Part I." *Journal of Political Economy* 81 (4): 813–46.

———. 1974. "A Theory of Social Interactions." NBER Working Paper 74, National Bureau of Economic Research, New York.

Blundell, R., and T. MaCurdy. 1999. "Labor Supply: A Review of Alternative Approaches." In *Handbook of Labor Economics vol. 3*, edited by O. Ashenfelter and D. Card, 1559–695. Amsterdam: Elsevier.

Chatterjee, U., R. Murgai, and M. Rama. 2015. "Job Opportunities along the Rural-Urban Gradation and Female Labor Force Participation in India." Policy Research Working Paper, 7412, World Bank, Washington, DC.

Cuberes, D., and M. Teignier. 2012. "Gender Gaps in the Labor Market and Aggregate Productivity." SEPR Working Paper 2012017, University of Sheffield, Department of Economics, Sheffield, U.K.

Currie, J., and A. Harrison. 1997. "Trade Reform and Labor Market Adjustment in Morocco." *Journal of Labor Economics* 15 (3): S44–71.

Diaz-Mayans, M., and R. Sanchez. 2004. "Temporary Employment and Technical Efficiency in Spain." *International Journal of Manpower* 25 (2): 181–94.

Do, Q. T., A. A. Levchenko, and C. E. Raddatz. 2014. "Comparative Advantage, International Trade, and Fertility." Policy Research Working Paper 6930, World Bank, Washington, DC.

Feenstra, R. C. 1994. "New Product Varieties and the Measurement of International Prices." *American Economic Review* 84 (1): 157–77.

Goldin, C. 1995. "The U-Shaped Female Labor Force Function in Economic Development and Economic History." In *Investment in Women's Human Capital and Economic Development*, edited by T. P. Schultz, 61–90. Chicago: University of Chicago Press.

Grossman, G. M. 1986. "Imports as a Cause of Injury: The Case of the U.S. Steel Industry." *Journal of International Economics* 20 (3-4): 201–23.

Hamermesh, D. 1993. *Labor Demand*. Princeton: Princeton University Press.

Harris, J., and M. Todaro. 1970. "Migration, Unemployment, and Development: A Two-Sector Analysis." *American Economic Review* 60 (1): 126–42.

Hausman, J. A. 1980. "The Effect of Wages, Taxes, and Fixed Costs on Women's Labor Force Participation." *Journal of Public Economics* 14 (2): 161–94.

Heath, R., and A. M. Mobarak. 2012. "Does Demand or Supply Constrain Investments in Education? Evidence from Garment Sector Jobs in Bangladesh." Report 81292, World Bank, Washington DC.

Heckman, J. J. 1978. "A Partial Survey of Recent Research on the Labor Supply of Women." *American Economic Review* 68 (2): 200–07.

ITA-OTEXA (U.S. International Trade Administration, Office of Textiles and Apparel). 2014. *Market Reports/Tariffs: Textiles, Apparel, Footwear and Travel Goods*. Washington, DC: ITA-OTEXA.

Jensen, R. 2012. "Do Labor Market Opportunities Affect Young Women's Work and Family Decisions? Experimental Evidence from India." *Quarterly Journal of Economics* 27 (2): 753–92.

Kabeer, N., R. Assaad, A. Darkwah, S. Mahmud, H. Sholkamy, S. Tasneem, D. Tsikata, and M. Sulaiman. 2013. *Paid Work, Women's Empowerment and Inclusive Growth: Transforming the Structures of Constraint*. New York: UN Entity for Gender Equality and the Empowerment of Women.

Klasen, S., and J. Pieters. 2012. "Push or Pull? Drivers of Female Labor Force Participation during India's Economic Boom." IZA Paper 6395, Institute for the Study of Labor, Bonn, Germany.

Levinsohn, J. 1999. "Employment Responses to International Liberalization in Chile." *Journal of International Economics* 47: 321–44.

Lopez-Acevedo, G., and R. Robertson. 2016. *Stitches to Riches? Apparel Employment, Trade, and Economic Development in South Asia*. Washington, DC: World Bank.

Revenga, A. 1997. "Employment and Wage Effects of Trade Liberalization: The Case of Mexican Manufacturing." *Journal of Labor Economics* 15 (53): S20–43.

Seddon, J., and R. Wacziarg. 2001. "Trade Liberalization and Intersectoral Labor Movements." Stanford GSB Working Paper 1652, Stanford Graduate School of Business, Stanford, CA.

Sivasankaran, Anitha. 2014. "Work and Women's Marriage, Fertility and Empowerment: Evidence from Textile Mill Employment in India." Harvard University Job Market Paper, Harvard University, Cambridge, MA.

Verick, Sher. 2014. "Female Labor Force Participation in Developing Countries." *IZA World of Labor*, September 2014. doi: 10.15185/izawol.87.

World Bank. 2014. World Development Indicators. Washington, DC: World Bank.

Need for Greater Emphasis on Trade Policies, Spatial Policies, and Firm Capabilities | 8

This report has focused on four main policy levers to boost South Asia's competitiveness. The first is policies to improve the business environment. This lever is relatively well known and multiple efforts are underway within the region to address some of the major shortcomings—although, as argued by the agribusiness industry case study at the end of chapter 3, more emphasis could be given to industry-specific business environment issues (product market regulations). The policy recommendations address the remaining three critical, and underused, drivers of competitiveness in the region: (1) better connection to global value chains (GVCs); (2) maximizing agglomeration benefits; and (3) support for innovation and productivity. We discuss each policy below.

Policies to better connect to global value chains

Trade-related issues have been found to be the most important constraints on competitiveness and productivity in the four industry case studies—for example, the difficulties exporters face in importing inputs in a timely manner at world-market prices (apparel and electronics), poor trade logistics (electronics), and high protection rates (automotive assembly and agribusiness).

With respect to trade and trade-related policies, South Asia does not compare favorably with the Association of Southeast Asian Nations (ASEAN) and Southern African Customs Union (SACU) countries. In 2010, trade costs within South Asia were almost double those in East Asia, and trade costs between the two regions were almost as high as those within South Asia.[1] Part 1 of this report described how tariffs, paratariffs,[2] nontariff measures (NTMs), and logistics inefficiencies boost trade costs. In GVCs—which by definition require that parts and components move back and forth across international borders—the effect of a marginal increase in trade costs is much larger than in "regular" trade flows. For example, most-favored nation (MFN) tariffs on intermediate apparel goods average from 15 percent to 21 percent in Bangladesh, Maldives, and Pakistan.[3] Duties exceed 30 percent on auto parts in Pakistan and MFN tariffs are high on final autos (from 23 percent to 100 percent) in all regional countries except Sri Lanka. The electronics sector is treated most favorably among the GVC sectors, with single-digit tariffs in most cases. NTMs in the region are also pervasive, including in GVC sectors: motorcycles and vehicles in Pakistan face the largest number of NTMs. Although both tariffs and NTMs matter for GVC participation (Ferrantino 2012a;

Ferrantino 2012b), Kee and Nicita (2013) finds that tariffs are the main policy-induced obstacle to regional trade.

Hence, gradually reducing import tariffs, paratariffs, and NTMs toward a common low baseline to increase exposure and access to global good practices is a policy priority that could reap substantial productivity gains. Tariffs should be gradually reduced when high tariffs shield industries from international good practices. High tariffs have been found and discussed in the automotive assembly industry as well as in the agribusiness industry (7 to 30 percent applied, 16 to 190 percent bound tariffs). Reducing tariffs on final goods would improve incentives for innovation and shift labor and capital from low-productivity firms that cannot survive in a more competitive environment to high-productivity firms. Tariffs on intermediate goods that are higher than those on final goods should also be reduced as this protection structure discourages domestic manufacturing.[4] The auto-parts industry in India shows that a gradual reduction in tariffs can lead to increased growth and competitiveness (figure 8.1).

There is also substantial room for improvement with regard to trade facilitation. The poor efficiency of customs and other clearance procedures for traded goods, as well as inadequate logistics services, are major impediments to firms' ability to sell to external markets and source inputs efficiently. In India, the average time reported to clear customs varied from 2 to 10 days for large firms and 14 to 21 days for small and medium enterprises (SMEs). Firms are often forced to hold higher-than-necessary inventories to compensate for lengthy and unpredictable delays in customs, and nevertheless may be forced to delay shipments, both of which can severely erode competitiveness.

However, external challenges are often dwarfed by internal ones. Indian firms reported that, although it takes 11 days for a container to travel from Shanghai to Mumbai, it takes 20 days to travel from Mumbai to Delhi. Firms in auto components, textiles, electronics, and heavy engineering report maintaining 27 percent higher inventories than necessary to cope with these internal obstacles. Poor infrastructure is one reason for these delays, but a survey shows that a quarter of the journey is spent at checkposts, state borders, city entrances, and other regulatory stoppages. In India, differences in tax regimes between states are important reasons for the need for, and time consumed by, internal clearances.

An improvement in all trade facilitation measures could raise South Asian exports by 40.3 percent—the largest increase among

FIGURE 8.1   Tariff reduction and faster growth of auto parts production in India went hand in hand

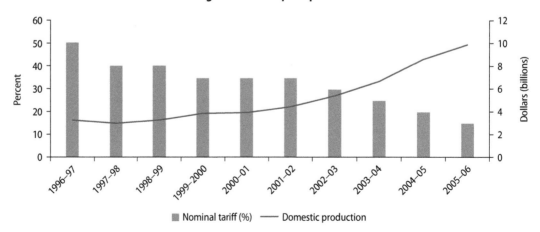

Source: World Integrated Trade Solutions database, http://wits.worldbank.org/; ACMA and McKinsey and Co. 2012; Narayan and Vashisht 2008.
Note: Domestic production is stated in current prices.

global regions, followed by Europe and Central Asia at 30 percent (Wilson, Mann, and Otsuki 2005). Within South Asia, India would have the highest increase in dollar terms ($10.4 billion), and Bangladesh the highest percentage increase (68.3 percent). These high export gains in the region would result more from improvements in port efficiency and service sector infrastructure than from improvements in the regulatory environment and the customs environment. Regional differences in trade gains (in percentage terms) are much smaller for imports, but South Asia remains one of the biggest beneficiaries.

Trade facilitation could be improved by reforming the duty and tax remission for export (DTRE) schemes to facilitate access to imported inputs for exporters. These schemes are supposed to enable exporters to import key inputs free of duties and taxes, but in practice they seldom work. Exporters are limited to exporting products made with locally sourced inputs, which greatly constrains their capacity to expand or improve quality. The apparel case study is the best illustration of the importance of such schemes, as shown by the superior performance of the Bangladesh apparel industry (the only industry that enjoys extensive access to bonded warehouses and accounts for almost 90 percent of Bangladesh's exports) and the Sri Lanka apparel industry (which does not require a DTRE scheme because it has no tariffs on textiles) compared to the apparel industries in India and Pakistan, where such schemes are plagued with red tape.[5] It is thus no surprise that India's and Pakistan's apparel export associations have put liberalizing the import regimes for inputs at the top of their list of policy recommendations.

A longer-term solution to trade facilitation issues must include strengthening the soft and hard infrastructure for domestic and external trade. Important steps to speed clearance at the border include providing for fully electronic submission of documents (the single electronic window); a risk-based inspection system for imported containers (reducing the need to physically inspect all of them); improving coordination of border management

agencies; and establishing an effective and quick grievance redress mechanism (the current administrative mechanisms are lengthy, and firms fear reprisals). Improvements in port efficiency and service-sector infrastructure will also be critical, in particular the capacity of ports to handle larger, more-sophisticated vessels. When asked why he was not investing in Bihar, where most of his labor comes from, a leading apparel manufacturer from Rajasthan answered, "Fix the Calcutta port."

Improvements in product market regulation are also critical. For example, in apparel, South Asia's GVC success story, the input mix is not fully consistent with global demand patterns. Although 32 percent of apparel globally is made from synthetic materials, the share of synthetics in South Asian exports ranges from 5 percent in Sri Lanka to 18 percent in India (figure 8.2). Synthetic fibers are increasingly in demand for high-performance garments, such as sports uniforms and protective gear, and require a greater degree of technological sophistication than products made from traditional fibers. Anecdotal evidence suggests that either high tariffs or NTMs may be reducing the supply of synthetics in South Asia. Such protection, to the extent it exists, could be driven by the interests of the cotton industry or of the small domestic synthetics industry in India that competes with imports. For example, in 2011–12 India produced 6.1 million tons of raw cotton fiber, compared to just 1.2 million tons of synthetic staple fibers (Saheed 2012).[6]

Firms also cite problems in domestic product markets, including controls on prices, inappropriate product standards, other constraints on markets, and administrative requirements for the transport of goods, as important constraints on production. Agribusiness firms state that restrictions on markets limit their operations. Outdated regulatory barriers hinder the development of storage and processing infrastructure. In particular, violations of stock limits and price caps carry penalties that can include jail sentences of up to seven years, which severely limits private sector interest in these markets.

FIGURE 8.2 **South Asia's apparel input mix is not fully consistent with global demand patterns**

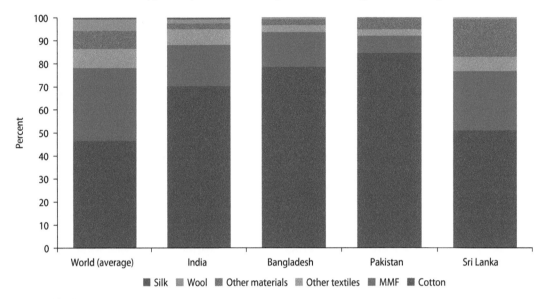

Source: World Bank 2016.
Note: MMF = manmade fiber.

Market committees impose strict controls on the marketing of agricultural produce. Produce can be traded only through the market; for some crops (such as sugar cane) direct purchases are allowed subject to a fee. As a consequence, there is no competition from private markets, services are poor, and the setting of fees is opaque. Price caps combined with minimum support prices on commodity products discourage investment in higher-quality products, and subsidies on fertilizer and water tend to benefit larger farmers and sustain low productivity and environmentally damaging practices.

Product market standards that are unnecessarily restrictive, do not reflect the latest technology, or are seriously out of line with international standards particularly limit productivity in sophisticated industries. For example, automotive firms in India are not required to use the latest international technical standards required by the European Union and the United States, reducing their incentives and capacity to compete in global markets. Moreover, frequent changes in regulations, such as those pertaining to

emission norms in India, force firms to change their technology, imposing heavy losses. The announcement in 2016 by the Indian government to adopt Euro 6 norms by 2020 (leaping over Euro 5 norms) is a welcome development.

Firms also call for greater representation of the private sector in the formulation and implementation of standards. In the agribusiness industry, processors and traders consulted for this report believed that food safety regulations often are rigid, not in accord with scientific advancements, and not in line with the World Trade Organization (WTO) Agreement on Sanitary and Phyto-Sanitary measures. Overlapping responsibilities among government bodies responsible for food safety, coupled with a lack of coordination, impair transparency and the ability of firms to comply with regulations in Bangladesh, India, and Pakistan. Enforcement of regulations is reportedly inefficient or lacking. Food safety laboratories are not recognized by international bodies and lack the capacity for certain tests, such as for pesticides, mycotoxins, and antibiotic residues. As a result, the system fails to effectively protect consumers and impedes firms' access to foreign markets.

The development of capabilities for GVC participation could help raise South Asian participation in GVCs beyond apparel. Simulations carried out in part 3 of this report show that, while South Asia is projected to more than triple its share in global exports of electronics and motor vehicles by 2030, countries other than India will remain small players in these industries. Even India in 2030 will only just approach China's current levels of exports of autos and electronics. To achieve more rapid growth in GVC products, countries in South Asia will need to substantially enhance GVC-relevant capabilities, for which they currently lag behind potential competitors in ASEAN and SACU. Improvements in logistics alone are unlikely to offset the challenges to competitiveness faced by the region; deeper institutional reform and human capital development will be equally crucial.

A pragmatic approach to increasing participation in GVCs is the development of the specific characteristics that lead firms look for when selecting suppliers. Surveys of global apparel buyers (Birnbaum 2014; Daher and Chmielewski 2013; Kurt Salmon Associates and Apparel Magazine 2007–13; Nathan Associates 2005) and interviews conducted for this report identify the following key factors:

- *Cost and quality*. These two firm-specific criteria ranked the highest in all buyer surveys reviewed over the last decade. Local firms can enhance their ability to meet the cost, quality, and timeliness standards of multinational corporations through investments in firm capabilities and innovation—whether of processes, products, organization or managerial capacity, and skills.
- *Lead time and reliability, including access to inputs*. The increasing importance of lead time is related to the shift toward lean retailing and just-in-time delivery, in which buyers reduce the inventory risks associated with supplying apparel to fast-changing, volatile markets by replenishing

items on their shelves in very short cycles (Abernathy, Volpe, and Weil 2006). Local, or at least regional, access to and availability of fabric inputs is also closely related. However, fabric production needs to be competitive in price, quality, lead time, and variety. In this context, the ability to import inputs duty-free is advantageous.
- *Full-package services*. Full-package capability refers to the ability of a firm to offer accompanying services that increase the value added of manufacturers. The buyer surveys show that the most important services include input and material sourcing and financing, and apparel product development services. Buyers' desire to reduce the complexity of their supply chains has spurred this shift from working with assembly suppliers (cut, make, and trim assembly) to full-package suppliers.
- *Social and, to a lesser extent, environmental compliance and political stability and predictability*. Because buyers play a limited role in the actual production process, country-specific factors are generally less important than firm-specific factors in the supplier selection process. However, social compliance has increased in importance in response to pressure from corporate social responsibility (CSR) campaigns by nongovernmental organizations (NGOs) and compliance-conscious consumers.

Policies to maximize agglomeration benefits

Agglomeration benefits, or the benefits that accrue to firms and workers from locating close together in cities or clusters, are important for productivity. Although measures of concentration are high in South Asia, concentration has not increased substantially over the past two decades, suggesting that more-productive locations have not generally been successful in attracting additional resources away from less-productive locations. This reflects significant barriers to the movement of goods, labor, and capital across internal borders in South Asian countries.

Indeed, impediments to efficient allocation of resources between districts are stronger than distortions within districts, creating significant barriers to firms' ability to reap the benefits of agglomeration.

The industry case studies confirm that, when it is allowed to happen, agglomeration is positively associated with firm performance in South Asia. For example, interviews suggest that automotive firms gain substantial benefits from being located in clusters because of the importance of frequent technical interactions, and location next to other automotive firms is highly correlated with productivity levels. Another interesting case is the light manufacturing cluster in Sialkot, Pakistan, where agglomeration benefits more than compensate for a challenging investment climate 1,000 kilometers from the Karachi port. The Sialkot cluster derives its competitive advantage from the ability of firms to hire workers from a large pool of skilled labor as well as from the ability to offer a one-stop solution to global buyers—the private enterprises in the cluster financed the development of an international airport, which provides direct connections to Dubai, and the development of new industrial zones to accommodate their growth and help comply with ever more stringent social and environmental norms.

Restrictions on land markets in South Asia discourage domestic and foreign investment and limit the benefits firms can gain through agglomeration and clustering. Firms mention the difficulty in accessing industrial land in Bangladesh as an important constraint on development. Inadequate space in well-serviced clusters also impairs productivity in apparel SMEs that are stranded in congested city centers across South Asia. Difficulties in the land market that take a long time to resolve (such as a lack of secure land titles), the need to provide infrastructure and overcome coordination issues, as well as the need to overcome negative externalities (such as pollution) and foster positive externalities (such as attracting leading investors and generating agglomeration economies and cluster effects) underline the importance of public intervention in improving access to land. Historically, public support has been provided in most countries through industrial zone developments. These have had a mixed record of success—many of the public zones were not in appropriate locations or have been poorly managed (for example, the Punjab Small Industries Corporation zones in Pakistan), while not enough quality industrial land was provided in the most suitable areas.

The lack of well-located and well-serviced industrial land limits export-oriented foreign direct investment (FDI) in electronics and apparel; investors can choose instead to invest in Vietnam, for example, which has readily available industrial land in prime locations. A notorious example is Samsung's decision to withdraw a planned $1.25 billion investment in Bangladesh, which would have employed 50,000 workers, because the company could not obtain 250 acres in an export processing zone. Samsung is now a major investor in Vietnam, where it contributed to the launch of the electronics industry. Conversely and unfortunately, Indian states have competed fiercely to attract major original equipment manufacturers (OEMs) with tax incentives and land deals, risking a "fiscal race to the bottom," suboptimal investment locations, and industry fragmentation. Ironically, governments are not providing sufficiently good land for export-oriented FDI (which can be made elsewhere), while providing too much land and incentives to market-oriented FDI, which would have been made in any case.

Cooperation with the private sector can play an important role in improving the efficiency and availability of clusters for industrial development. Industrial zones can enable SMEs to cluster around their main customers (for example in automotive and electronics) as well as to have access to common facilities for research and development (R&D) and testing, waste disposal, and recycling. The Combined Effluent Treatment Plants in the upcoming leather and apparel parks in Punjab, Pakistan, are an example. An important lesson for South Asia can be drawn from

China's cooperation with private firms to develop "plug and play" industrial zones, which provide SMEs with ready-to-use standardized industrial buildings and provide decent worker housing close to the factories.

India has developed an interesting public-private partnership solution to address the coordination and financing issues associated with moving an urban SME cluster to an industrial estate outside the city. In the Scheme for Integrated Textile Parks, Infrastructure Leasing and Financial Services Ltd. (ILFS) (a company of mixed public and private ownership) helps SME clusters set up special purpose vehicles, find appropriate land, and secure the required financing. ILFS also provides managerial and technical training to the members of the cluster.

It is interesting to note that many of the modern industrial clusters in South Asia remain located within or near large urban centers—for example, Dhaka and Chittagong for apparel in Bangladesh, Delhi/Noida and Chennai for electronics in India, and Karachi and Lahore for automotive in Pakistan. This helps explain the result at the aggregate level that agglomeration benefits in South Asia come primarily from urbanization rather than specialization effects; the industry case studies show that most specialization happens in large cities. The case studies also show, however, the emergence of specialization within smaller or specialized cities—for example, the light manufacturing cluster in Sialkot, Pakistan, and the automotive clusters in Pune and Aurangabad, India. This may signal the next wave of economies of agglomeration, which should be driven by smaller or specialized cities, as has happened in China and more developed regions as primary cities become too congested and expensive.

To enable this natural and desirable evolution, and as discussed in Ellis and Roberts (2016), South Asian governments should continue to invest in infrastructure to better connect and equip secondary cities and pursue decentralization. One critical aspect of this decentralization will be the delegation of authority over land markets (including over property taxes) to elected local governments to provide them with the authority, resources, and incentives they need to promote industrial development by facilitating private sector–led industrial zones. This is the path followed by China, which started with five Special Economic Zones launched by the central government followed by thousands of industrial zones launched by the private sector with the support of local governments, which financed the infrastructure and facilitated access to land.

In addition to land market reforms, improving the flexibility of markets for labor and capital is likely to facilitate further gains from agglomeration. In particular, policies to increase the flexibility of labor markets, especially for women, who face particularly high discrimination in South Asia's labor markets (World Bank 2012), are likely to substantially reduce misallocation of labor and improve productivity. Additional flexibility could also improve labor mobility, which is relatively low in the region. Chauvin, Glaeser, and Tobio (2011) found that only 0.4 percent of the population in South Asia had moved to a different state within the previous five years, compared with 9 percent in the United States. Labor market policies in the region remain an important constraint, especially as per capita incomes rise (figure 8.3). Although hiring rules in the region are rather flexible, dismissal procedures in South Asia are among the most onerous in the world (World Bank 2011).

Minimizing the misallocation of labor and capital and maximizing the benefits of agglomeration economies, therefore, go hand in hand. Policies directed at improving urban governance and bridging the region's infrastructure gap will ensure that firms and workers will be matched more easily. Achieving this will require tackling congestion issues head-on (box 8.1). In particular, investments in improved urban connectivity (going beyond roads to invest in public transit),[7] provision of quality affordable housing and other basic infrastructure services, and reducing the negative social impact of

FIGURE 8.3 **Labor regulations are a more important constraint in South Asia than in other regions**

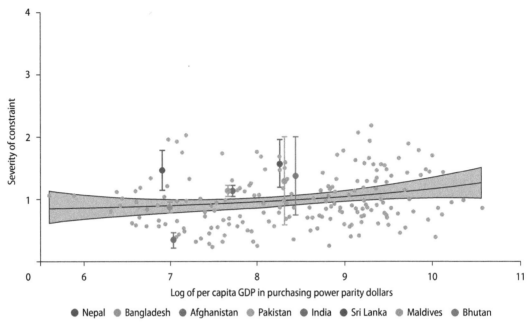

Source: World Bank 2011.
Note: The cross-country regression lion shows the relationship between the reported severity of the constraint for a benchmark firm and the log of per capita GDP. The shaded area is the 95 percent confidence interval band around the regression line. Vertical bars show confidence intervals of 95 percent around the reported severity of the constraint for countries in South Asia. The lack of overlap between the South Asian country confidence interval and the regression line confidence interval is a conservative test of the statistically significant difference between the reported severity of a constraint for the South Asian country and the average reported severity of constraint for countries at the same level of per capita GDP. The reported severity could still be significantly different even with overlap. Analysis is based on pooled sample of enterprise survey conducted between 2000 and 2010. The severity of constraint is rated by firms on a 5-point scale, with 0 being no obstacle, 1 being a minor obstacle, 2 being a moderate obstacle, 3 being a major obstacle, and 4 being a very severe obstacle.

BOX 8.1 Leveraging urbanization in South Asia

Ellis and Roberts (2016) urge policy action to reduce the high costs of urban congestion in the region. To address key congestion constraints, they call the attention of policy makers to three fundamental urban governance deficits: empowerment, resources, and accountability.

- *Empowerment.* Most urban local governments in South Asia suffer from unclear institutional roles, limited functional and revenue assignments, and limited control over human resources. Empowering urban local governments will require a dedicated commitment to

clarifying intergovernmental fiscal legal frameworks—amending existing laws, enforcing them, and, in some cases, enacting new and simpler laws. Significant effort will also be required to establish and align incentives for urban management, governance, and finance.
- *Resources.* Revenue mobilization and management are difficult for most urban local governments in South Asia. Revenue mobilization is constrained by established fees and tax rates, narrow tax bases, and weak administrative capacity to fully use existing revenue opportunities. Budgetary transfers, while

(continues next page)

BOX 8.1   Leveraging urbanization in South Asia (continued)

officially unconditional, often come with higher-level rules and "guidance" on use. Improved design, implementation, and effectiveness of intergovernmental fiscal transfers are required to close the resource gap.

• *Accountability.* Many of the formal administrative accountability systems in the region are weak or little used. Even though audits are legally mandated, poorly performing local governments continue to receive transfers without penalty. Bridging the accountability deficit requires the development of better systems and practices and the building of capacity of both government (at all levels) and citizens, including nurturing the social contract between local governments and citizens and clarifying fiscal relations between local and higher tiers of government.

Ellis and Roberts (2016) also raise three additional, and interrelated, areas for policy action:

• *Connectivity and planning.* Decision makers should focus on strengthening transport links to improve connectivity between urban areas (for example, between large and secondary cities and between secondary cities and towns), adopt forward-looking planning approaches to guide expansion on city peripheries (where it is most rapid), revitalize city cores by investing in better-quality public urban spaces to enhance pedestrian walkability and livability, and adopt granular spatial planning approaches that permit greater variation in land use and intensity of development.

• *Land and housing.* City and suburban governments need to go beyond the upgrading of slums and embrace measures to stimulate the supply of affordable housing and offer more options to both low- and middle-income households. The supply of affordable housing can be increased over time through more permissive land-use and development regulations. Also needed is infrastructure investment to open land for residential development, easy-to-use land titling and registration systems, and greater access to construction and mortgage finance. In addition, government regulations need to be revised to foster the provision of more affordable rental housing.

• *Resilience to disasters and climate change effects.* Cities in South Asia are particularly exposed to disaster shocks. The first step in developing a resilience strategy is to accurately identify and quantify the national, subnational, and city risks, and build national geo-referenced hazard exposure databases. With the help of urban planners, engineers, and academics, cities should revisit the design and enforcement of building codes and land-use plans to avoid further building in risk-prone areas and to reinforce structures so they are resilient to various hazards. In addition, national disaster risk-financing frameworks need to be developed on the basis of risk layering to match risks with appropriate financing instruments.

Source: Ellis and Roberts 2016.

agglomeration (such as crime),[8] should be high on the policy makers' agendas.

Policies to strengthen firm capabilities

Many firms in South Asia are at a disadvantage compared to competitors in other countries with respect to innovation, managerial capabilities, technology adoption, and worker skills, even though evidence shows that relaxing these constraints can lead to substantial improvements in productivity. The findings of this report suggest different approaches to innovation policy for both countries that are innovation leaders and countries that are laggards. For leaders, the critical challenge is how to generate novel and, if possible, radical innovations. Enhancement of complementary factors—skills and finance—is warranted, but more important is breaking the pattern of inward innovation development by supporting cooperation with other firms and institutions. For laggards, policies need to concentrate on increasing the number of firms engaged in incremental innovation.

Public support for innovation can take various forms. Investment in R&D is an important determinant of innovation and productivity. There are many examples of public R&D interventions catalyzing firm growth in the region, especially in agribusiness, where research needs to be localized and spread widely among a large number of farmers (box 8.2). Yet, overall, public and private investment in R&D in South Asia is low (figure 8.4) and has remained relatively unchanged over the past decade, while Latin America and East Asia in particular have increased their investment in R&D. The growing gap is particularly worrisome in light of empirical evidence that shows that social returns from R&D are at least twice as high as private returns (Bloom, Schankerman, and Van Reenen 2013) and may be even higher in developing countries further away from the technological frontier (Griffith, Redding, and Van Reenen 2004). However, as shown by Goni and Maloney (2014), returns to formal R&D are likely to be extremely low in the absence of complementary factors such as education and the quality of the private sector, including managerial capabilities. Therefore, authorities should focus on enhancing the inputs that are complementary to R&D investments—technology, skills, and finance. Given the varying rates of technology adoption in the region, increasing the limited adoption of the Internet and the use of computers among private firms, and then turning to increasing the use of information and communication technology (ICT) to improve management and performance is particularly important in Nepal and Bangladesh. In contrast, the use of ICT is common in Indian firms, so efforts should be devoted to increasing e-commerce, the use of the Internet for the commercialization of products.

Public support for improving firm capabilities through technology extension, access to

---

BOX 8.2   Public support for the development of Pusa-1121 basmati rice in India

At the turn of the twenty-first century, managers at KRBL Ltd. (KRBL) attended a demonstration by the Indian Agricultural Research Institute (IARI) at which a new "evolved" variety of basmati rice, numbered 1121, was presented. KRBL staff were shown its extraordinary cooking characteristics, which resulted in the longest cooked grain of any basmati type. Subsequently, KRBL acquired a 3.5-kilogram sample of variety 1121 from IARI, and in 2001 began growing it for eventual seed multiplication even before the line had entered national trials. Three seasons later, when the variety was officially released as Pusa-1121, KRBL had 20,000 tons ready. Over the next three seasons a portion of the crop was saved for multiplication and a portion milled for test marketing. KRBL had already established a network of farmers through their attempts at contract production. The knowledge that KRBL would buy Pusa-1121 in the local wholesale markets eliminated the marketing risk for farmers growing the new variety. The results of testing were overwhelmingly positive, both from growers, who recognized higher returns from higher yields on a shorter growing cycle with a lower water requirement, and from the consumers in the Persian Gulf markets who found that a cup of milled rice gave 4.5 cups of boiled rice instead of the more typical 4 cups. From there, adoption of the new variety spread rapidly to cover 84 percent of basmati plantings in Punjab and 68 percent in Haryana by 2013.

FIGURE 8.4   South Asia invests relatively less in R&D

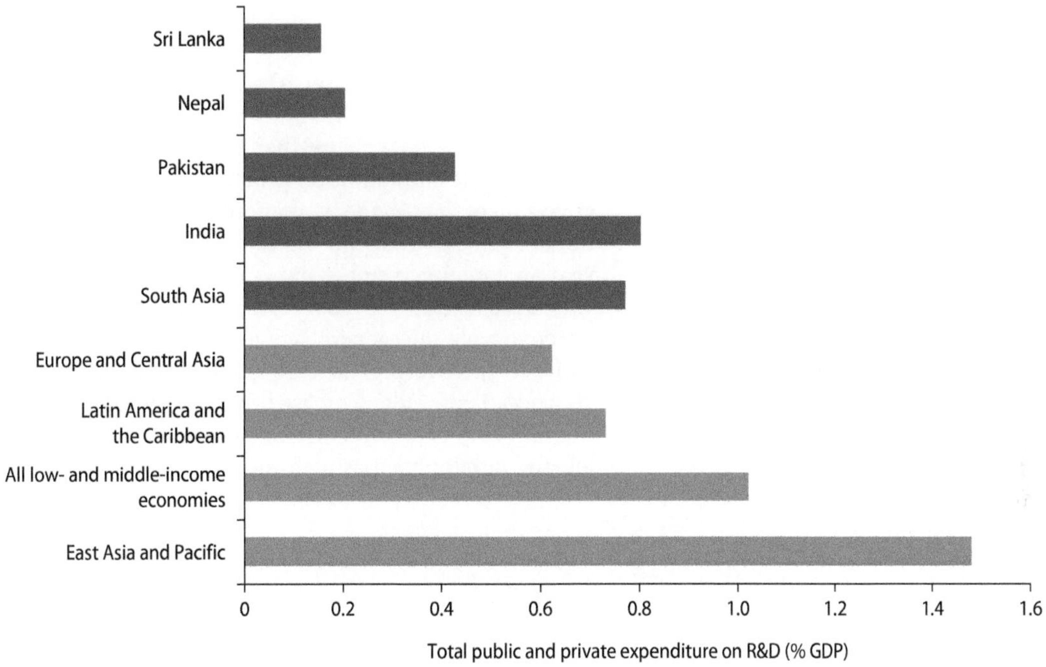

Total public and private expenditure on R&D (% GDP)

Source: World Bank calculations based on World Development Indicators for 2004–13.

consulting services, networking, and information has a long history in high-income countries, in which returns on investment in these services to SMEs have been estimated to be as high as 10–30 times (Ezell and Atkinson 2011). Although most of these programs have not been evaluated using randomized controlled trials, a recent rigorous evaluation in Indian textiles found an 11 percent increase in productivity over one year in response to management consulting (Bloom et al. 2013). Recognizing the importance of these investments, governments in Latin America and Africa are piloting interventions that provide SMEs with access to individualized consulting services, as well as the more novel approach of group consulting services, which can be delivered at lower cost and leverage group-learning dynamics (similar to agricultural extension services). Much of the original research and experimentation into the importance of managerial capabilities for firm performance originates in East and South Asia, affording authorities opportunities to

learn from ongoing efforts and implement their own pilot initiatives.

Skills matter critically for technology adoption in South Asia, and worker skills are an important complement to firm investment in technology, research, and management capabilities. The share of high school graduates among firm employees is positively and significantly associated with ICT adoption in the region as a whole, and in every country except Pakistan. Many of the lead firms interviewed for the industry case studies cited low skill levels as a major constraint on productivity. For example, skills were viewed as a key factor in the success of firms in the automotive industry. The lack of adequate managerial skills was seen as a serious problem. For example, only 43 percent of nonproduction workers in the automotive sector in India are formally trained, compared to nearly 70 percent in China.

Governments can and should play a leading role in the development of technical, managerial, and vocational skills.

BOX 8.3   China's approach to workforce skills

China has taken effective steps to deal with the demand-side challenges associated with training and providing skills to its industrial workforce. Over the years, the Chinese government has invested extensively in vocational education. As a result, nearly 50 percent of the secondary school–level students in China have access to vocational education. The quality of training in Chinese vocational institutions is good, mainly because of extensive industry participation, favorable government policies, and a flexible curriculum. The key stakeholders in the system work hand in hand. Chinese courses require that students undergo one year of training to get a diploma, ensuring faster absorption into the job market.

Similarly, to make sure that the faculty keeps abreast of the latest industry practices, the Chinese government has made it compulsory for vocational trainers to spend at least a month every year in manufacturing companies. Additionally, China has made it very easy for vocational students to move back into general academic programs by sufficiently covering general academic skills in vocational curricula. Chinese firms take employee training seriously, spending twice as much on training and development as their Indian counterparts.

Source: BCG 2013.

Establishing educational partnerships, as well as upgrading university and vocational curricula for procurement, supply chain, and marketing competencies, including e-marketing and e-commerce, will be important for creating a generation of business managers who can successfully communicate with global firms. Firms should forge more robust links with local and technical universities. Training, however, cannot be limited to preservice training from public technical and vocational education and training institutes, which have shown mixed success in India and Pakistan compared to China, where vocational training benefits from extensive industry participation (box 8.3). On-the-job training (including apprenticeships) is also a very effective way to acquire skills (often superior to government-led programs or a worker's own investment) although it has some bias toward existing skill needs. Company-led training programs by Samsung, LG, and Intel in Vietnam and by Daewoo in Bangladesh have addressed important skills gaps. Large Pakistani apparel firms report that they conduct in-house training for most of their workers (Nabi and Hamid 2013).

LESSONS FROM THE FOUR INDUSTRY CASE STUDIES

Drivers and constraints of competitiveness as seen by the managers of leading firms

This section summarizes the experiences of the more than 80 leading firms in South Asia interviewed for the four industry case studies in this report. Many of them are from South Asia and include major apparel exporters (such as US Apparel in Pakistan, Orient Craft in India, Pacific Jeans in Bangladesh, and MAS in Sri Lanka), leading auto-parts manufacturers (such as Bharat Forge, Hi-Tech Gear, Motherson Sumi Systems Ltd. [MSSL] and Hi-Tech Gear Ltd. in India), notable agribusiness firms (such as Fauji Foundation in Pakistan, Dilmah Tea in Sri Lanka, and KRBL Ltd. in India), and emerging world-class firms in the relatively new electronics sector (such as Dixon Technologies and Micromax in India). Most of these firms started from very modest beginnings—Dilmah, for example, started in 1974 with 18 staff but now has 35,000 employees, while US Apparel started with four sewing machines in the 1930s.

Foreign firms continue to play an important role in complex, capital- and knowledge-intensive activities such as car assembly (Maruti-Suzuki in India and Hyundai in Pakistan), electronics (Samsung in India and Tos Lanka, a subsidiary of Toslec of Japan, in Sri Lanka), and agribusiness (Hindustan Lever, Nestlé, and Pepsico, which have transmitted leading-edge knowledge to tens of thousands of farmers).

Beyond their direct contributions, leading firms have important positive effects through the knowledge and support they provide to suppliers and the competitive pressure they put on all firms in the industry. Their example and competition compel other firms to improve and signal to the international investor community what can be achieved in their country.

These leading firms have demonstrated that world-class levels of efficiency and quality could be achieved in South Asia across all the studied industries. This section presents their experience with respect to the drivers of and constraints on competitiveness.

Technology adoption and innovation

Leading firms are demonstrating that world-class and innovative products can be developed in South Asia by South Asian firms—Dilmah and KRBL are recognized, respectively, as premium tea and rice brands globally, and MAS has developed a range of high-performance sportswear using its innovative synthetic fabric. Some of these firms are becoming global through the acquisition of other leading firms abroad—Bharat Forge has acquired automotive companies in Germany and now engages in design, engineering, R&D, testing, and calibration. In electronics, Dixon is leading a new generation of productive and innovative Indian firms in home appliances, with two R&D centers located in Delhi.

In some cases, the government played an important facilitating role. For example, Pacific Jeans in Bangladesh said that the system of bonded warehouses and back-to-back letters of credit provided by the government in the 1970s promoted the industry by providing it access to critical imported inputs. In the case of KRBL, the Indian government played a critical role in the development of the Pusa-1121 basmati rice.

Agglomeration economies and diffusion of knowledge through clustering

Agglomeration economies are the benefits that arise when firms and people locate near one another, either in cities or industrial clusters. There are five sources of agglomeration economies: access to and sharing of inputs and services (increasing returns to scale); labor market pooling (better matches between employers and employees); knowledge spillovers (exchanges of ideas);

market effects (the concentration of demand encourages agglomeration); and economies of consumption (because consumers enjoy variety).

The biggest benefits from agglomeration economies were found in the electronics and automotive industries, in which geographic proximity to the customer has supported efforts to upgrade product, process, and function. Quoting a senior executive from MSSL, a lead automotive firm in India: "We make the decision to co-locate based on several factors. Is the job big enough in size to justify co-location? Is the OEM reputed enough to learn from? Is there potential to increase share of wallet? Is there potential to learn something new completely?" In fact, the Indian and Pakistan automotive industries are concentrated in major clusters in Karachi, Lahore, Chennai, and Pune. It is already possible to see agglomeration effects in South Asia's nascent electronics industry in clusters in Bangalore, Chennai, and Delhi, India. But these effects can also be seen in the rapidly growing electronics industry in Vietnam.

Leading firms (such as the Mahr Group and Wol Plus Incorp.) and their suppliers in the leather apparel cluster in Sialkot benefit from close proximity, which facilitates labor pooling and knowledge diffusion and provides international buyers a critical mass of offerings to encourage travel to this remote location in Pakistan. Buyers' access was further facilitated by the development of an international airport and exhibition center privately financed by the cluster.

Leading firms' links with local suppliers also provide a positive impact on firms in the agribusiness industry. For the Pusa-1121 variety of basmati rice, KRBL transferred crucial market information to farmers by ensuring that they produced the "right" product for the overseas markets. In Bangladesh, Aftab Bahumuki Farms Ltd. introduced contract farming with poultry farmers; contracted farmers recorded a significantly higher level of output (at 11,783 kilograms per year) than noncontract farmers (at 6,763 kilograms per year) (Begum 2008). In Bhutan, Mountain Hazelnut Ventures was established in 2010 to plant and process hazelnuts. The company imports hazel tissue–cultured plantlets and seeds from a related operation in China, which are distributed among farmers. After three years of operation, 2,000 hectares had been planted and 5,000 farmers trained. In India, Nestlé has helped 190,000 farmers increase the quality of their milk and access and develop formal dairy markets in urban areas.

Learning from the best and improving continuously by linking to GVCs

Some of the leading South Asian entrepreneurs, such as the founder of Dilmah, acquired their knowledge by studying and working abroad. The Desh-Daewoo joint venture, which included the intense technical and managerial training of 130 Bangladeshis in Daewoo's Pusan plant in 1979, established the foundation for the next generation of Bangladeshi entrepreneurs. Similarly, many of the leading Indian auto-part companies acquired their knowledge as suppliers to foreign companies, for example, Bharat Forge and MSSL from Maruti-Suzuki and Hi-Tech Gear from Hero MotoCorp. (formerly Hero-Honda). The same is true of MAS through its close partnership with its main customer, Victoria's Secret.

These companies developed their capabilities over time by participating in export markets (such as apparel) or very competitive domestic markets (such as auto parts and electronics following the reduction in import tariffs). Quoting a senior executive at Hi-Tech Gear: "From an operational perspective, exports challenge companies to design, develop, manufacture and supply products to discerning customers in global markets. This in turn motivates companies to scale up the value chain, I wanted to find the most discerning customers, whether in India or abroad. I would bend over backwards to work with them because I found I learnt the most when I worked with OEMs who held very high standards."

Developing trusted relationships with leading international customers also provided a platform for further expansion. MSSL, for example, expanded from making basic plastic components to building tooling and injection-molding machines.

To compete in global markets, these firms made significant investments in acquiring skilled manpower at all levels and meeting international standards. Workers at Tos Lanka undergo training in Japan for a period ranging from three months to one year. Just as many of these leading firms acquired their capabilities as suppliers to leading OEMs, they in turn are having a major positive impact on their own suppliers. For example, MSSL's chief technology officer visits suppliers and works closely with them to define and guide product specifications.

The main constraints reported by leading firms

Industry-specific policies, in the form of product market regulations, are the main constraints found across the four industry case studies. These policies include restrictions on trade, prices, products (through standards), and markets that have protected firms from exposure to global good practices (automotive and agribusiness) or have limited firms' capacity to adopt these practices (apparel and electronics). These constraints are summarized as follows and in table 8.1:

- Trade-related issues were the most important constraints mentioned by the leading firms:
  - Difficulties apparel exporters face in importing inputs at world market prices: Orient Craft (India) and US Apparel (Pakistan) identified the difficulty of importing synthetic fiber as their number

one constraint, echoing the apparel export associations in these two countries. Instead they focused on cotton-based textiles and integrated vertically to ensure quality textiles—a costly solution not available to SMEs in the sector. Conversely, Pacific Jeans (Bangladesh) and MAS (Sri Lanka) reported that the ability to import fabric duty-free was critical to their success.
  - Poor trade logistics and inverted tariffs: In electronics, Samsung mentioned the inverted tariff structure in India, and very high effective protection rates were identified in the automotive and agribusiness sectors. Trade-related issues also include major barriers to regional trade as well as barriers to internal trade within India, which affects all industries.
- Industry-specific product market regulations are important constraints in the automotive industry (through standards) and agribusiness (through standards, subsidies, and restrictive regulations on prices and markets).
- The lack of managerial and technical skills is a constraint in automotive, electronics, and agribusiness. When asked to identify the main challenge to growth, the chairman of Bharat Forge said, "Talent," echoing other leading auto-part manufacturers.
- Difficulties in accessing well-located and well-serviced industrial land is a very serious issue for FDI (especially in electronics and apparel in Bangladesh) and for clusters of SMEs in apparel stranded in city centers in all countries. Samsung could not invest in Bangladesh because it could not find 250 acres for itself and its suppliers around Chittagong.

TABLE 8.1 Major constraints to competitiveness identified in the industry case studies

	Apparel	Electronics	Automotive	Agribusiness
Trade barriers	Very important	Very important	Very important	Important
Product standards and market restrictions	Less important	Less important	Important	Very important
Lack of technical and managerial skills	Less important	Important	Very important	Important
Difficulties in accessing well-located industrial land	Important	Important	Important	Less important

Notes

1. World Bank calculations using data from the U.N. Economic and Social Commission for Asia and the Pacific–World Bank International Trade Costs database. South Asia is represented by India, Pakistan, and Sri Lanka. East Asia is represented by China, Japan, Malaysia, Thailand, and Vietnam.
2. For information on paratariffs, see Sattar (2014).
3. In some cases, these may be offset by duty drawbacks.
4. In Nepal, an inverted tariff structure was found in yarn. Bangladesh, Maldives, and Pakistan impose 15 to 21 percent tariffs on intermediate apparel goods. Tariffs of more than 30 percent were imposed on auto parts in Pakistan. In India, a 7.5 percent tariff was imposed on materials for medical equipment while final goods faced a tariff of 5 percent. In Pakistan, finished poultry products are imported at zero duty from Malaysia and at 16 percent duty from China, yet duties on the inputs for local poultry processors are 15 to 30 percent, in addition to the goods and services tax of 17 percent. In the Indian electronics sector, producers face high tariffs on materials designated as dual-use under the WTO Information Technology Agreement, and the process for obtaining exemption from duty is cumbersome. And in the Indian automotive sector, final goods are subjected to no tariffs under bilateral trade agreements (such as that with Thailand) while intermediate inputs still face tariffs.
5. Difficulties with duty drawback schemes were also found to affect the electronics industry in India (the extremely cumbersome procedures around notification 25/99 discourage firms from using it) and the auto-parts industry in Pakistan.
6. Globally, apparel manufactured from synthetic fibers grew at a rate of 6.7 percent over the 2005–12 period, and its share of the world apparel trade increased from 26 percent to 32 percent, while cotton's share of the global market decreased from 51 percent to 46 percent over the same time period. United Nations Statistics Division (database), United Nations, New York (accessed June 20, 2014), http://wits.worldbank.org.
7. Duranton and Turner (2011) find that in U.S. cities, improved road provision eases traffic congestion only in the short run, which means that expansion of roads is unlikely to relieve congestion in the long run. Public transport improvements appear to be the most powerful tool for alleviating the inconvenience of commuting in urban areas.
8. Using Brazilian city-level data, Lage de Sousa (2014) showed that migration is negatively affected not only by local crime rates but also by those in neighboring areas.

References

Abernathy, F., A. Volpe, and D. Weil. 2006. "The Future of the Apparel and Textile Industries: Prospects and Choices for Public and Private Actors." *Environment and Planning* 38 (12): 2207–32.

ACMA (Automotive Component Manufacturers Association of India) and McKinsey & Co. 2012. *Auto Component Industry—Ready for the Transition*. New Delhi: ACMA.

BCG (Boston Consulting Group). 2013. "People Productivity. Key to Indian Manufacturing Competitiveness." Boston Consulting Group. http://www.bcgindia.com/documents/file130179.pdf.

Begum, I. A. 2008. "Prospects and Potentialities of Vertically Integrated Contract Farming in Bangladesh." Department of Agricultural Development Economics, Hokkaido University, Japan.

Birnbaum, D. 2014. "Comment: Bangladesh's Garment Trend Lines Look Pretty Poor." *Just-style.com*, June 8. http://www.just-style.com/comment/bangladeshs-garment-trend-lines-look-pretty-poor_id121926.aspx.

Bloom, N., B. Eifert, A. Mahajan, D. McKenzie, and J. Roberts. 2013. "Does Management Matter? Evidence from India." *Quarterly Journal of Economics* 128 (1): 1–51.

Bloom, N., M. Schankerman, and J. Van Reenen. 2013. "Identifying Technology Spillovers and Product Market Rivalry." *Econometrica* 81: 1347–93.

Chauvin, J. P., E. Glaeser, and K. Tobio. 2011. "Urban Economics in the U.S. and India." Paper presented at the Economic Geography Conference, Seoul, Republic of Korea, June 29.

Daher, M., and J. Chmielewski. 2013. *Private Label Sourcing Strategies to Differentiate and Defend: Insights from the 2012–2013 Private Label Sourcing Survey*. New York: Deloitte Consulting LLP.

Duranton, G., and M. A. Turner. 2011. "The Fundamental Law of Road Congestion: Evidence from U.S. Cities." *American Economic Review* 101 (6): 2616–52.

Ellis, P., and M. Roberts. 2016. *Leveraging Urbanization in South Asia: Managing Spatial Transformation for Prosperity and Livability.* World Bank: Washington, DC.

Ezell, S. and R. D. Atkinson. 2011. International Benchmarking of Countries' Policies and Programs Supporting SME Manufacturers. The Information Technology & Innovation Foundation.

Ferrantino, M. 2012a. "Using Supply Chain Analysis to Examine the Costs of Non-Tariff Measures (NTMs) and the Benefits of Trade Facilitation." Staff Working Paper ERSD-2012-02, World Trade Organization, Geneva.

———. 2012b. "Supply Chains and Behind-the-Border Trade Barriers: Implications for Developing Nations." Centre for Economic Policy Research. http://voxeu.org/article/why-non-tariff-measures-matter-more-world-sliced-supply-chains.

Goni, E., and W. F. Maloney. 2014. "Why Don't Poor Countries Do R&D?" Policy Research Working Paper 6811, World Bank, Washington, DC.

Griffith, R., E. Huergo, J. Mairesse, and B. Peters. 2006. "Innovation and Productivity Across Four European Countries." *Oxford Review of Economic Policy* 22 (4): 483–98.

Griffith, R., S. Redding, and J. Van Reenen. 2004. "Mapping the Two Faces of R&D: Productivity Growth in a Panel of OECD Industries." *Review of Economics and Statistics* 86 (4):883–95.

Kee, H. L., and A. Nicita. 2016. "Trade Frauds, Trade Elasticities, and Non-Tariff Measures." Paper prepared for 5th IMF-World Bank-WTO Trade Research Workshop, Washington, DC, November 30.

Kurt Salmon Associates and Apparel Magazine. 2007–13. Excellence in Global Sourcing Survey: Annual Apparel Research Study & Analysis.

Lage de Sousa, F. 2014. "Does Crime Affect Migration Flows?" *Papers in Regional Science* 93 (S1): S99–S111.

Nabi, I., and N. Hamid. 2013. *Garments as a Driver of Economic Growth: Insights from Pakistan Case Studies.* Lahore, Pakistan: International Growth Centre.

Narayan, B. G., and P. Vashisht. 2008. "Determinants of Competitiveness of the Indian Auto Industry." Working Paper 201, Indian Council for Research on International Economic Relations, New Delhi.

Nathan Associates. 2005. "Survey of U.S. Apparel Buyers: Sourcing from Sub-Saharan Africa in the Post-Quota Era." University of Sussex.

Pursell, G., and F. M. Ziaul Ahsan. 2011. "Sri Lanka's Trade Policies: Back to Protectionism." ASARC Working Paper 2011/03, Australian National University, Canberra.

Reis, J.G., and D. Taglioni. 2013. "Pakistan: Reinvigorating the Trade Agenda." Policy Paper Series on Pakistan PK 15/12, World Bank, Washington, DC.

Saheed, H. 2012. "Prospects for the Textile and Clothing Industry in India." *Textile Outlook International* 156: 86–127.

Sattar, Z. 2014. "Challenges of Export-Led Growth: Breaking Into New Markets And Products." Presentation for Bangladesh Economists' Forum, Dhaka, June 21–22.

Wilson, J., C. Mann, and T. Otsuki. 2005. "Assessing the Benefits of Trade Facilitation: A Global Perspective." *World Economy* 28 (6): 841–71.

World Bank. 2011. *More and Better Jobs in South Asia.* Washington, DC: World Bank.

———. 2012. *World Development Report: Jobs.* Washington, DC: World Bank.

———. 2016. *Stitches to Riches?: Apparel Employment, Trade, and Economic Development in South Asia.* Washington, DC: World Bank.